The Lost Supper

The Lost Supper

Revisiting Passover and the Origins of the Eucharist

Matthew Colvin

LEXINGTON BOOKS/FORTRESS ACADEMIC
Lanham • Boulder • New York • London

Published by Lexington Books/Fortress Academic
Lexington Books is an imprint of The Rowman & Littlefield Publishing Group, Inc.
4501 Forbes Boulevard, Suite 200, Lanham, Maryland 20706
www.rowman.com

6 Tinworth Street, London SE11 5AL, United Kingdom

Copyright © 2019 by The Rowman & Littlefield Publishing Group, Inc.

Cover image: Image(s) may not be further reproduced from software. For reproduction application must be made to the Head of Digital Resources and Imaging Services, by post to Trinity College Library Dublin, College Street, Dublin 2, Ireland; or by email at digitalresources@tcd.ie.

All rights reserved. No part of this book may be reproduced in any form or by any electronic or mechanical means, including information storage and retrieval systems, without written permission from the publisher, except by a reviewer who may quote passages in a review.

British Library Cataloguing in Publication Information Available

Library of Congress Cataloging-in-Publication Data

ISBN: 978-1-9787-0033-8 (cloth : alk. paper)
ISBN: 978-1-9787-0034-5 (electronic)

♾️ The paper used in this publication meets the minimum requirements of American National Standard for Information Sciences—Permanence of Paper for Printed Library Materials, ANSI/NISO Z39.48-1992.

To Naomi

מה-תשתוחחי נפשי ומה-תהמי עלי

הוחילי לאלהים כי-עוד אודנו ישועת פני ואלהי

Contents

Preface		ix
Abbreviations		xiii
1	The Historical Project	1
2	The Passover Background	11
3	Evidence from Jews and Greeks	37
4	Layers of Meaning	71
5	Mechanics and Misinterpretations	93
6	Rereading John 6	111
7	The Festal Meal in Corinth	119
8	Experiencing the Lord's Supper Today	139
Bibliography		151
General Index		161
Index of Ancient Literature		167
About the Author		173

Preface

The debate over eucharistic origins combines enormous stakes with an almost uniquely muddled *status quaestionis*. The conclusions of any such investigation have implications for Christian eucharistic practice in the present day, for our understanding of the historical Jesus, and for the relationship of the Christian faith to the Judaism from which it sprung. Combine these high stakes with the variety of scholars' religious persuasions, and you have a formula for theological *parti pris* and biased interpretation.

The aim of this book is to argue that scholars of eucharistic origins have wrongly rejected an explanation for Jesus' words and actions in the Last Supper narratives that was set out in 1925 by Robert Eisler and again in 1963 by David Daube. Although Daube's and Eisler's thesis has never compelled the assent of the majority of scholars, it has nonetheless exerted a continual fascination on a minority with its elegance and its "ring of truth." It deserves another hearing. My hope is that a third defense of the idea, at greater length than earlier ones, will cause other scholars to re-evaluate it and see its strengths. I believe that it has been rejected for bad reasons, mistakes of philology and history that have been repeatedly cited as facts. Part of the aim of this book is to return to the sources and interrogate them anew.

In urging another look at this hypothesis, I recognize that I am swimming against the current that has prevailed in the last thirty years of scholarship on eucharistic origins. Since Jeremias' attempted vindication of the origin of the eucharist in the final Passover meal of Jesus,[1] research has swung away from Jewish comparisons and background. It is claimed that the question of

---

[1] Joachim Jeremias, *The Eucharistic Words of Jesus* (Minneapolis, MN: Fortress, 1966).

whether the Last Supper was a Passover meal is "unknowable."² The NT's accounts of that meal are criticized as mutually contradictory unhistorical retrojections of the practices of the early Christian community.

If the NT accounts of the Last Supper are unhistorical, there is less reason to have patience for parsing and etymologizing of the words of those accounts, and scholars have accordingly sought elsewhere for light and understanding. In opposition to traditional and institutional Christian claims of a single dominical institution, scholars since the turn of the twenty-first century have argued that the evidence of the early Christian communities shows a diversity of eucharistic practices. As far back as H. Lietzmann and O. Cullmann, the existence of variation in early eucharistic meals has been taken as evidence that not all of the early church's eucharists were derived from the Last Supper.³ Lietzmann pointed out that the Alexandrian liturgy and the Didache do not contain any reference to the words of institution which the NT accounts ascribe to Jesus at the Last Supper; he thus posited a two-source theory of eucharistic origins. Cullmann went further by pointing to the bread-and-salt eucharists of the pseudo-Clementine epistles and the representation of the eucharist by the symbolism of fish in early Christian art. He traced these traditions to the post-resurrection appearances of Jesus, especially the participle συναλιζόμενος, "taking salt together" in Acts 1:3–4, and the meals of fish that the risen Lord had with his disciples (Lk. 24:42). More recently, Andrew McGowan's *Ascetic Eucharists* has presented evidence of early Christian meals using bread and cheese, bread and fish, and especially bread and water, and argues that these ascetic meals, eschewing wine because of its association with the "cuisine of sacrifice," ought to be taken as evidence "of just how diverse early Christian meal practice really was."⁴ A genetic account of the eucharist's

---

²The noted scholar of Christian liturgical history, Paul Bradshaw, writes, "the question of whether the Last Supper was a Passover meal does not seem particularly crucial. Even if it *were* a Passover meal, no exclusively paschal practices appear to have been retained in the primitive Church's eucharistic celebrations" (Bradshaw, 65). I find this an untenable opinion. What are we then to make of 1 Corinthians 5:7 and Melito of Sardis' *Peri Pascha*—to name only the most obvious Paschal associations and practices? Similarly, the Roman Catholic liturgiologist Louis Bouyer: "The undoubtedly insoluble argument whether the last meal Jesus took with his followers was the Passover meal or not need not delay us too much, since it focuses on a secondary point...All these arguments...are of no importance for the interpretation of the Last Supper and the eucharist to which it was to give rise" (Louis Bouyer, *Eucharist*, 99). Note the difference between Paul's claim that Jesus instituted the eucharist at the Last Supper and Bouyer's idea that the Last Supper somehow "gave rise to" the eucharist. The idea of "development" has a fascination for liturgical scholars out of all proportion to its explanatory power.

³Hans Lietzmann, *Messe und Herrenmahl—Eine Studie zur Geschichte der Liturgie* (Berlin, Verlag Walter de Gruyter, 1926), English translation by Dorothea Reeve as *Mass and Lord's Supper: A Study in the History of the Liturgy* (Leiden, E.J. Brill, 1979), and Oscar Cullmann, "La signification de la Sainte-Cène dans le christianisme primitif," *Revue d'Histoire et de Philosophie religieuses* (Strasbourg, 1936), translated in O. Cullmann and F.J. Leenhardt, *Essays on the Lord's Supper* (Atlanta, GA: John Knox Press, 1958).

⁴Andrew McGowan, *Ascetic Eucharists* (Oxford, 1999), 255.

origin in the Jewish Passover cannot account for such a diversity of eucharistic practices, but rather would tend to uniformity.

This emphasis on diversity has led many scholars to turn away from analysis of the Jewish cultural and linguistic background of the NT's institution narratives and to turn instead to sociological analysis of the more general phenomenon of meals in the Greco-Roman world, casting their nets wider in the hope of reaching less hotly contested conclusions, on the basis of more widely agreed evidence. The work of Dennis Smith, Hal Taussig, and the symposium on meals in the Greco-Roman world has brought to bear insights from first-century culture to highlight the roles of class, sex, power, and the social meanings of different foods and practices.[5] This literature draws on such texts as Plutarch's *Moralia*, Xenophon's *Memorabilia*, Petronius' *Satyricon*, Athenaeus' *Deipnosophistae*, and the poems of Martial, Horace, Catullus, and Juvenal to generalize about the social context of the meals in the early church.

At the same time, other scholars concerned not with the origins of the eucharist, but with the origins of Passover, have cautioned against the retrojection of later Rabbinic material concerning the Passover seder (order of service) back into the Second Temple period. Baruch Bokser and, more recently, Joshua Kulp have attempted to trace the development of the early Rabbinic Passover seder to decisive events in the history of Judaism that took place after the ministry of Jesus and the origins of Christianity, especially the fall of the Temple.[6] Since these events all happened after the time of Jesus, they can have played no role in the Passover meal which he celebrated with his disciples before his death. The appeals to rabbinic materials made by Eisler and Daube (as well as by later scholars such as Deborah Bleicher Carmichael, Alistair Stewart-Sykes, and others) are therefore discounted as anachronistic. Kulp even denies that there was a seder properly so called at the time of Jesus.

Given this *status quaestionis*, the present book may be fairly described as swimming upstream. It seeks to do three things: to lay out the history of Daube's and Eisler's idea; to examine the criticisms of it and show that they are mostly unfounded; to suggest that this explanation fits well with the current direction of research on the historical Jesus; and to sketch some of its consequences for Christian theology of the eucharist.

The first chapter, "The Historical Project," argues for the propriety, in principle, of using early Rabbinic sources to shed light on the New Testament.

---

[5] A. McGowan, *Ascetic Eucharists*; Hal Taussig and Dennis Smith, *Many Tables*; and the essays in Taussig and Smith, ed. *Meals in the Early Christian World*.

[6] Baruch Bokser, *The Origins of the Seder* (Berkeley, CA: University of California Press, 1984) and Joshua Kulp, "The Origins of the Seder and Haggadah" in *Currents in Biblical Research* 4.1 (2005), 109–134.

The second chapter, "The Passover Background," explains the importance of the Passover background and introduces Eisler's and David Daube's proposal concerning the bread at the Last Supper. Chapter 3, "Evidence from Jews and Greeks," adduces philological and historical evidence in confirmation of Daube's proposal, drawing on the Gospels, Paul, the Passover Haggadah, Melito of Sardis, and Jerome. Chapter 4, "Layers of Meaning," explores the likely meaning of the wine in light of three levels of increasingly specific context in the Hebrew Bible, in the covenant between YHWH and Israel, and in the Passover as it is attested in the Mishnah and Talmud. Chapter 5, "Mechanics and Misinterpretations," is likely to be the most controversial, since it contrasts the New Testament's very Jewish view of the Last Supper and Lord's Supper with the explanations of later Christian traditions. The chapter is not intended to be a comprehensive survey of Christian eucharistic theologies, but only an examination of the most prominent and influential views in light of Eisler's and Daube's thesis. Chapters 6 and 7 ("Rereading John 6" and "The Festal Meal in Corinth") argue that Eisler's and Daube's view fits well with the other important "eucharistic" texts of the NT outside the synoptic Gospels, namely, John 6 and 1 Corinthians 10–11. The eighth and last chapter, "Experiencing the Lord's Supper Today," sketches the implications of the book's thesis for twenty-first-century Christian praxis.

It is my hope that the work presented in this volume will be of help to scholars in NT studies, for whom I write as an outsider to their guild. My training, like that of Eisler and Daube, has been in an allied field (Classics), but not in NT studies. That comes with advantages and disadvantages: it may be that a fresh pair of eyes may see things that insiders have dismissed; but it may also be that as an outsider, I will blunder in ways that the guild would not. All errors are of course my own.

I am thankful to my editors at Fortress Academic, Neil Elliott and Gayla Freeman, and to my anonymous peer reviewer for suggestions which I have striven to incorporate; to my friends Mark Butler and Steve Schlissel for years of encouragement; to Samuel Bray for his frequent and generous assistance; and to Bishops Peter Manto and Daniel Morse of the Reformed Episcopal Church, for their partnership during my years as a missionary in the Philippines and Indonesia, when most of the manuscript was written. I owe the greatest debt of all to my wife, Sora, who first introduced me to Passover in our first year of marriage.

Abbreviations

b.	Babylonian Talmud (Bavli)
BCP	Book of Common Prayer
CAD	Chicago Assyrian Dictionary
CWDD	Collected Works of David Daube
HALOT	Hebrew and Aramaic Lexicon of the Old Testament
HThR	Harvard Theological Review
IG	Inscriptiones Graecae
JPS	Jewish Publication Society
JSNT	Journal for the Study of the New Testament
KJV	King James or Authorized Version of the Bible
LSJ	Liddell, Scott, Jones, and MacKenzie, A Greek-English Lexicon (9th edition)
LXX	Septuagint
m.	Mishnah
MT	Masoretic text
NT	New Testament
OT	Old Testament
t.	Tosefta
SBL	Society of Biblical Literature
TDNT	Theological Dictionary of the New Testament
y.	Palestinian Talmud (Yerushalmi)
ZNW	Zeitschrift für die Neutestamentliche Wissenschaft und die Kunde der älteren Kirche

Chapter One

The Historical Project

We are attempting "to put the Last Supper in its true Jewish setting, and to seek a meaning for the Words of Institution which harmonises with the actual situation in the Upper Room, and the thoughts and feelings natural to Jesus and his disciples on that occasion."[1] Understanding the NT accounts of the Last Supper is not only a matter of decoding the signification of various words and actions, but also of thinking our way into the heads of Jesus and His disciples.

This implies, of course, that we have any access to the historical words and actions of Jesus in the Upper Room. Some have doubted this. For instance, Bruce Chilton's study of the eucharist takes as its methodological assumption the idea that "the texts reflect the conscious practice of distinct and often separate circles of usage. . . . At each stage, the meaning attached to eucharistic practice corresponded to the social context of the circle concerned."[2] Chilton assumes that each book of the NT has a discrete Christian community ("the Johannine community" or "the Petrine community") as its intended audience. In a similar manner, some scholars refer to the gospels and Paul's accounts of the Last Supper as "liturgical texts," by which they mean that the formulas and phrases of the early church's eucharistic celebrations have been put in the mouth of Jesus. The methodological assumption that the gospels are products of, and written for, different local Christian communities has been called into question by the work of Richard Bauckham.[3] He points out that the church in the apostolic age was highly mobile and interconnected, with traveling missionaries

---

[1] T.H.W. Maxfield, *The words of institution; a study of the Hebrew background of the Holy communion service* (Cambridge: W. Heffer & Sons, 1933).

[2] Bruce Chilton, *A Feast of Meanings* (Leiden: E.J. Brill, 1994), ix.

[3] Richard Bauckham, ed. *The Gospels for all Christians: Rethinking the Gospel audiences*. (Grand Rapids, MI: Eerdmans, 1997).

and apostles moving around the Mediterranean world and sending letters from one church to another in full expectation that such letters would be copied and disseminated more widely. We cannot assume that the eucharistic theology of 1 Corinthians is peculiar to the Pauline churches; still less that the account of the Last Supper in the synoptics is an aetiological myth created by the "Matthaean" and "Marcan" and "Lucan" communities. Chilton's method is to identify differing eucharistic theologies from "the circle of Peter," "the circle of James," "the Pauline and synoptic positions," and "the Johannine circle." Bauckham's judgment is apropos: "Those who no longer think it possible to use the Gospels to reconstruct the historical Jesus compensate for this loss by using them to reconstruct the communities that produced the Gospels."[4]

One of the challenges that besets this approach is the need to distinguish between the historical utterances and actions of Jesus in the upper room and the tendency of early Christian sources to project onto that historical moment ideas that have their proper *Sitz im Leben* only in the early church after Jesus, and not in the circle of Jesus and his disciples. Rudolf Pesch attempted to distinguish between the Pauline narration of the Last Supper in 1 Corinthians 11, which he characterized as a *Kultätiologie* expressing the founding of the early Christian community's rituals, and the *berichtende Erzählung*, historical reportage, of Mark's gospel.[5] Similarly Maurice Casey, an advocate of Marcan priority as a solution to the Synoptic question, sees Mark's gospel as containing credible historical eyewitness testimony, complete with telltale signs of Aramaic interference in its Greek, but he considers the Pauline account of the Last Supper to be "rewritten to meet the situation with which he was faced in Corinth."[6] This is not to say that 1 Corinthians 11 is a wholly unhistorical myth, but that it is a retelling of the synoptic tradition of the Last Supper, adapted for the occasional and pastoral purposes of Paul's letter. Casey, however, is correct that the account in Mark is the closest to the events: "This source was written by an Aramaic-speaking Jew from Israel, who was writing for people who shared *his* cultural assumptions."[7] What is more, Mark's account of Jesus' final Passover "shows no signs of rewriting in the interests of the early church in general, or of the community to which Mark belonged."[8]

---

[4] Richard Bauckham, "For Whom Were the Gospels Written?" in *The Gospels for All Christians* (Grand Rapids, MI: Eerdmans, 1997), 20.

[5] Rudolf Pesch, *Das Abendmahl und Jesu Todesverständnis* (Basel: Editiones Herder, 1978), 32–34 and 90–101. Pesch especially traces the meaning of the bread-word to the Mishnah's description of the matzah as "Brots der Bedrängnis," "bread of affliction" (לֶחֶם עֹנִי)

[6] Casey, *Jesus of Nazareth*, 437.

[7] Casey, *Aramaic Sources*, 237; cf. also Maurice Casey, "No Cannibals at Passover," *Theology* 96 (1993), 200.

[8] Casey, *Jesus of Nazareth*, 437.

HISTORICAL DETAILS OF MARK'S ACCOUNT

It is true that Mark's account omits most of the details of the actual Passover meal. There is no mention of the bitter herbs, the prayers, the narration of the Exodus, or even the consumption of the lamb itself. These omissions, however, are not dispositive: it is as though a critic of the movie *Die Hard* were to object that John McTiernan's movie did not depict the singing of Christmas carols or the exchanging of presents, and therefore could not really have been set during Christmas. That is, the omissions are all things that both the author and his Jewish readers would have known without being told. The fact that it was Passover is scene-setting, and it is accordingly stated explicitly in exactly the places where we should expect such scene-setting: in 14:1, where the intent of Jesus' enemies to destroy him is disclosed; and again, two days later, in 14:12, when the action introduced by 14:1 is resumed after being interrupted by the episode of the woman anointing Jesus with perfume (14:3–9). Mark 14:12 uses an adverbial clause to place the action of the chapter precisely in time: τῇ πρώτῃ ἡμέρᾳ τῶν ἀζύμων, ὅτε τὸ πάσχα ἔθυον. . . . The verb ἔθυον should be taken in the most straightforward progressive sense, to indicate that the slaughtering of the Passover lambs was taking place when Jesus' disciples asked him where to prepare a room for him.[9] It should not be taken as denoting the repeated or habitual action ("when Jews usually sacrificed the Passover"), since this lends no specificity at all, and would be wholly otiose in light of 14:1. The slaughtering of lambs at the Temple was a major part of the Second Temple Passover. Casey lays great stress upon the sensory power of this aspect of the feast: the smells, the blood, the sounds of victims and of slaughter.

Why had no room been procured already? Earlier arrangements were impossible because short-notice preparations were necessary in order to avoid the plot that had already been set in motion (14:1–2) by the chief priests and scribes to arrest Jesus and put him to death; likewise, the elaborate instructions (14:13–16) involving (1) entry into the city, (2) encounter with an unmistakable person, (3) an utterance that will gain the desired object, and (4) the interlocutor's compliance with the request are not only an echo of the story of the anointing of Saul (1 Sam. 10), but are a device to avoid being waylaid or ambushed by Jesus' enemies. These details have a clear *Sitz im Leben* within the ministry of Jesus, and not in the early church's later celebrations.

---

[9]Casey further suggests, more speculatively, that this detail is given because the proper time to sacrifice the Passover lamb was a live issue of halakhic debate in the first century, citing the Mishnah account of disagreement between R. Joshua ben Hananiah and Ben Bathyra (*m.Zev.* 1.4). Casey, *Aramaic Sources*, 223–225.

The term πάσχα is Aramaic, פסחא. In 14:1, it denotes the feast as a whole, and is followed by an explanatory gloss: ἦν δὲ τὸ πάσχα καὶ τὰ ἄζυμα. In 14:12 it denotes the one-year-old lamb. It is "part of the evidence that the background to the oldest Gospel narratives is Aramaic rather than Hebrew."[10] The word used for "the feast of unleavened bread," the neuter plural ἄζυμα, is also an Aramaism since it is derived from the Aramaic determinative form פטירא, which appeared to a Greek-speaking ear to be a neuter plural ending in -α. (The same phenomenon explains why the NT uses σάββατα in the plural to denote the Sabbath: the determinative שבתא likewise appeared to Greek ears to be neuter plural, and indeed, the singular σάββατον is likely a back-formation from this false plural.) The numerous Aramaisms in Mark 14 are clear indications that its account of the Last Supper comes from a Jewish source close to the events or even a participant in them. Casey argues persuasively for a date earlier than 40 CE.

The narrative distinguishes between the Twelve and the disciples (μαθηταί). As Jeremias notes, the need to rent a room was typical of Passover, when the city of Jerusalem was inundated with pilgrims. Mark expressly designates the room as an ἀνάγαιον μέγα—surely an accommodation larger than necessary for thirteen men, and intended rather for a larger crowd of disciples of indeterminate number. It is some of these disciples, not the Twelve, who had inquired about the room (14:12), and Jesus instructs some of these disciples ("you") to make ready for "us." Mark 14:17's notice that "he came with the Twelve" is to be understood in contrast to the other disciples who had procured the room and prepared it. Similarly, Jesus' response to the inquiry about who would betray him is phrased in a way that makes good sense in the context of a larger gathering than just thirteen people. Verse 17 specifies the betrayer as "one of you who eats with me"; this is not specific enough, so there is further discussion, and Jesus specifies further: "It is one of the twelve, who dips with me in the dish." (14:20) We may thus understand the scene to involve more than thirteen persons.

There follows an account, not of the Passover meal itself so much as of the things that Jesus did and said during it. The bitter herbs are not mentioned. The consumption of the lamb is omitted. There is no account of the prayers and recitations that would probably have accompanied the meal. From these omissions, some have concluded that the meal was not a Passover meal. But these details are omitted because they were not significant, and would only have distracted from the main point of the narrative: to relate the things that Jesus said and did in relation to his impending death. It was the bread and wine that he singled out for special treatment and words of interpretation. That is why those elements are mentioned, and not others.

---

[10]Casey, *Aramaic Sources*, 221.

Scholars have assumed that the reference of Jesus' word "this" in "this is my body" is ascertainable by historical reconstruction (i.e., by envisioning in their minds' eye the scene in the upper room). This is the correct approach, but far from simplifying the problem, it indicates the difficulty of the task: make the attempt for any modern meal, and you will see that "common sense" is the last thing that dictates *mores* at the meal table. I know a high school that offers a protocol class to help its students learn the right way of proposing a toast and how to tell the salad fork from the lobster fork. If the meal table were governed by plain common sense, it would not be such an arena of confrontation between parents and toddlers ("Eat your peas, or no dessert for you!"). Rather, we want others to eat "properly" and in the "polite" way, especially at the table. Almost no area of human life is so ritualized and mannered as our meals. And the Last Supper was not just a meal, but a festal meal, laden with symbolic meaning, and therefore even more wrapped in protocol and manners. Then, too, it was an ancient Jewish festal meal, so that its protocol and manners are alien to us in the modern English-speaking world. The details of the New Testament's accounts of the Last Supper cannot be approached as though common sense could tell us what they mean. Instead, we must try to think our way into the worldview of Jesus and his disciples in first-century Israel.[11]

ON THE USE OF RABBINIC SOURCES

Here we are faced with a daunting set of difficulties. We are not, most of us, Jewish. And even the Jews among us are still separated from the events in the Upper Room by two thousand years of history, and by the huge changes that occurred in the Passover as a result of the destruction of the Temple. How, then, are we to think our way back into the mindset or worldview of Jesus and his disciples? Some would give a counsel of despair at this point: the project is impossible because the necessary data are not available. But this is too pessimistic. In the 1950s, David Daube "lamented the pettiness of Jewish scholars who excluded the New Testament from their studies and Christian scholars who carried on a tradition of what he called 'theological anti-Semitism.'"[12] By contrast, while I was doing research for the present volume,

---

[11]The term for this enterprise of mutually correcting rereading and rethinking is "the hermeneutical spiral." For discussion of the epistemological issue and the proper solution to it, cf. N.T. Wright, *The New Testament and the People of God* (London: SPCK, 1991), chapter 2, as well as Ben F. Meyer, *Critical Realism and the New Testament* (Eugene, OR: Pickwick Publications, 2009), and more recently, Grant Osborne, *The Hermeneutical Spiral: A Comprehensive Introduction to Biblical Interpretation* (Downers Grove, IL: Intervarsity Press, 2010).

[12]Daube's protégé Calum Carmichael in the preface to *Collected Works of David Daube II: New Testament Judaism*. (Berkeley, CA: The Robbins Collection, 2000). p. xvii.

Hebrew Union College (Cincinnati, OH) instituted the New Testament as required reading for its Rabbinics students. Nonetheless, the number of Jewish scholars with a thorough knowledge of the New Testament remains small.[13] The proportion of Christian scholars with a thorough familiarity with the Talmud and other Judaica is probably even smaller. The late David Daube's insights—one of which is the foundation for the thesis of this book—were the product of his expert knowledge of both literatures, Jewish and Christian. Robert Eisler also was Jewish, and spent fifteen months in Buchenwald and Dachau before being released and settling in England.

Much remains to be done. The standard five-volume commentary on the New Testament from ancient Jewish sources, Strack and Billerbeck's *Kommentar zum Neuen Testament aus Talmud und Midrasch*, remains unavailable in English. Even though it is widely viewed as outdated and unreliable, it has not been replaced by anything better.[14] Jewish literature in general is relatively inaccessible to English readers, though this problem is gradually improving. The so-called "New Perspective" on Paul in academic studies of the New Testament has put aside some of the more unfortunate caricatures of Judaism that have influenced Christian theology in the past, replacing them with a more accurate and sympathetic portrait of Judaism in the Second Temple period. Nonetheless, most Christian seminaries require students to read only the Bible and intertestamental Jewish literature (e.g., Philo, the Apocrypha, apocalyptic literature, and the documents from Qumran). They pay little attention to Rabbinic literature because it is deemed to be chronologically irrelevant to the New Testament. Since this book advances an interpretation of the New Testament based on this later Rabbinic literature, it would be well to establish the propriety of that method at the outset.

What sources are we concerned with? After the destruction of Jerusalem by Titus in 70 CE, and the crushing defeat of Bar Kochbah's revolt in 135, Roman persecution prompted the Jews to act to preserve their cultural and religious heritage. Rabbi Judah the Prince directed the compilation of the Mishnah, a summary and selection of Jewish law. The work was probably finished around 220 CE (though the traditional date is 189 CE). One of his pupils, R. Ḥiyya, completed a second collection, the Tosefta, around 250. The roughly 120 rabbis from 50–200 CE whose opinions are cited in the Mishnah and Tosefta are known as the Tannaim ("those who repeat or learn"), and material ascribed to them is commonly called Tannaitic. The next period, from 200 to 500 CE is the period of the Amoraim ("those who tell over"), rabbis

---

[13]See R. Zoll, "Reform Rabbi Michael J. Cook Says Jews Are Handicapped by Not Knowing New Testament" (Associated Press, April 8, 2006).

[14]David Instone-Brewer's multi-volume *Traditions of the Rabbis from the Era of the New Testament* supplies some of the needs met by Strack-Billerbeck, but in the opposite direction, commenting on the Rabbis and using the NT as evidence. In particular, he attempts to provide a better chronology.

who commented on the opinions of the earlier Tannaim. Their discussions were compiled into two massive collections of commentary on the Mishnah, known as the Jerusalemite or Palestinian Talmud (or Talmud Yerushalmi) and the larger, more authoritative Babylonian Talmud (or Talmud Bavli). These date from around 420 CE and 520 CE respectively. The contents of the Mishnah and Talmud are relevant to the study of New Testament narrative (the gospels and Acts) because they are compendia of Rabbinic rulings and opinions about *halakhah*, practical morality, which can be observed to be at work in the NT's narratives.

In addition to the Mishnah and Talmud, we have various early Jewish commentaries. The most important is the Midrash Rabba, a collection of separate commentaries on the five Books of Moses, the Song of Solomon, Ruth, Lamentations, Ecclesiastes, and Esther. Like the Talmud, the Midrash Rabba contains chronologically diverse strata. Also like the Talmud, it contains much that is Tannaitic in date. Finally, there is the Mekhilta, a commentary on Exodus that may date from the 1st century CE. The Mekhilta and Midrash Rabba are relevant to the study of the New Testament because they preserve early Jewish exegesis, which can be compared to the exegesis of Jesus and Paul.

All these Rabbinic sources contain material useful and relevant to the study of the New Testament. Unfortunately, there are some scholars who defend the propriety of Christian ignorance of post-Christian Jewish literature, even asking outright, "Why should Christians care what the Talmud says?" This attitude is sometimes justified by the observation that the Talmud contains nothing other than the "oral law" that Jesus condemned (Mt. 15:9). Worse, the earlier Talmud, the Yerushalmi or Palestinian, was not compiled until 420. How, then, can it shed any light on the New Testament?

Such objections rest upon a mistaken understanding of the early Rabbinic documents. Precisely because it transmits the Jewish legal and religious tradition, the Talmud turns out to contain many things that go back to times even before the New Testament. Thus, readers of the Talmud are not like archaeologists who discover a papyrus of Aeschylus or Epicurus. Rather, they are more like Heinrich Schliemann excavating Troy: they deal with strata of material, of various ages. The fact that the final form of the Talmud is from the middle ages is no reason to think that it tells us nothing about the time of Jesus and Paul. After all, "before the Qumrân discoveries we also had no copy of a Hebrew text of the Bible prior to the 9th century."[15]

The gospels of the New Testament show us Jesus and his disciples, their friends and their enemies, all living and acting in an ancient Palestinian social

---

[15]Louis Bouyer, *Eucharist: Theology and Spirituality of the Eucharistic Prayer* (South Bend, IN: University of Notre Dame Press, 1968), 23.

context that was governed by earlier stages and parts of *halakhah*. For instance, when Jesus is rebuked by the Pharisees for allowing his disciples to pluck and eat grain on the Sabbath (Mk. 2:23–28), his adversaries would have had no case to argue unless they had had some precise definition of "work" on the Sabbath that would cover what his disciples were doing. As it turns out, shucking wheat kernels falls under the Mishnah's prohibition against grinding on the Sabbath (*m.Shabbath* 7:2). Thus, although the Mishnah is later than the New Testament, we can see that this prohibition, or a similar one, was in force in Pharisaic circles at the time of Christ. The handling of Rabbinic sources in this book will follow this pattern of reasoning.[16]

I am most concerned with traditions concerning Passover, which is attested in the earliest Jewish sources available: the Mishnah (c. 220 CE), the Tosefta (c. 250), and the two Talmuds, Yerushalmi (420) and Bavli (520). That these were all compiled much later than the New Testament is no reason for excluding them from comparison with it. We would do well to keep in mind that the Talmud includes traditions, rules, and ways of looking at the world that were operative at the time of Jesus, and can be demonstrated to be at work in the narratives of the gospels and the letters of Paul.

For instance, while Jesus is praying in Gethsemane, his disciples fall into a deeper and deeper sleep. The Talmud distinguishes between a doze and a proper sleep. The former does not bring about the dissolution of a company (*ḥaburah*) celebrating the Passover, the latter does. Jesus and his disciples are still constituting a *ḥaburah* as they go out from the upper room. He asks them to "watch and pray." David Daube comments:

> R. Ashi, at the beginning of the 5th cent., defines the meaning of "a doze," which does not bring about a dissolution of the *ḥaburah*, as opposed to "a proper sleep," which does. A man, he says, merely dozes "if, when addressed, he replies but does not know how to answer sensibly." This late comment is curiously reminiscent of Mark's description of the state in which the disciples were when Jesus returned the second time: "neither wist they what to answer him."[17]

---

[16] N.T. Wright surveys the current state of Rabbinic sources in a footnote: "For a while many drew back from using the rabbis (see, still, e.g. Schnabel 2009, 488) because it was so hard to be sure which material could be dated when. The work of Instone-Brewer 1992 advanced different claims; and in Instone-Brewer 2004 (see e.g. 28–40), the beginning of a massive project, he claims to provide more clarity and chronological discernment. Reviewers have not (to put it mildly) been convinced (see e.g. Hezser 2005). Segal 2003, 162 suggests that in the place of a project like Strack-Billerbeck, going through the NT and providing rabbinic 'parallels,' one might better write a commentary on the Mishnah finding parallels in the NT and using them to date early traditions—not totally unlike Instone-Brewer's project, and one suspects equally unwelcome to many." N.T. Wright, *Paul and the Faithfulness of God* (London: SPCK, 2013), 81 n. 20. This, in a nutshell, is precisely what Daube does: where the NT shows a Talmudic custom or law evidently being practiced, we may conclude that something like it dates from NT times.

[17] David Daube, "Two Incidents after the Last Supper" in *Collected Works of David Daube vol. 2: New Testament Judaism*, ed. Calum Carmichael (Berkeley, CA: the Robbins Collection, 2000), 444.

Jesus' remark upon finding the disciples asleep a third time is ambiguous: καθεύδετε τὸ λοιπὸν καὶ ἀναπαύεσθε. This has usually been translated and punctuated as a question: "Are you still sleeping and taking your rest?" or else as an exasperated imperative: "Sleep, now, and take your rest." But neither of these options accounts for the word τὸ λοιπὸν.[18] Indeed, it is omitted from most English translations. In light of the Talmud's evidence, and the Paschal circumstances of the events in Gethsemane, it becomes more likely that the most literal translation is the most accurate: "you are sleeping the remainder and taking your rest"—meaning, "You have passed from dozing to slumber, and are now properly sleeping." We need not imagine that R. Ashi's rule was in force in his own words at the time of Jesus; obviously, this is chronologically impossible. But it is unlikely to be a coincidence that a similar criterion of slumber plays a role in the gospels' narratives of the vigil in Gethsemane. Rather, the narrative of the prayer in Gethsemane presupposes that the Jews were concerned with the relation of sleep and observance of holy days, and that some similar criterion of sleep was at work.[19]

The Mishnah's tractate Niddah informs us that in CE 66, as Jewish nationalism and separatism intensified before the coming Roman onslaught, the radical Shammaite sect of Pharisees gained control of the assembly and enacted a rule that all Samaritan women "are menstruants from their cradle." (*m.Nidd.* 4.1) Another tractate of the Mishnah, Kelim (*m.Kel.* 1.1ff) deals with uncleanness being conveyed from an unclean person to a vessel. Keeping these passages in mind, we turn to John 4, the story of Jesus and the Samaritan woman at the well. Already you will see the application I wish to make, but there is a more specific point: many English translations render the verb συγχρῶνται in 4:9 by "Jews have no dealings with Samaritans" (e.g., the Authorized Version). The meaning of the verb is difficult to settle by Greek philology alone; indeed, the standard Greek lexicon (LSJ) actually includes the meaning "to have social dealings with one" under συγχράομαι, citing John 4:9 as its only example. But the Mishnah's evidence makes it certain that the proper translation is the woodenly literal one: "Jews do not use [sc. vessels] in common with Samaritans." This translation is confirmed by the Samaritan woman's reply to Jesus, "Sir, you have nothing to draw with"—implication: you cannot use my pitcher, since your Jewish cleanness rules prevent you.

---

[18] It is true that LSJ give the latter option as a meaning under λοιπὸν, citing Mark 14:41 and Matthew 26:45: "sleep now . . ." However, since these are the very passages at issue, and since no other passages in Greek literature are given to support this meaning, it seems best to look for another in the present case.

[19] Lachs objects to Daube's interpretation on the grounds that "the Mishnah has reference to those at table, not those who were outside." Samuel Tobias Lachs, *A Rabbinic Commentary on the New Testament* (Hoboken, NJ: Ktav, 1987), 414. This is not persuasive, in light of the rules concerning what counts as "under one roof" and the evident desire of Jesus for the continuation of his company's fellowship.

As in the case of the slumber in Gethsemane, the evidence of the Talmud regarding Samaritan women and their pitchers does not overthrow our understanding of the passage. Jesus' point is that the worship of God in spirit and truth will soon spell an end to the ethnic and religious conflict between Jews and Samaritans, and this point remains clear whether we have the Mishnah or not. But the circumstances and details of the story become clearer and more vivid. Instead of general avoidance of social intercourse, the story's premise turns out to be the uncleanness of Samaritan women and its specific transmission via vessels of water.

The two examples I have given here, about slumber and about uncleanness, demonstrate the general usefulness of the Jewish background, even when it cannot be recovered except from Rabbinic sources that postdate the NT by several centuries. In each of these cases, there is a puzzling aspect that cannot be solved without the Rabbinic sources. In Gethsemane, why does Jesus check twice and then give up? Why does the text bother to say, "They knew not what to answer him?" In John 4, what is the precise meaning of συγχρῶνται? And why does the Samaritan woman say "You have nothing to draw with"? In both cases, the explanation from Talmudic sources rings true because it explains these otherwise mysterious or intractable difficulties. In general, the more such details or linguistic difficulties can be accounted for, the more persuasive the interpretation or explanation. I have taken the time to go through these examples from David Daube because I hope they will remove some of the stumbling-blocks that might prevent some readers from accepting the similar case I want to make about the Last Supper.

With this methodology, then, let us turn to the Last Supper and attempt to consider it through first-century Jewish eyes.

Chapter Two

The Passover Background

In his seminal 1996 study of the historical Jesus, N.T. Wright urged that scholars studying the NT must make a special effort to understand symbolic actions as a crucial part of the worldview of Second Temple Judaism and of Jesus and his disciples:

> Modern westerners, who live in a world that has rid itself of many of its ancient symbols, and mocks or marginalizes those that are left, have to make a huge effort of historical imagination to enter into a world where a single action can actually say something. Unless we make the effort, however, we become the prisoners of our own culture, and should give up even trying to be historians. Words focus, limit and sharpen symbolic actions, but do not replace them. And the central symbolic action which provides the key to Jesus' implicit story about his own death is, of course, the Last Supper.[1]

The ritual is a Jewish one, to be explained in Jewish terms. The mechanics of its working must be Jewish no less than its symbolic meaning. Unfortunately, the Christian theological tradition from the Church Fathers to the present day has had almost no concern for describing the Supper in terms available to 1st century Jews eating Passover. And this is true of the narrative meaning of the Last Supper no less than of the metaphysics of the eucharist. To read most Christian sacramentology, one would never suppose that the meal had anything much to do with Israel's story except insofar as it concerns Jesus, who happens, almost incidentally, to be Israel's Messiah rather than the king or ruler of some other people. The point of the meal is sought in the individual's union with Christ, or in the Church's unity and discipline, or in the elements as (a re-presentation of) a sacrifice offered to God. There is barely a word of

---

[1] N. T. Wright, *Jesus and the Victory of God* (London: SPCK, 1996), 554.

the story of Israel in theologians' writings on the Supper. This is a staggering omission. If we believe that Jesus instituted the eucharist in the course of celebrating the Passover with his disciples, it ought to be inconceivable that the meal could be separated from the Israel-narrative within which it was conceived. Yet that is precisely what is done in many churches.

The same mistake, or worse, is made concerning the metaphysics of the Supper. It is a rare Christian theologian who asks how, say, the apostle Peter would have explained how the eucharist worked. Yet the danger here is acute, for Aristotelian metaphysics, Augustinian language about visible signs and invisible grace, or even the Reformers' theories about "eating by faith" all purport to *explain* the Supper, and explaining means supplying more readily understood terms for less well understood terms. And once we have done that, there is a great temptation to suppose that the more well understood terms of these second-order theological and metaphysical explanations are the basic reality behind the narrated description of the New Testament. But could not Jesus have had his own intended explanation for what he was doing? And could not the apostle Paul likewise?

AGAINST FALSE HUMILITY

The stakes are high because theories and mechanisms and metaphysics have bloomed into liturgy, practice, and devotion. Some have therefore tried to avoid the question. Perhaps the most famous statement of this strategy are the verses attributed to Elizabeth I in Richard Baker's *Chronicle* (1643):

> Christ was the word that spake it.
> He took the bread and brake it;
> And what his words did make it
> That I believe and take it.[2]

This is an expression of the virgin queen's quite understandable impatience with the theories of theologians. And to be sure, it sounds very humble to say, "We have no theory. We just believe Jesus' words, 'This is my body' without positing any further explanation." But this is not really a humble or neutral response. It is in fact an audacious claim about Jesus' communication to his disciples in the Upper Room. It is a claim that Jesus was deliberately saying something that his disciples could not understand; that, in fact, they did not understand it; that Jesus offered no further explanation to alleviate

---

[2] For a full discussion of this possibly apocryphal quatrain (also attributed to John Donne in the 1635 edition of his poems), see Elizabeth Hageman and Katherine Conway, *Resurrecting Elizabeth I in Seventeenth-Century England* (Vancouver: Fairleigh Dickinson University Press, 2007), 55–57.

their incomprehension; and finally, that the disciples said nothing to express their bewilderment on this occasion. For that is what we are commenting on: not a ritual or a miracle yet. Even if it might turn out to be those things on further investigation, we will only discover it to be so by first examining Christ's words as an utterance, an act of communication. If our account of the meaning of Jesus' words renders them incomprehensible to his disciples, or renders the disciples' reaction a non-sequitur, then we may be sure that we have not understood him correctly.³

CRITERIA AND THEMES

The right interpretation should offer a meaning that was (1) chronologically and culturally available to Jesus and his disciples (i.e., the sort of thing that Jews of that period could have understood, not a retrojected anachronism or modern theology read back into the historical account). This meaning should be (2) clearly and distinctly intended by Jesus and heard by the disciples, not drowned out by the comparative volume of other themes in the semiotic surroundings of the Upper Room. Finally, it should also (3) provide a solution to other puzzles. A good interpretation will remove misunderstandings, lay bare obscured meanings, and have a "ring" of truth to it.

What, then, did Jesus mean, and what did his disciples understand him to be saying? The semiotic ambience in which they sat on that night presented them with three themes above all others: the exodus from Egypt, eschatological expectation, and the Messiah. The first two both arose naturally from the disciples' time and place that night: they were gathered together in the Upper Room to commemorate Israel's redemption from Egypt, and with the expectation that God would take the same time of year as the occasion for the eagerly awaited restoration of the kingdom to Israel, and deliverance

---

³In a similar way, I must dissent from the usual account of the eucharist as a "mystery"—a label that is used both to excuse the incredible claims made for its mode of operation and to obviate the need to explain the metaphysics or mechanism of these claims. ("How can Christ be in or under the bread?" "It's a mystery!") This type of language is quite old, going back to the Fathers of the early church. Nonetheless, the New Testament nowhere calls either baptism or the Supper a "mystery." 1 Corinthians 4:1 is sometimes thought to do so, calling the apostles "stewards of the mysteries of God" (οἰκονόμους μυστηρίων θεοῦ), but examination of just what the "mysteries" of God were reveals that Paul has in mind such facts as the transformation of our bodies for life in the resurrection (1 Cor. 15:51), the consummation of the marriage between Christ and his church which earthly marriages symbolize (Eph. 5:32) and the inclusion of the Gentiles in the body of the church (Eph. 3, passim). In short, it denotes great events in the history of Israel, whether past or future, which it has been given to the apostles to disclose to the church. These, and not the sacraments, are the mysteries that the apostles are charged with stewarding (Eph. 3:1,9; Col. 1:25; 1 Cor. 9:17). Nor is the idea of the sacraments as inscrutable puzzles consistent with the rhetoric of the NT. When Paul asks, "The bread which we break, is it not (οὐχί) a sharing in the body of Christ?" (1 Cor. 10:16), he does not expect his Corinthian readers to reply, "Maybe, but I can't understand how."

from foreign domination. The third theme, the Messiah, was a subset of the second, since the Messiah's coming was itself one of the most looked-for eschatological events.

These three themes, then—Passover, eschatology, and the messiah—constituted the main interpretative background of the disciples as they sat with Jesus around the table. His utterances were understood by his disciples in terms of these themes, and not in terms of substance and accidents, material transformations, the initiatory rites of Greek mystery religions, or any other concept alien in time and space from the upper room in Jerusalem in 33 CE.

BAKED INTO ISRAEL'S STORY

And understand it they did. Not only is there no evidence that Jesus had to do any further explaining, but the Bible even says that when he later appeared to two disciples on the road to Emmaus, Jesus "was known to them in the breaking of bread" (Lk. 24:31). Why? Was it because Jesus had a peculiar way of breaking bread? No. Rather, Richard Hays helpfully explains the thought process of these disciples:

> Cleopas and his anonymous companion on the road to Emmaus are well acquainted with all the stories and traditions about Jesus' life, including the report of the empty tomb and the angelic proclamation of the resurrection, but they are nonetheless departing Jerusalem in a state of gloomy disappointment: "But we had hoped that he was the one to redeem Israel" (v. 21a). This is a moment of wrenching irony: Jesus, the redeemer of Israel, stands before them, yet they fail to recognize him. . . . The resurrection of Jesus will remain a mute, uninterpretable puzzle unless it is placed firmly within the OT's story of Israel. The disciples on the way to Emmaus had already heard it reported that Jesus was alive, but because they did not know how to locate this report within Israel's story, it seemed a curious and meaningless claim.[4]

What Jesus does for the two disciples on the way to Emmaus is expressed by Luke in these words: "Then beginning with Moses and all the prophets, he interpreted to them the things about himself in all the scriptures." Breaking bread with them was part of this explanation—indeed, it was the the final and most effective part of the explanation, the bit that turned the trick, removing the temporary blindness that had kept them from recognizing him (24:16): "their eyes were opened and they recognized him" (Lk. 24:31). Recognition was the goal—and not mere recognition ("That's Jesus!"), but recognition *in terms of Israel's story* ("This is Israel's Messiah, about whom all the prophets

---

[4]Richard Hays, *Reading Backward* (Waco, TX: Baylor University Press, 2014), ch. 1.

spoke!"). For the disciples were not thinking about "substance" or "vessels of grace" as they walked and then ate with Jesus. As their own words show, they were thinking in terms of Israel's story: ". . . we were hoping that he was the One who was going to redeem Israel."

The gospels are forthright and unashamed in telling us when the disciples did not understand Jesus' meaning on various occasions. "Is it because we forgot to bring bread?" (Mk. 8:14); "They did not know what to answer him." (Mk. 14:40) "He [Peter] did not know what he was saying." (Lk. 9:33). Had the words of our Lord at the Last Supper been incomprehensible to the disciples, the gospels would tell us. But this was not a time when Jesus intended to hide his meaning, but to reveal it. The breaking of bread and giving it to his disciples was a way of placing Jesus in Israel's story, with the result that "their eyes were opened and they recognized him." Explanation and food go together.[5]

THE IMPORTANCE OF THE PASSOVER CONTEXT

What is needed, wrote T.H.W. Maxfield in 1933, is "a meaning which harmonises with . . . the thoughts and feelings natural to Jesus and his disciples on that occasion."[6] Immediately, the project becomes different. No longer is it merely a matter of figuring out the signification of various words and actions,[7] but also of thinking our way into the perceptions of Jesus and his disciples. This means, above all, determining the role that the existent Passover rituals, and the theology of them, played in the Upper Room on that night.

---

[5] A similar process is at work later in the same chapter. These same two disciples have hastened back to Jerusalem to report Jesus' appearance to them. There they find the other disciples excited over the report of Jesus' resurrection and appearance to Peter. Then Jesus himself appears in the room, and uses again the combination of food and verbal explanation: "While they were still not believing from joy and were marveling, he said to them, 'Do you have anything to eat here?' And they gave him a piece of broiled fish, and he took it and ate it in front of them. And he said to them, 'These are my words which I spoke to you while I was still with you, that it is necessary for all the things to be fulfilled which are written in the law of Moses and the prophets and psalms concerning me.' Then he opened their mind to understand the Scriptures" (Lk. 24:41–45). Here the food is not bread, but fish. To investigate the reason for this difference would take us too far afield, but we may note that Jesus gave fish along with bread in the feeding of the two multitudes (δύο ἰχθύες in the feeding of the 5000 in Mt. 14:17, Mk. 6:38, Lk. 9:13; δύο ὀψάρια in Jn. 6:9; ὀλίγα ἰχθύδια in the feeding of the 4000 in Mt. 15:34 and Mk. 8:7), and ate fish after his resurrection when he appeared to his disciples at the Sea of Tiberias (ὀψάριον . . . καὶ ἄρτον in Jn. 21:9).

[6] Maxfield, *The Words of Institution*, x.

[7] Still less is it a matter of underlining "est" in "*hoc est corpus meum*" or insisting that "'is' means 'is.'" Analysis of this sort does not begin to meet the demands of the historical project and its necessary hermeneutical spiral: we must engage in the difficult and recursive process of revisiting our interpretation of the text in light of history, and of history in light of the text.

The reconstruction of the scene in the Upper Room[8] reached an apparent *ne plus ultra* in the work of the great twentieth-century German New Testament scholar, Joachim Jeremias. His masterful *Das Letzte Abendmahl Jesus* (trans. *The Eucharistic Words of Jesus*) brought to bear a level of erudition not previously seen in treatments of the Last Supper. Before Jeremias, there was a considerable contingent of scholars who doubted whether the Last Supper was a Passover meal. Jeremias' argument is an inductive one: the cumulative weight of numerous details is such as can only be explained by the Last Supper being a Passover meal. Unfortunately, some scholars have treated Jeremias' evidences as though they were intended to be deductive proofs, so that if one particular piece of evidence can be explained in some other way, the conclusion about Passover is thereby undermined. This is a methodological error, and a failure to appreciate the cumulative and inductive nature of Jeremias' argument.[9]

Jeremias adduces, among other things, the specifically designated drinkings of wine ("cup of blessing," "cup after supper"), the singing of the Hallel psalms, the reclining at table, the consumption of the meal at night (Jn. 13:30), and the speaking of "words of interpretation" over the bread and wine—all of which mark the meal as the Passover rather than an ordinary Jewish meal.[10] To these, we can add the apparent regulation of the gathering by the *halakhah* concerning the unity of sacred gatherings, or *haburot*,[11] which I discussed earlier. Above all, the synoptic gospels are unanimous and unequivocal about the date of the Last Supper: it was Passover.

---

[8]It is now the scholarly fashion within the mainstream academic guild to deny that this approach will be fruitful and to seek for the origins of the eucharist in the customs governing Roman convivia and Greek symposia; for instance, Andrew McGowan ("Rethinking Eucharistic Origins," *Pacifica* 23 (June 2010)) positions himself against traditional Christian scholarship on eucharistic origins by denying that "the earliest Christian communities celebrated their sacramental meal in direct imitation of the Last Supper of Jesus." Likewise, Paul Bradshaw, *The Search for the Origins of Christian Worship: Sources and Methods for the Study of Early Liturgy* (London: SPCK, 2002) 65 and *Eucharistic Origins* (London: SPCK, 2004), passim) denies that a single origin can explain the diversity he claims to find in early Christian eucharistic practice; Bradshaw also paints the landscape of 2nd temple Jewish liturgical practice as a bewildering diversity incapable of providing any explanation for eucharistic origins. Similar skeptical approaches are found in Dennis Smith and Hal Taussig, *Many Tables: The Eucharist in the New Testament and Liturgy Today* (London: SCM Press, 1990) and in Bryan Spinks, *Do This in Remembrance of Me: the Eucharist from the Early Church to the Present Day* (London: SCM Press, 2013).

[9]More recently, cf. Andreas Köstenberger, "Was the Last Supper a Passover Meal?" in T. Schreiner and M. Crawford, ed. *The Lord's Supper* (Nashville, TN: B&H, 2011), 6–30 and Scot McKnight, *Jesus and His Death*, 244–25; also I. Howard Marshall, *Last Supper and Lord's Supper* (Grand Rapids, MI: Eerdmans, 1980), 62–64.

[10]Cf. Jeremias, *Eucharistic Words*, 41–62.

[11]Cf. Daube "Two Incidents," 330–335.

JOHANNINE CHRONOLOGY OF THE PASSION WEEK VS THE SYNOPTICS?

Yet for over a century, some scholars have alleged that the fourth gospel conflicts with this chronology of the Passion week. The eye around which this tempest revolves is the phrase in John 19:14 stating when Christ was crucified: ἦν δὲ παρασκευὴ τοῦ πάσχα—"it was the preparation [day] of the Passover," which is taken by some critics to mean that it was the day before Passover when Christ was crucified. After all, if Friday was the "preparation of the Sabbath," then "the preparation day of the Passover" must have been the day before Passover. Thus, Franz Delitzsch translated the phrase into Hebrew as עֶרֶב פֶּסַח—"Erev Pesach," Passover Eve.[12] The Last Supper thus would have been two days too early to be a Passover seder proper, taking place on the evening before the day before Passover. William Oesterley believed that the allegedly discrepant Johannine chronology was proof that the Last Supper was not a Passover meal, and he accordingly attempted to find its antecedents in the "Kiddush meal." But this is a mistake. The correct translation of the phrase, put forth by Theodor Zahn in 1908,[13] is "it was the preparation [day] in the [week-long] Passover [feast]"—sc. the preparation day for the Sabbath, which is the denotation of παρασκευὴ when used substantively for this very day in all the synoptic gospels (Mt. 27:62, Mk. 15:42 ἦν παρασκευή, ὅ ἐστιν προσάββατον, Lk. 23:54, ἡμέρα ἦν παρασκευῆς) and for Friday generally in other 2nd Temple Judaic Greek sources (e.g. Josephus, *Antiquities* 16.6). The date of the Last Supper is thus unanimously fixed as the evening on which Passover itself arrived. (Jewish dates begin at sundown, and Passover was an evening meal.) There is no difference between the Synoptics and John on this point.[14]

---

[12]Franz Delitzsch, *The Delitzsch Hebrew Gospels* (Marshfield, MO: Vine of David, 2011) ad loc. The translation represents the text of Delitzsch revised after his death in 1890 by his pupil Gustaf Dalman.

[13]Theodor Zahn, *Das Evangelium des Johannes* (Leipzig: A. Deichert, 1908), 639. "Nun aber wollte Jo[hannes] durch den Zusatz τοῦ πάσχα zu dem in sich vollständigen Begriff παρασκευὴ 19, 14 ausdrücklich darauf aufmerksam machen, daß dieser Tag ein in die Passazeit fallender Freitag war." That the term πάσχα could denote either the day or the week-long feast was noted as early as the Venerable Bede's commentary on Luke. Cf. Migne, ed. *Patrologia Latina* 54, 592B.

[14]But for further discussion and proposed solutions of the alleged chronological discrepancy, cf. Etienne Nodet, "On Jesus' Last Supper" in *Biblica* 91 fasc. 3 (PIB 2010), 348–369 and Annie Jaubert, *The Date of the Last Supper* (Staten Island: Alba House, 1965), who posits that Jesus followed a divergent, sectarian calendar. The most influential discussion of the issue in the first part of the twentieth century was W.O.E. Oesterley's *The Jewish Background of the Christian Liturgy* (Oxford, 1925), 156–193. More recently, cf. Barry Smith, "The Chronology of the Last Supper," *Westminster Theological Journal* 53:1 (1991), 29–45, which vindicates the harmony of John's chronology with that of the synoptics. For discussion of the conflicting chronologies in connection with the evidence of Josephus, cf. Federico Colautti, *Passover in the Works of Josephus* (Leiden: E.J. Brill, 2002), 178.

Unfortunately, Zahn's explanation was summarily dismissed by Gustaf Dalman, who claims that the phrase is "never the Friday in the festive week, as Zahn suggests."[15] In support of this sweeping statement, Dalman cites *m.Pes.* 4.1, 8.8, and 10.1—none of which, however, uses the expression "preparation of the Passover" but only and always the unambiguous locution "the eve of the Passover" (עַרְבֵי פְסָחִים). The onus, then, remains on those who believe that παρασκευή can mean "the day before" just any day, rather than only Friday, the day before the Sabbath, when the Torah's prohibitions against work made it necessary to "prepare" for the Sabbath. More than a century later, no evidence has been offered.

Old scholarly problems die hard. In recent years, several scholars have continued to take the Johannine chronology as Dalman did, basing their opinion primarily on the same misunderstanding of the phrase παρασκευὴ τοῦ πάσχα in John 19:14.[16] But if we translate the phrase correctly as "Friday in the Passover week," then it turns out to express precisely the same chronology as the synoptic gospels: the Last Supper took place on Thursday; it was a Passover meal; and Jesus died on Friday. The entire problem is illusory, generated by mistaken philology and mistranslation.

The other considerations alleged to support a divergent Johannine chronology—John 13:1's use of the temporal phrase "before the Feast of the Passover" to mark the occasion when Jesus washed his disciples' feet, and the priests' wanting to remain clean so that they could eat τὸ πάσχα (Jn. 18:28)—are not decisive indicators one way or the other, since the maintenance of a state of purity would have been desirable throughout the week of the feast, and "before" is vague enough to admit of all possibilities ("How much before? Earlier the same evening?"). Josephus records that throughout the entire week-long festival "two bulls are killed, and one ram, and seven lambs. Now these lambs are entirely burnt, besides the kid of the goats which is added to all the rest, for sins; for it is intended as a feast for the priest *on every one of those days*." (Ant. 3.10.5) Thus the fact that Caiaphas and his fellow priests did not want to enter Pilate's court is not evidence that the

---

[15] Gustaf Dalman, *Jesus-Jeshua*, trans. P. Levertoff. (New York: MacMillan, 1929), 88.

[16] Thus, McKnight states that "When Jesus died, it was 'the day of Preparation of the Passover,' the sixth hour. This means the last supper could not have been Pesah." S. McKnight, *Jesus and His Death* (Waco, TX: Baylor, 2005), 271. Similarly, Jonathan Klawans, "Was Jesus' Last Supper a Seder?" *Bible Review*, October 2001 consistently chooses to make John conflict with the synoptics in a tour de force of anti-harmonizing, even citing the Jesus Seminar in an effort to discredit the testimony of the canonical gospels. Likewise, Bryan Spinks, *Do This in Remembrance of Me* (London: SCM Press, 2013), 5 rejects Jeremias' identification of the Last Supper as a Passover meal on the grounds of the alleged chronological conflict with John's gospel. Christoph Niemand, likewise: "Hier wird Jesus schon einen Tag früher, am Vorbereitungstag des Festes . . ." Christoph Niemand, "Jesu Abendmahl. Versuche zur historischen Rekonstruktion und theologischen Deutung," in *Forschungen zum Neuen Testament und seiner Umwelt* LPhThB 7, Bern: Lang, 2002, 81–122 at 87. It is truly remarkable how so simple an omission of philological due diligence has grown legs and traveled through the scholarship.

sacrifice of lambs on the first night of Passover had not yet happened; there were further sacrificial meals on subsequent nights which would have been consumed especially by the priests.[17]

Moreover, the idea that the Johannine chronology places Jesus' death on the day before Passover, before the feast had begun, is actually belied by John's gospel itself: Pilate is depicted offering to release a prisoner, since "it is a custom for you that I release one to you *during the Passover feast* (ἐν τῷ πάσχα—a temporal locution that might mean "on any of the days of the week-long feast," but cannot mean "before Passover")." (Jn. 18:39) The scene agrees in every detail with the corresponding scene in the synoptic gospels: Pilate presents the crowd with the choice of which prisoner to release, Jesus or Barabbas, and this is said to be a custom "on the occasion of the feast" (κατὰ ἑορτῆν), not before it. We may be skeptical of how close John's account of Jesus' death is to the events; we may prefer the account of Mark, which has more verifiable Semitisms and is generally agreed to be earlier; but once philology has done its proper work on the phrase παρασκευὴ τοῦ πάσχα, there remains no adequate basis in the text of John's gospel for the claim that its chronology of the death of Jesus conflicts with that of the synoptics. Therefore, the fourth gospel's chronology cannot be set against the synoptics in order to undermine their clear presentation of the Last Supper as a Passover meal.

Jeremias' treatment of the telltale indications that the Last Supper took place at Passover is fairly persuasive: details like the renting of a room, the going in and out of the city to another house in Bethany, the use of wine and the reclining posture—these are not the sorts of things that could be easily invented by a later writer who was ignorant of Passover customs in the Second Temple period. The objections that other scholars have made to Jeremias' argument from all these cumulative details have been unpersuasive. Maurice Casey correctly assesses the situation: "It is methodologically unsound to take small points like reclining one at a time, argue that there are circumstances where each separately might take place, declare verses 12–16 are really from somewhere else, and find ourselves left without the Passover meal so carefully prepared for in the beginning of this passage [sc. Mk. 14.12–26]."[18] Without attempting any thorough vindication of the historicity of the synoptic gospels' accounts of the event, we may take it as uncontroversial that they present the Last Supper as either itself a Passover meal, or at the very least as a meal within the Passover milieu.[19] Attempts to explain the

---

[17]In defense of this possibility, cf. the essay of Mitch Glaser, "Passover in the Gospel of John" in Bock and Glaser, ed. *Messiah in the Passover* (Grand Rapids, MI: Kregel, 2017), 70–72.

[18]Maurice Casey, *Aramaic Sources of Mark's Gospel*, 229.

[19]Scot McKnight, while demurring from Jeremias' Paschal date, nonetheless finds the semiotic ambience of Passover determinative for the meaning of the Last Supper, since he rightly recognizes that all meals during the week of the feast would have been full of the same sort of overtones as the

NT accounts of Jesus' words at the Last Supper must therefore reckon with the gospels' presentation of that meal as Passover.[20]

A POLITICALLY CHARGED FESTIVAL

If the meal was Passover, and if the Exodus, eschatology, and the Messiah were the three main topics on which first-century Jewish minds dwelt during a Passover feast, how do Jesus' words fit into these themes? Passover, being a celebration of the origins of the nation of Israel in the events of the Exodus, was inescapably *political*. For a nation under foreign rule, the celebration of their past deliverance from Pharaoh intensified their hopes for eventual deliverance from Rome. This hope was bound up with the human agent of this deliverance, the Messiah, who was expected to arrive on Passover, and to restore the kingdom to Israel.[21] This messianic expectation apparently survived the destruction of the Temple, and is echoed in Rabbinic sources. The earliest commentary on Exodus, the *Mekhilta*, gives it as a dictum of Rabbi Joshua ben Hananiah (c. 90) that "In that night they were redeemed, and in that night they will be redeemed."[22] This expectation persisted for a millennium: the tenth–twelfth-century Exodus Rabbah likewise declares: "Let this sign be in your hands: on the day when I wrought salvation for you, on that very night know that I will redeem you."[23] Jerome in his commentary on Matthew (c. 398) notes that "It is a tradition of the Jews that the Messiah will come in the middle of the night, in the likeness of the time in Egypt when the Passover was celebrated."[24] The Exodus was the paradigm of national salvation, so its

---

Passover meal itself: "The meals of Passover week, not excluding *Pesah* itself, would have been joyous occasions celebrating God's past liberation and anticipating God's future liberation. In the middle of such a meal Jesus suddenly shifted the mood from joyous celebration of God's liberation to morose contemplation of his own death." McKnight, *Jesus and His Death*, 273.

[20]"Whatever conclusions may ultimately be reached in the current attempt to find a parallel for the institution of the Lord's Supper—if not its actual origin—in the solemn community meals of the Qumran sectaries, from a *formgeschichtliche* point of view there remains the very strong likelihood that, at any rate, the writers of the Synoptic Gospels saw the origin of this institution in the *seder* service of the Jewish Passover." Jakob Josef Petuchowski, "'Do this in remembrance of me' (1 Cor. 11:24)," *Journal of Biblical Literature* 76.4 (Dec. 1957), 293.

[21]Contrary to McKnight, *Jesus and His Death*, 334, there is abundant evidence that this was in fact the case. Even if we did not have historical evidence of repeated nationalist uprisings fueled by eschatological expectation, the conduct of the inhabitants of Jerusalem who welcomed Jesus on Palm Sunday would be inexplicable apart from such eschatological expectations. On top of this, the rabbinic evidence for eschatological expectations at Passover is as early as 90 CE. Skepticism on this point is untenable.

[22]Mekhilta ad Exodus 12:42. Cf. Jeremias, *Eucharistic Words*, 206. Cf. also Targ. Jer. I Ex. 12:42.

[23]Ex. R. 18.12 on 12:42. For other Jewish sources reflecting this expectation that the messiah would come on Passover, cf. Jeremias, *Eucharistic Words*, 207, n. 2.

[24]Jerome, *Commentary on the Gospel of Matthew* 25:6, from Migne, PL 26, 192. (My translation.)

details were scrutinized and pressed into service to determine the shape of the coming deliverance by the messiah.

Accordingly, we find that many leaders of Jewish rebellions chose Passover as the day on which to put their plans into action. The choice was a strategically shrewd one: for any leader hoping to rally popular support and play upon Jewish nationalism, Passover offered the chance to exploit nationalistic zeal at its annual zenith. We can see that these passions were at work, seething and ready to erupt also in Jesus' day: "Then the chief priests, the scribes, and the elders of the people assembled at the palace of the high priest, who was called Caiaphas, and plotted to take Jesus by trickery and kill him. But they said, 'Not during the festal procession (ἐν τῇ ἑορτῇ), lest there be an uproar among the people.'" (Mt. 26:3–5) But this was not the first or last time. On Herod's death in 4 BCE, a revolt began on Passover, provoking reprisals and suppression by his son Archelaus.[25] In 6 CE, the father of Zealotry, Judas of Galilee, chose to launch his revolt on Passover.[26] Under Cumanus, Pilate's successor as procurator of Judea (48–52), there was a riot at Passover in which 20,000 Jews were killed, attacks by brigands were made against the Romans, and there was further looting of the Temple by Roman troops.[27] Agrippa chose Passover as the time to execute James, the brother of John and head of the Jerusalem church (Acts 12:2), perhaps singling him out as the likeliest heir to the mantle of messianic pretensions that he, as the reigning Herodian monarch, thought it best to snuff out. Indeed, so frequently did this pattern of Jewish unrest at Passover repeat itself that Josephus even remarks upon it as a general trend: "But when [Alexander] had made slaves of the citizens of all these cities, the nation of the Jews made an insurrection against him at a festival; *for at those feasts seditions* (στάσεις) *are generally begun*. . . ."[28] The fatal siege of Jerusalem by Rome also began during the week of Passover in 65, trapping inside the besieged city a vast multitude of Jewish pilgrims who would not otherwise have been in Jerusalem.[29]

To disciples already occupied with these themes of national deliverance and the Messiah, Jesus spoke words over the unleavened bread. Here is the act of communication that we must understand.

---

[25]For accounts of the revolt, cf. Josephus, *Ant.* 17.206–18; *War* 2.1–13.

[26]Josephus, *Ant.* 18.1.

[27]The riot was supposedly caused by a Roman soldier stationed on the roof of the Temple portico exposing himself to the Jews in the courtyard below. Cf. Josephus, *Ant.* 20.105–12; *War* 2.224–7; *Ant.* 20.113–17; *War* 2.228–31.

[28]Josephus, *War* 1.88.

[29]Josephus, *War* 6.9. The Romans were well aware of the Jews' heightened nationalistic fervor during festivals. Josephus also informs us that the Romans customarily "were armed, and kept guard at the festivals, to prevent any rebellion which the multitude gathered together might attempt" (Josephus, *War* 2.12.1).

THIS IS . . .

Jesus' words are *deictic*: they begin with a demonstrative, "This is . . ." This form has been rightly recognized as a typically Jewish utterance over the food at Passover; it was available to Jesus in 33 CE. The medieval Haggadah records a formally similar utterance in Aramaic, likewise spoken over the unleavened bread: "Behold, *this is* the bread of affliction, which our fathers had to eat as they came out of Egypt. Whoever hungers, let him come and eat. . . ."[30] We also possess instruction from Rabban Gamaliel,[31] who enumerates the elements that must be mentioned when one speaks words of interpretation over the Passover meal, thus proving that such a practice was usual in the time of Jesus. As a piece of communication, then, Jesus' words were not wholly unexpected at this point in the meal.

But were his words comprehensible to his audience? Astoundingly, Jeremias thinks they were not. He argues for two hundred pages that the Last Supper was indeed a Passover meal; he distills the various reports down to the putative *ipsissima verba* of Jesus; he back-translates these Greek words into Aramaic and Hebrew; and yet despite all this erudition, Jeremias in the end fails to account for the words of interpretation—the titular "*Eucharistic Words of Jesus*"—in a satisfactory manner. He is still compelled to say that the words of interpretation are "in themselves puzzling"[32]; that "according to Mark/Matthew, the bread word completely lacks any detailed explanation of its meaning"; that "Jesus must have said more than has been preserved in our brief, liturgical texts;"[33] and that "essential to any such attempt is a recapitulation of the ideas which Jesus' contemporaries associated with the breaking of bread and the blessing of the cup." He approvingly quotes M. Goguel: "The essential word, 'This is my body,' is strictly unintelligible to the uninitiated reader."[34]

---

[30]This saying is still repeated in the modern Jewish Passover Seder today. Cf. Jeremias, *Eucharistic Words*, 54, n. 3–5.

[31]"Rabban Gamaliel used to say: 'Whoever does not mention these three things at Passover has not fulfilled his obligation: the Passover lamb, the unleavened bread, and the bitter herbs" (m.Pes. 10.5). Jeremias, Daube, and Casey all believe that this was probably Gamaliel I, c. 30 CE, and not his grandson Gamaliel II, the first *nasi* or leader of the Sanhedrin after CE 70. There is much confusion because both are given the honorific title "Rabban." The consensus view of modern Jewish scholars favors identifying the Gamaliel of the Haggadah and m.Pes. 10.5 with Gamaliel II, but note that this only pushes the date to perhaps 30–40 years later, and at any rate, it is overwhelmingly likely that the foods enumerated by the saying in question were traditional long before they were made the subject of this rule: otherwise Rabban Gamaliel would have been legislating without good precedent in past Jewish usage. Cf. M. Casey, *Aramaic Sources of Mark's Gospel*, 237–238.

[32]Jeremias, *Eucharistic Words*, 87–88.

[33]Jeremias, *Eucharistic Words*, 224.

[34]Jeremias, *Eucharistic Words*, 133. Jeremias' mystery-religion approach to the gospel of John (in which the Fourth Evangelist "omitted the account of the Lord's Supper because he did not want to reveal the sacred formula to the general public"—*Eucharistic Words*, 125) seems doubtful. The

Jeremias' solution to this problem is to posit that Jesus delivered an unrecorded (!) Passover meditation for his disciples, in which he more fully explained the meaning that he would then sum up in the words of interpretation. But there is no trace in the gospels or Paul of this discourse. Worse, Jeremias claims that Jesus spoke this explanatory discourse "during the distribution, which *normally took place in silence*"[35]—in other words, the meal normally happened just as the gospels actually record it. The theory of a missing explanatory Passover meditation is wholly conjectural, and ought to be dismissed as a black box explanation.

Jeremias' hypothesis of an unrecorded Passover discourse is similar to Maurice Casey's claim that "at some stage [of the meal], there will have been the story of the deliverance of Israel from Egypt, possibly recited from Exodus 12. Symbolic interpretations of the main elements of the Passover meal will have been included."[36] (Note Casey's use of the future-perfect.) This claim rests partly upon the fact that two Rabbis nearly contemporary with Jesus, Gamaliel and Hillel, are quoted in the Mishnah as requiring oral interpretation of the foods of the Passover meal: "Rabban Gamaliel used to say, 'Whoever has not spoken of these three things during Passover has not discharged his share of obligation, namely, these: the Passover [sc. lamb, פֶּסַח], unleavened bread [מַצָּה], and bitter herbs [מָרוֹר]" (m.Pes. 10.5). Second, the custom of Hillel is also alleged to presuppose interpretation of the foods: "as was taught in a baraita: They said concerning Hillel that he used to wrap them [sc. the bitter herbs and unleavened bread] together and eat them, as it is stated, 'They shall eat it with matzot and bitter herbs' (Num. 9:11)" (b.Pes. 115a, cf. t.Pes. 2.22). It is true that these Rabbis are from the right period. The Hillel in question is certainly Hillel the Elder (110–10 BCE), since the source is a *baraita*. The Gamaliel may be either Gamaliel I (†52) or his grandson Gamaliel II († sometime after 95, since he was part of an embassy to Domitian[37]). But neither anecdote really warrants the assumption that the Passover in Jesus' day consistently involved oral explanations spoken over the ceremonial foods or the renarration of the Exodus story in full. It is true that these customs developed before the Mishnah, and that they are grounded on commandments in the Torah (e.g., Ex. 13:8, "And you shall tell your son . . ."). But the precise chronology of the development of the haggadah is not clearly enough defined to permit us to say for certain what words of interpretation Jesus "will have" uttered without being recorded in the gospels, and which were simply

---

Passover, though certainly a closed meal inasmuch as it was restricted to Jews, was by no means a secret one.

[35] Jeremias, 109. Emphasis mine.
[36] Casey, *Aramaic Sources*, 237.
[37] For the Talmudic sources referring to this embassy by four leading Rabbis, cf. E. Mary Smallwood, *The Jews Under Roman Rule* (Leiden: E.J. Brill, 1976), 383, n. 99.

not yet customary in his day. In light of this uncertainty, it is going too far to claim, as Jeremias does, that a full explanatory discourse has been omitted from the gospels; or to say, with Casey, that "We must infer that Jesus gave traditional interpretations of the lamb or goat, and of the bitter herbs."[38]

EISLER AND THE FIRST PROPOSAL OF THE THESIS

Into this gap, I must insert the thesis that is the subject of this book. It was first proposed by Robert Eisler in 1925, but lay rejected and buried until it was resurrected by David Daube in his 1966 lecture in the crypt of St. Paul's Cathedral, entitled "He That Cometh." The thesis is this: that the bread over which Jesus said "This is my body" was already known to the disciples and already bore a symbolic association with the Messiah.

Eisler had pointed to the Passover ritual of the *afiqoman*,[39] in which a piece of unleavened bread is broken off from one of a group of three matzoh and hidden, to be restored later, sometimes after a quest by the children of the gathering, and had attempted to associate this ritual in many of its details with the Last Supper as it stands recorded in the testimony of the NT. Although his central contention was correct, Eisler overplayed his hand, attempting to retroject into the Upper Room of 33 CE too many features of related but later rituals from the medieval Passover seder. Some of these are suggestive indeed, and we will discuss them in their proper place. But because of the chronology, they cannot be made the central proof of the thesis. For our present purposes, we are concerned only to show that *some ritual already associated a piece of unleavened bread with the Messiah before Jesus and His disciples ever ate the Last Supper.*

Eisler, writing at a time when regnant orthodoxy in NT studies traced the origins of the eucharist to an alleged Pauline adoption of meals from pagan mystery religions, proposed an alternative account, deliberately seeking the sources of the Catholic mass and early Christian communion in the Jewish Passover. Appealing to the significance of sharing bread ("com-mensa-lism," "com-pany"), Eisler looked to the medieval Passover Seder with its three named pieces of matzah: the "Israel," "Levi," and "Kohen." To interpret this ritual, he argued, first, that there was precedent in the OT for bread as a

---

[38]Casey, *Aramaic Sources*, 238.
[39]Robert Eisler, "Das Letzte Abendmahl" in two parts, *ZNW* 24 (1925), 161–192 and *ZNW* 25 (1926), 5–37. The latter issue also contains refutations by Marmorstein and Lietzmann, the editor of the journal, as well as an editorial note from Lietzmann declaring that the second half of the article was published only under duress after threats from Eisler's lawyer. For a summary of the entire sordid affair, see Deborah Bleicher Carmichael, "David Daube on the eucharist and the Passover Seder" in *JSNT* 42 (1991), 45–67.

symbol of a people. Focusing next on the "Levi" matzah, Eisler recounts the Jewish custom of breaking off a piece of this second cake and hiding it, to be found by children and "redeemed" by the father or host who had hidden it. The medieval name for this hidden piece of matzah was the *'afiqomen*, which Eisler identifies as a Greek loanword. He rejects the derivation of it from the Greek word ἐπίκομον, as well as from ἐπικομίζειν "to fetch" or from ἐπικώμιον in the sense of "what follows after the feast." These etymologies are, he rightly claims, impossible. (We will investigate the *vorlage* behind *'afiqomen* in chapter 3.) A noun formed from ἐπικομίζειν would need to be ἐπικόμισμα and would mean "bringing something"; ἐπίκομον could only mean "hairy"; and as for ἐπικώμιον, it means a festive song in celebration of, e.g. an Olympic victor being escorted to his house in a celebratory procession (κῶμος). Instead, Eisler proposed that *'afiqomen* is a transliteration of the Greek ἀφικόμενος, corresponding to the Hebrew *leḥem habā,*' Aramaic *lahma 'athē*, meaning "the bread of the age to come," messianic bread. With this etymology, Eisler suggested that the mysterious action of hiding the *'afiqomen* could be explained as the symbolic enactment of the arrival of the Messiah, who is called "the Coming One" in various passages of the NT (Mt. 11:3, Lk. 7:19, Heb. 10:37, Jude 14). Eisler explained the taking of the *'afiqomen* from the "Levi" matzah as consistent with Jewish expectation that the Messiah would be, not a Judahite like Jesus, but a second Moses from the tribe of Levi. This ritual was, he claims, used by Jesus himself when he broke and distributed the matzah to his disciples at the Last Supper, and this was an "acted parable" of the sort often found among the OT prophets.

Eisler points out that the words "this is my body" accompanied by the act of breaking bread cannot be a *vaticinium post eventum* because it does not fit crucifixion as a mode of death: Jesus' body was emphatically *not* broken on the cross; Luke's gospel especially goes out of its way to remind us that not a bone of Jesus' body was broken. There was no σκελοκοπία, the breaking of the legs of a crucified person, as John 19:23 explicitly tells us. Eisler claims that Jesus expected to die by the sword, cut to pieces by his enemies. This meant more than the mere announcement of death and suffering: it was a self-identification." "hā, τοῦτο"—pointing to the *'aphiqomen*—"*gufi*, τὸ σῶμα μοῦ ἐστιν"—is tantamount to: "ὁ ἀφικόμενος—ἐγώ εἰμί, the unrecognized messianic king who has 'arrived' on earth—I am he."

Eisler then traces a clear line from this understanding of Jesus' words at the Last Supper to the language of the apostle Paul in 1 Corinthians 10:17 and 5:6, both of which use the one bread as a symbol of the unity of the church. He explains Paul's use of the metaphor of body parts (μέλη τοῦ Χριστοῦ) as probably influenced by a Jewish re-interpretation of *leḥem abhirim* ("angels' bread") in Psalm 78:23 as *leḥem 'ebārim*, "bread of the limbs." He also suggests that the expression τὸν ἐπιούσιον ἄρτον corresponds well with the term *'aphiqomen* as a reference to the "bread for two days" which according to Exodus 16:22, was collected on Friday evening for the following sabbath.

Eisler's article provoked two responses in the very next issue of *ZNW*: one from Hans Leitzmann, the preeminent Christian scholar of eucharistic origins, and one from the great Hungarian rabbi, Arthur Marmorstein.[40]

Marmorstein's reply is a historical investigation of the custom of the three cakes of matzah. He concludes that even R. Eisak Tyrnau, living in the fifteenth century in France, does not yet know the three matzot by the names "Kohen, Levi, and Israel," but only as "aleph, bet, and gimel." He traces the custom of breaking the middle matzah "for *'afiqomen*" to the sixteenth century. Marmorstein points out that the Palestinian Talmud does not depict three matzoth, and that the "cup for Elijah" to which Eisler has appealed, is a seventeenth-century invention, first mentioned by the Czech rabbi Jacob Rauscher.

Lietzmann surveys the Rabbinic explanations of the term *'afiqomen* in the Mishnah and Talmud, dividing them into, first, the views given in the Babylonian Talmud: (1) the opinion of Rab (†247) that "they should not go from one table-company to another"; (2) the opinion of Shemuel (†254) that the word *'afiqomen* means truffles and (3) that of Abba, that it means "young doves"; (4) that of R. Chanina bar Shela and R. Yoḥanan (†279) that it means "dates, toasted grains, and walnuts." From there, Lietzmann passes on to the Talmud Yerushalmi and finds further opinions: (5) that of R. Simon on behalf of R. Inainy bar R. Sisai that *'afiqomen* means "kinds of song" (but on this more, later); (6) that of R. Yochanan that it means "kinds of sweets"; (7) a reiteration of (4) from the Babylonian Talmud; (8) the teaching by R. Ḥiyyah: "And you shall teach him also about the Passover rules: that one does not dismiss after the Passover אפיקומן, that one does not stand at this table-company and (afterwards) enter another table-company." Finally, Lietzmann includes the Tosefta (*t.Pes.* 10.11), which gives another definition (9), "for instance, walnuts and dates and roasted grains." On the basis of this survey, Lietzmann concluded that the identification of ὁ ἀφικόμενος as a messianic term is "ein Phantasiegebilde"; that in the Mishnaic and Amoraic periods (first–sixth centuries), no one used אפיקומן as a technical term for a piece of matzah in the Passover ritual; and that its application to a piece of matzah today is a consequence of the misunderstanding of the word as "dessert." Lietzmann faulted Eisler for relying on the "rite of the three matzot" with symbolic designations and the custom of hiding a piece of the middle matzah, since in the absence of any proof of the messianic significance of the אפיקומן, this ritual must be

---

[40]Hans Lietzmann, "Jüdische Passahsitten und der ἀφικόμενος" in *ZNW* 25 (1926), 299–303 and Arthur Marmorstein, "Miscellen I: Das letze Abendmahl und der Sederabend" in *ZNW* 25 (1926), 249–253.

assumed to be later. He concluded with an attempt to nail the coffin lid on Eisler's theory: "Womit den jede Möglichkeit, das Abendmahl von dort aus verstehen zu wollen, beseitigt ist."[41]

Thus, from a leading Jewish scholar and a leading Christian one, Eisler stood condemned for anachronism. From our vantage point, it is hard to sympathize with him: his use of the Rabbinic sources fits the description of him by Gershom Scholem: "Eisler's eloquence was as amazing as his education. It was impressive, but not quite serious. I, at any rate, had never seen such a display of learning—brilliantly riveting, sparkling and at the same time suspect. . . . For all unsolved problems he had in readiness brilliantly false solutions of the most surprising kind."[42] He was, as Daube puts it, "impossible." Born a Jew in Vienna, he had converted to Christianity in order to marry the daughter of the well-known Austrian painter Franz Xaver von Pausinger. He managed to obtain two different doctorates from the University of Vienna: one in philosophy and the other in art history. He was unable to receive his *Habilitation* and become a professor because, says Scholem, "the Gentiles were made uneasy by his markedly Jewish appearance, and the Jews by his apostasy." With assistance from Martin Buber, he founded a society for research on the Kabbala, and submitted an essay on this project to *Der Jude*, which Buber refused to print until such time as he might receive confirmation of Eisler's de-conversion from Christianity. His other publications are equally outlandish. They include such titles as *Bees in Jewish and Christian Mysticism*, another on *Terminologie und Geschichte der jüdischen Alchemie*, and an authoritative study of werewolves, *Man into Wolf*. These subjects "had one thing in common: they were all rich in unsolved problems which left the amplest scope to the combinatory mind. Anyone who heard his lectures was overwhelmed by his rhetorical gifts. If one read his writings, one was rendered speechless by the wealth of quotations and the references to the most unimaginable and most remote sources."[43] It is hardly surprising that the argumentation and evidence produced by such a mind were found inadequate by Lietzmann and Marmorstein. Nonetheless, Eisler's thesis struck a chord that has continued resounding in later scholarship.

---

[41]Lietzmann, "Jüdische Passahsitten und der ἀφικόμενος," 303.

[42]Gershom Scholem, *From Berlin to Jerusalem*, trans. Harry Zohn (New York: Schocken, 1980), 129–130. Cited in David Biale, *Gershom Scholem: Master of the Kabbalah* (New Haven, CT: Yale University Press, 2018), 76.

[43]Scholem, *From Berlin to Jerusalem*, 130. Also notable is this anecdote (ibid, 129): "Eisler invited me to visit him in his little villa on Lake Starnberg, which dated from his days as a millionaire's son. . . . For a few minutes I was taken into a library crammed to the ceiling with the most scholarly works about everything under the sun. My attention was attracted by ten quarto volumes bound in green morocco and bearing the inscription *Erotica et Curiosa*. Without a moment's hesitation I pulled out one of the volumes: it was just a dummy for cognac glasses and bottles behind it."

DAVID DAUBE AND THE DEFENSE OF THE THESIS

In 1966, the great German Jewish scholar of the history of law, David Daube, revived the central claim of Eisler's thesis. He termed the ritual of the messiah-bread "The Coming One," for reasons that I will discuss in the next chapter. Daube's most important contribution was to place Eisler's thesis, shorn of anachronistic extravagances and imaginative excesses, on a firm historical foundation.[44] He considers the question first as a problem of *communication*:

> There is, however, further evidence that the eucharist was modeled on, made use of, an earlier Jewish rite. In my opinion, it is the best evidence, which Eisler unfortunately missed; it is, so to speak, internal evidence, from the New Testament account itself. What I mean is that the institution of the eucharist as recorded in the New Testament of necessity presupposes a ritual essentially (not in details, to be sure, but essentially) like that of "The Coming One." *Jesus could not at the same time have introduced both the general idea of eating a cake of unleavened bread as the Messiah and the specific identification of that cake with himself.* That is just not how rites come into being. The ceremony—some ceremony—of eating a piece of unleavened bread as the Messiah must have been practiced before; the new thing was the identification, the self-revelation, the proclamation that the Messiah had now found bodily, human presence—"This is my body" (or even, at an Aramaic stage, "This is me").
>
> . . . [H]ad no ritual of the kind preserved in the Jewish Passover eve service existed, and had Jesus suddenly distributed a cake of unleavened bread and said of it, "This is my body," his disciples—to put it mildly—would have been perplexed. With such a ritual referring to "The Coming One" already in existence, the self-revelation made sense.[45]

The italicized sentence focuses the issue very precisely. It shows that Daube approached the question of the words over the bread at the Last Supper from a perspective almost the opposite of Eisler's scattershot conjuring with sources freely associated in his "combinatory mind." Daube's mind worked quite differently: like Eisler, he is attracted to puzzles, but unlike him, he approaches problems in an almost forensic manner. Sir Alan Rodger, a pupil of Daube's at Oxford, sums up his method:

---

[44]Daube's work was taken up and expanded further by Deborah Bleicher Carmichael's 1991 article, "David Daube on the eucharist and the Passover Seder" in *JSNT* 42 (1991), 45–67. The additional corroborating evidence she provides will be discussed in more detail in chapter 3, when we consider the evidence of the earliest subapostolic Christian writings.

[45]David Daube, "He That Cometh," repr. in *Collected Works of David Daube* vol. 2, ed. Calum Carmichael (Berkeley, CA: the Robbins Collection, 2000), 438–439.

Daube's work provides endless models of how we should proceed. For it matters little whether the text is a statute, a Digest text or a line of Ovid or Homer. In all cases the crucial thing for Daube is to notice precisely what expressions are used. And then you have to ask yourself why. Why did the draughtsman or author use this word rather than another? Why does that item come at the end of the list rather than at the beginning? Does this text actually make sense or has it been modified and has something gone wrong in the process of modification? These are the kinds of issues which regularly present themselves, or should present themselves, when a reader is trying to understand a modern text just as much as an ancient text.[46]

Ernest Metzger suggests that "Daube's method of reading texts produces the explanations it does because it does not rely on *inferences* from the text so much as *prior guesses* about what the text means."[47] By approaching the question from the perspective of a historian trying to figure out what Jesus' words must have meant to his disciples,[48] Daube was able to determine that the words of institution are high-context speech that has been analyzed inappropriately as if it were low-context speech. Luther's and Zwingli's parsing of "is" in "this is my body" at the 1529 Marburg colloquy was inappropriate as a method of determining the meaning—not only because the word "is" would not have been in the Aramaic spoken at the Last Supper, as Oecolampadius pointed out,[49] but even more importantly, because the preponderance of the words' meaning lies, not in a minute analysis of their diction and grammar, but *in their ritual context*. To readers who approach them without the benefit of this context, they remain opaque, and in their opacity, they have become a canvas for theologians to paint with pigments or figments of philosophy and mysticism. Such paintings may be brilliant and profound, but

---

[46] Alan Rodger, "Law For All Times: the Work and Contribution of David Daube" in *Law for All Times*, ed. Ernest Metzger (Lawrence, KS: University of Kansas School of Law, 2009), 12.

[47] Ernest Metzger, "*Quare?* Argument in David Daube, after Karl Popper" in *Law for All Times*, ed. Ernest Metzger (Lawrence, KS: University of Kansas School of Law, 2009), 27.

[48] Daube is remarkable among scholars for his distinctive approach, aptly expressed in a quotation from *Pilgrim's Progress*: "Wouldst thou read puzzles and their explanations?" That is, he reads a text closely and identifies puzzling features, then asks, "Why was this expression chosen? What were the conditions that determined it?" The answer to such questions about a particular feature often sheds new light on the entire work under study. For more on Daube's methods, cf. Alan Rodger, "Law for All Times" in *Roman Legal Tradition* 2 (Glasgow: 2004), p 3–23 and Ernest Metzger, "*Quare?* Argument in David Daube, After Karl Popper" in *Roman Legal Tradition* 2 (Glasgow: 2009), 27–58, and Calum Carmichael's preface to *Collected Works of David Daube I: Taldmudic Law* (Berkeley, CA: the Robbins Collection, 1992).

[49] This linguistic fact was first noticed by Oecolampadius against Luther at the Marburg colloquy. Cf. Katherine Gill, "Transcript of the Marburg Colloquy," *Great Debates of the Reformation*, (New York: Random House, 1969), 77–107. On Oecolampadius' doctrine of the eucharist, cf. Nicholas Piotrowski, "Johannes Oecolampadius: Christology and the Supper" in *Mid-America Journal of Theology* 23 (2012), 131–137, who argues that Oecolampadius "did not simply follow Zwingli in his doctrine of the Supper, but deviated in a significant way that made him a forerunner to Calvin's doctrine of the spiritual presence of Christ."

they conceal, and do not reveal, the meaning that was experienced by Jesus' disciples in the upper room.

Jeremias had mistakenly concluded that the missing meaning must have been supplied to the disciples in an explanatory discourse now lost to us. Daube, on the other hand, correctly perceived that the missing meaning was located in the context: namely, in the Passover meal with which the disciples were already familiar.

SELF-DISCLOSURE AND ARAMAIC *GŪPH*

In Daube's analysis, the central point of the words Jesus spoke over the bread was not to set up a new and miraculous transformation of the bread in question, but to use an existing ritual with an already known significance as a means of identifying himself as Israel's long-awaited Messiah. If messianic self-identification was the point of the bread ritual, then the Last Supper turns out to be of a piece with the rest of Jesus' earthly ministry: his miracles, his parables, his questions to others—nearly everything he said and did was aimed at this meaning.[50] That Daube's interpretation makes the Last Supper fit with this larger pattern of self-disclosure by Jesus is a powerful argument in its favor.

Indeed, self-disclosure has long been recognized as the contextually appropriate communication, for it has been the *desideratum* motivating one of the main proposed Aramaic *vorlage* behind the Greek τοῦτο μού ἐστιν τὸ σῶμα: namely, the word *gūphā*, which was combined with personal suffixes in much the same way as the English "self," so that *gūphī* can mean "myself."[51] The

---

[50]For some of the most helpful expositions of this point, cf. Wright, *Jesus and the Victory of God*, especially chapters 11 and 12, which lay out the many ways in which Jesus staked his claim to be Israel's Messiah. When, after discussing many of Jesus' miracles and parables, Wright comes to the Last Supper, his words are fully in accord with Daube's view: "Jesus' last meal with his followers was a deliberate double drama. As a Passover meal (of sorts), it told the story of Jewish history in terms of divine deliverance from tyranny, looking back to the exodus from Egypt and on to the great exodus, the return from exile, that was still eagerly awaited. But Jesus' meal fused this great story together with another one: the story of Jesus' own life, and of his coming death. It somehow involved him in the god-given drama, not as a spectator, or as one participant among many, but as the central character." N.T. Wright, *Jesus and the Victory of God* (Minneapolis, MN: Fortress, 1996), 554.

[51]G.R. Driver identifies *gwph* in the Hebrew Bible as a poetical synonym of *pgr* drawn from Aramaic. G.R. Driver, "Hebrew Poetic Diction," *Congress Volume: Copenhagen 1953, Supplements to Vetus Testamentum* vol. 1 (Leiden: E.J. Brill, 1953), 26–39 at 30. The word is Aramaic, used in Targum Jonathan (1 Sam. 31:10) to render the Hebrew גְּוִיָּתוֹ (denoting the dead body of Saul that the Philistines fastened to the wall of Beth Shan). Note that the Hebrew גְּוִיָּה also can be used in the sense of "self" Gen. 47:18, Neh. 9:37 (HALOT). The date and origin of Targum Jonathan is contested, with some seeing it as a 2nd century Palestinian production on the basis of affinities with the Aramaic of the Qumran documents, but others date it as post-Islamic (seventh century) on the basis of a supposed echo of the Muslim Shahada. On this issue, cf. Eveline van Staalduine-Sulman, *The Targum of Samuel* (Leiden: E.J. Brill, 2002), 35–40.

proposal is tentative. The word is not used in this sense in the Peshitta, which has *pagrā* for σῶμα (1 Cor. 11:24 and Lk. 22:19), and might have been expected to preserve Jesus' original Aramaic words from this occasion, even though it is a translation from the Greek (just as Jeremias suggests it preserves the Lord's Prayer); nor does *gūph* appear with this meaning in Jewish Literary Aramaic.[52] So far, it is primarily a Babylonian Aramaic usage: evidence for the use of *gūph* with pronominal suffixes in the sense of "oneself" can be found in *m.Avot* 4.6:

> R. Jose says: "Whoever honors the Torah—his body (= himself) will be honored by created beings (גּוּפוֹ מְכֻבָּד עַל הַבְּרִיּוֹת). Whoever dishonors the Torah, he himself will be dishonored by created beings (גּוּפוֹ מְחֻלָּל עַל הַבְּרִיּוֹת).

(The R. Jose in question is R. Jose ben Halafta, the disciple of Akiba, placing the saying perhaps c. 135.) Dalman also cites *Avot de-Rabbi Nathan* 27, which is difficult to date. R. Nathan himself is likewise from the 2nd century, but the final recension of *Avot de Rabbi Nathan* is from the Geonic period (700–900). The use of *gūph* in the sense of "self" or "person" is also found in Targum Sheni (Esther) 1.8, where "the drinking was according to each person's usage (גּוּפָא מנהג)," but Targum Sheni is post-Talmudic and possibly even from the post-Byzantine or Islamic period.[53]

The Mishnah and Tosefta do not use גּוּפוֹ with the meaning "self," but they do use it to designate the body of the Passover lamb in distinction from the feast: "And in [time of] the Temple, it used to be that the body of the Passover lamb (גּוּפוֹ שֶׁל פֶּסַח) would be set before [the leader of the company]." (*m.Pes.* 10.3 and *t.Pes.* 10.9 with identical phrasing) As Brant Pitre points out, these sayings refer expressly to the Second Temple period.[54] This is another encouragement to date this usage of גּוּפוֹ to the time of Jesus.

---

[52]Instances of *gūph* in Palestinian Targumic Aramaic: Targum Neofiti Genesis 47:18 ("there is nothing left for our lord except our bodies (גופינו) and our land"; an alternative reading in the margin, גופיהון, makes it "their bodies," i.e. the bodies of the dead cattle; interestingly, LXX has τό ἴδιον σῶμα); Targum Neofiti Leviticus 1:8 ("Then the priests. . . . shall lay the parts, the head, and the body (הפוג) in order on the wood . . ."); ibid Leviticus 1:12 and 8:20 in similar contexts; Targum Jonathan on 1 Samuel 5:4 (Dagon's "head and hands had been broken off and were lying on the threshold; only his body (גופיה) remained") and on 1 Samuel 31:10, 12 (of the "body (גופיה)" of Saul fastened to the wall of Beth Shan); Targum Jonathan Isaiah 8:6 (purifying the body with water) and Isaiah 58:11 (the Lord "will revive your soul and body נַפְשֶׁךָ וְגוּפָךְ").

[53]The date of this targum is highly uncertain, being possibly as early as the 4th century and as late the 11th. In favor of an early date is the fact that it is written in Galilean Aramaic and contains several Greek words. Grossfeld dates it to the Byzantine period, since it represents Rome as the power to be supplanted by the Messianic kingdom. Flesher and Chilton offer some caveats about this dating, however, pointing out that Targum Sheni may borrow from an earlier Esther targum of Amoraic date. Bernard Grossfeld, *Two Targums of Esther* (Edinburgh, T&T Clark, 1991), 19–21, 23–24. Paul V.M. Flesher and Bruce Chilton, *The Targums: A Critical Introduction* (Leiden: E.J. Brill, 2011), 246–252.

[54]Brant Pitre, *Jesus and the Last Supper* (Grand Rapids, MI: Eerdmans, 2017), 408.

Dalman too suggests that Jesus used *gūphī* to make a reference to himself as the Passover lamb, but he also acknowledged that "the fact that the Early christians did not take it in this sense [sc. 'I myself'], as well as our Lord's reference to his blood at the administration of the wine, necessitate the translation, 'My Body'"[55] rather than 'myself.'" Methodologically speaking, this is an unreasonably cautious scruple. As Casey points out, "We should not demand that this particular reference be found in examples from before the time of Jesus, because too little Aramaic is still extant for such a detailed demand to be reasonable. It is sufficient that the word [sc. not the particular sense of the word] is clearly attested in earlier sources, and that the [use of it in a particular sense] both is clear in later sources and emerges naturally when [a passage] is reconstructed."[56]

Similarly, Meyer endorses *gūphā* and cites *b.Qid.* 37a, where the *mitzvah* against idol worship is "an obligation of the body" (חובת הגוף), meaning that it was obligatory for every person as such, as opposed to an obligation that applies only within the land of Israel.[57] Pesch, likewise, notes that both *biśrā'* and *gūphā* can be used with personal suffixes to denote "oneself": "mit dem Suffix der 1. Person die Person des Sprechers bezeichnen: das bin ich selbst!"[58] Of the two, Pesch prefers *gūphā*. Jeremias rejects *gūphā* in favor of *biśrā'* or the Hebrew *baśar,* on the grounds that the LXX more frequently renders this word by the Greek σῶμα, but as Meyer notes, *biśrā'* can also be used with personal suffixes to mean "oneself."

Maurice Casey proposes *gshem* as the word for "body" here, appealing to its use in Daniel 3:27–8 of the bodies of Shadrach, Meshak, and Abednego. He renders "this is my body" as *'dnah hu' gishmi.'*[59] The word *gshem* appears in a fragment from Qumran (4Q531 fg 40:1) with the meaning "body," but it must be noted that the word is not complete in that text. It also occurs in Targum Neofiti on Ex. 22:12 to denote the body of an animal that has been killed while on loan from a neighbor: "he shall take him the body (גושמת) of the mangled animal and he shall not make recompense."[60] This word seems to me far less likely than *biśrā'* or *gūphā*, because it denotes "body" in distinction from "living animal." It is semantically confusing to imagine Jesus associating the bread with both himself and with the Passover lamb at the same time and in the same sense. Johannes Behm recognized this and drew the necessary conclusion: "[A] more important point than the absence of the copula (by Aram. usage) is that the word which he probably used for 'body,'

---

[55] Dalman, *Jesus-Jeshua*, 143.
[56] Casey, *Aramaic Sources*, 234.
[57] Meyer, "σάρξ" in *TDNT* 7.116 and Schweizer, "σῶμα κτλ." in the same volume, 7.1059.
[58] Pesch, *Das Abendmahl und Jesu Todesverstandnis*, 91.
[59] Casey, "No Cannibals at Passover!" 201; Casey, *Aramaic Sources*, 239.
[60] Martin McNamara, *Targum Neofiti 1: Exodus* (Collegeville, MN: Liturgical Press, 1994), 95–96.

i.e. גוּף, means not only 'body' but also 'self' or 'person.' In the figure Jesus was hardly referring to his body as such. There is no point of comparison for the equation of bread and body. The obvious sense is that 'this (the bread) I am myself.'"[61] Unfortunately, Behm went on to claim that this identification of Jesus' self with the bread is "the pledge of his personal presence in their fellowship." This is equally out of place, since Jesus' personal presence at the meal was already obvious apart from the bread and required no such symbolic pledge.

The observation that *gūph* was especially used to refer to the body of the Passover lamb adds a curious double-entendre to Jesus' utterance. To speak of the Messiah-bread as a *gūph* when everybody could see the *gūph* of the Passover lamb at the same time, was a pointed act. It is tempting to see it as a claim that the Messiah would be a new sacrifice. But since *gūph* is conjecture in the first place, we cannot put any weight on this suggestion.

Ultimately, any Aramaic reconstruction must be tentative. Nonetheless, we note the trend that so many of the scholars who have posited Aramaic words behind the Greek σῶμα have suggested words that double as self-referential pronouns when combined with the personal suffix suggested by μού. These scholars have recognized that the circumstances of the utterance make such a self-reference appropriate and comprehensible.

Scot McKnight objects to this widespread suggestion by asking why, if Jesus' intent was to "disclose privately to his followers that he was, in fact, the Messiah who was signified by the *aphikoman*" he should have waited until then to tell them?[62] This is a two-fold objection. The mention of *aphikoman* (*'afiqomen*) can be set aside, since Daube never claims that the name *'afiqomen* was used of the messiah-bread ritual he posits. The main point of McKnight's question, however, must be addressed: if the context and probable Aramaic of Jesus' words over the bread have led so many scholars to interpret his words as a self-identification, and if Eisler and Daube are correct that the antecedent meaning of the bread meant that this was self-identification as Israel's Messiah, then why should Jesus have waited until this moment to make such a self-disclosure? McKnight no doubt intends his question in a rhetorical sense: he does not think there is an answer to it. But there is a good answer available, and it tends to confirm the correctness of the explanation. Namely: Jesus' use of the Passover ritual as an act of symbolic self-disclosure is in accord with his usual behavior: he never advertises his messianic identity openly and frankly, but always tacitly invites his disciples and the crowds which his ministry attracted to identify him as such *in terms of their prior knowledge*. The messianic symbolism of the bread was a piece of such prior

---

[61] Johannes Behm, "κλάω" in *TDNT* 3.736.
[62] McKnight, *Jesus and His Death*, 281.

knowledge. Nowhere in the synoptic gospels do we find Jesus asserting his messiahship explicitly. Instead, when asked by John's disciples, he points (Lk. 7:22, Mt. 11:4) to the correspondence between his recent works and the signs enumerated by the prophet Isaiah. His response when questioned outright by both Pilate and the Sanhedrin is not, "Yes, I am the Messiah," but "You have said it" (*'amarta*, σὺ εἶπας)—a Semitic idiom which disavows responsibility for the statement while acknowledging its correctness.[63] Perhaps the closest thing we find to an explicit assertion is Jesus' answer to Simon Peter's confession (Mt. 16:16–17, Mk. 8:29–30; Luke's account, interestingly, has Jesus immediately bind his disciples to secrecy). Likewise, his use of "the Son of Man" (ὁ υἱὸς τοῦ ἀνθρώπου) as a self-reference is a consistent part of the same strategy: the Aramaic idiom (בר (א)נשא) is originally a very generic term for human beings as a whole, sometimes used with reference to the speaker, often when the circumstances involve the speaker in claiming an embarrassingly lofty or humiliating position.[64] Jesus' use of this generic idiom as an unmistakeable self-reference is a form of indirection, a way of making astonishing claims—that the Son of Man is lord of the Sabbath, has power on earth to forgive sins, will come with the clouds, and so forth—without immodestly using the first person. It is a way for him to identify himself as the Messiah without saying, "I am the Messiah." It places a semiotic buffer between him and that title, with all its crushing implications. It invites his disciples to use their own knowledge. Jesus exhibits a similar indirection and reticence in identifying Judas as his betrayer: he does not name him in so many words, but responds to Judas' question, "Is it I?" with the deflecting "You have said it" (Mt. 26:25), and sets up a symbolic piece of bread which he hands to Judas, enabling his other disciples to make the connection for themselves without needing any explicit verbal identification.

In light of Jesus' reticence regarding open self-identification as the messiah, and his preference for cryptic indications, indirection, and symbolism, I submit that it would be completely in character for him to use the Passover's messiah-bread in this manner. Doing so would also have had the added advantage of likening his impending death to the events of the Exodus.

Seeing the words over the bread as a cryptic statement of messianic self-identification also fits the historical consequences: Long before controversies

---

[63] Jesus uses this response several times in the gospels in answer to such direct questions: "Are you the Christ, the Son of the Blessed One?" by the High Priest (Mt. 26:64); and "You are the king of the Jews?" by Pilate (Mt. 27:11, Mk. 15:2, Lk. 23:3, Jn. 18:37). Daube argues convincingly that Jesus' response of "You have said it" (σὺ εἶπας) is not to be construed as an affirmative response, but as something more akin to "I take no responsibility for the proposition you have just put. It came out of your mouth, not mine. To say more would be to cross a line into impropriety." David Daube, "Judas" in CWDD vol. 2, 795–799.

[64] On the "Son of Man" idiom, see the study by Maurice Casey, *The Solution to the Son of Man Problem* (London: T&T Clark, 2009).

over the "real presence" or transubstantiation ever arose, the question of Jesus' identity as Israel's messiah was at the center of the strife between the church and the synagogue. As we shall see, both Christians and Jews altered their liturgies around this claim, for the bread ritual has left its mark not only in the pages of Scripture and the church fathers, but also in the Passover Haggadah. To that text we now turn.

Chapter Three

Evidence from Jews and Greeks

COHERENCE AND HISTORICAL PLAUSIBILITY

Daube considered the "best evidence" for his view to be the very nature of ritual actions as such: "Jesus could not at the same time have introduced both the general idea of eating a cake of unleavened bread as the Messiah and the specific identification of that cake with himself. That is just not how rites come into being."[1] This is an important difference between his view and most Christian understandings of the eucharist and Last Supper: many Christians have a view of the effect of Jesus' words of institution that actually renders them incomprehensible to the disciples in the Upper Room. If Jesus' words were effecting a metaphysical change in the elements of bread and wine, this was a *sensus plenior* that could not have been understood by the disciples at the time. It is, of course, possible that Jesus intended something that would only be understood by his disciples later. We note, however, that there are no expressions of incomprehension at the Last Supper, despite the fact that the gospels are frequently quite free about noting such puzzlement (Mt. 17:4, Mk. 8:14, Jn. 13:8, etc). But Daube's view makes the words instantly comprehensible to Jesus' disciples; he places them within a historically plausible Jewish ritual setting paralleled by other similar ritual utterances from the same period (e.g. Hillel's custom of eating bread and bitter herbs together).

Above all, Daube's thesis makes the words of institution cohere thematically with the Jewish ritual setting of the Passover. This is a difference from most traditional Christian views, in which the eucharist is related to the Passover only as antitype to type. Most Christian eucharistic liturgies have little or nothing to say about Israel or the Passover. The eucharist has been

---

[1] Daube, "He That Cometh," repr. in CWDD vol. 2, p. 438–439.

de-paschalized. More striking still, for most traditional Christian views of the eucharist, the Last Supper itself is the very occasion on which this de-paschalization took place. Ephrem the Syrian's *Hymns on Unleavened Bread* 6.4 puts this view most dramatically:

> Our Lord ate the Passover with his disciples;
> Through the bread that he broke, he abolished the unleavened bread.[2]

Ephrem can speak this way with the benefit of three centuries of hindsight, but it is clear from the NT's narratives of Jesus' last Passover with his disciples that he did no such thing. Still less did he announce the replacement of the Passover with a new ritual. Any such replacement would have been impossible on that occasion: the powerful themes and rich symbolism of the Passover meal would have been hindrances and obstacles to the creation of a different ritual with new themes and symbolism. If it had been Jesus' project to set up a new rite, he could have done so more easily if he had instituted it on another occasion, free from the densely layered and overwhelmingly powerful semiotic milieu of Passover. But it was not his aim to set up a new rite. He was, rather, using an already existing ritual to speak about himself.

Daube's words about "how rites come into being" should also serve as a corrective against a common mistake in historical scholarship on eucharistic origins. Form critics have frequently judged the historicity of words and actions ascribed to Jesus by whether they have a plausible *Sitz im Leben* within the Judaism of Jesus' day; if an idea or utterance has a *Sitz im Leben* within the early church, that is thought to be proof that it is not historical, but is a projection of the church's ideas back onto Jesus. In particular, the addition of the Lucan and Pauline accounts' inclusion of Jesus' command to repeat the ritual ("do this"), and the explanation of it as retrospective ("in remembrance of me") are stripped away by Maurice Casey as inauthentic because he believes that they have no *Sitz im Leben* in Jesus' ministry, but only in the early church. Thus, for Casey, "the notion that the eucharist was instituted on this occasion was invented by St. Paul."[3] But the words "this is my body" and "this is my blood" would have been understood by Jesus' disciples as invitations to share symbolically in Jesus' impending death by eating and drinking. This in itself underwrites repetition because it was done *before* the arrest and execution which Jesus was expecting. His intention was proleptic: he expected to die, and his concern was for the preservation of his followers: hence his prediction with quotation from the Psalms, "All of you will

---

[2] *H. Azym.* 6.4 in Ephrem the Syrian, *Hymns on the Unleavened Bread*, trans. J. Edward Walters (Piscataway, NJ: Gorgias Press, 2012), 38.
[3] Maurice Casey, *Jesus of Nazareth: An Independent Historian's Account of His Life and Teaching* (London: T&T Clark, 2010), 436.

be made to stumble because of me this night, for it is written, 'I will strike the shepherd, and the sheep will be scattered'" (Mk. 14:27); hence also his instructions to his disciples to "stay awake and pray, lest you enter into trial" (Mk. 14:38); and this concern is also reflected, perhaps at a later remove and in the memory of the disciples, in John 18:8 and 17:9–19. But if the bread and wine were given to the disciples at the Last Supper with an intent that they should share vicariously in Jesus' sacrificial death, then the way is clear for them to continue to understand it in this way thereafter.

If Paul "invented the institution of the eucharist," then he was falsely claiming that Christ had instituted it. This is not plausible, for several reasons. First, there is a "no outcry" argument against it. Paul had plenty of enemies: the "circumcision" party in Galatia, the ὑπεραπόστολοι in Corinth, and above all, his opponents in the Jerusalem church ("the Pharisees who believed," Acts 15:5), many of whom were likely in a position to correct his account, especially if any of them had been present at the Last Supper. But though Paul's opponents attacked his teaching and authority in many ways, we have no evidence that they charged him with falsifying the eucharist. And the eucharist was also practiced in non-Pauline churches.[4]

Second, the transition from Mark, based on Aramaic-speaking sources, to Matthew and Luke, which smooth out Mark's Greek and correct many of his Aramaisms, is marked by the omission of many Jewish details. Luke especially alters narratives to leave out details that would have been significant to a Jewish audience, but which Gentiles would have struggled to understand because they lacked the necessary cultural knowledge. The changes in the Last Supper accounts from Mark to Luke to Paul should be understood in terms of this change of audience. This accounts also for the omission of the conjectured messianic bread-ritual posited by Eisler and Daube: it was not seen as necessary for Gentiles to know, provided that they grasped the idea that the eucharist was a sharing in Christ. Rather than claim, as Casey does, that the Pauline account of the Last Supper is an instance of the "Christ of faith," while Mark's gospel gives us the historical Jesus, so that "the eucharist originated in falsehood," it would be better to ask whether the Pauline eucharist can be understood as a presentation and contextualization of the historical actions presented by Mark.

Third, part of Casey's objection is that the Pauline eucharist of 1 Corinthians 11 has "nothing to do with Passover."[5] That claim is mistaken, for as we shall see in chapter 7, Paul's conception of the meal is communicated in diction and imagery taken from Passover.

---

[4]This fact is acknowledged even by those who posit radical changes in theology in the "communities" of the early church. Cf. Chilton, *Feast of Meanings*, 143 on the clearly Paschal imagery of Revelation.

[5]Casey, *Jesus of Nazareth*, 436.

I would suggest that we have this sequence: Mark gives us a very faithful, early, and detailed account of the Last Supper, preserving many Aramaic features, but omitting the narration of the Passover meal except for those portions of it which were of interest in explaining Jesus' death; Luke represents a later version of the same, but edited for a Gentile audience and therefore omitting or correcting some of Mark's Semitisms. Paul then represents a further tradition of this same account to a Gentile church context. The Lucan and Pauline additions include "do this in remembrance of me" and "shed for the forgiveness of sins" or "for many." These are either further reminiscences from witnesses who were present at Jesus' last Passover meal, or else they are epexegetic additions added by Paul and Luke to make explicit to a new audience what the original audience would have understood. That is to say, they are not retrojections of a later practice, but traces of the fitting of an original and Dominical practice to a new audience, supplying things which the original Jewish Christians knew, but which Gentile Christians might not have known.

Another objection to the idea that the Last Supper was the institution of the eucharist is that it was an annual Passover meal, so that even if Jesus commanded its repetition, that repetition would have been annual, not weekly or more often as the eucharist was. As Brant Pitre points out, this virtually implies the similar idea that Jesus did not intend to establish a renewed Israel, so that any language pointing to the church as a renewed Israel, and to the eucharist as the ritual meal of that renewed Israel must have its *Sitz im Leben* in the early church, and not in the ministry of Jesus.[6] This is in fact Casey's position. But even Casey acknowledges that the original words of Jesus over the cup make explicit reference to "the covenant." Even if we grant that the words "new covenant" (1 Cor. 11:25) are a Pauline epexegetic addition, the mention of the covenant strongly suggests repetition of the meal. Throughout the Hebrew Bible, the idea of covenant (*berîth*) serves precisely to bridge the temporal gap between Israel's past and present. This is so regardless of whether the covenant is viewed prospectively or retrospectively: thus, the Exodus was a matter of God "remembering" (*wayyizkor*) his past "covenant with Abraham, Isaac, and Jacob" (Ex. 2:24), and the Passover is "a memorial" (*zikkarôn*) to be kept "as a feast to the Lord throughout your generations" (Ex. 12:14). The command to "do this" also has its proper place in commands concerning repeated cultic rites (Ex. 29:31–35, Num. 15:8–15).[7] For Jesus to take up this same language of covenant and remembrance in con-

---

[6] Pitre, *Jesus and the Last Supper*, 26–28.

[7] Brant Pitre has given a convincing argument that "we can legitimately speak of Jesus' words over the bread and wine . . . as words of institution. In these words of interpretation and command, Jesus is establishing a new cultic act, a new Passover sacrifice and meal." He also adduces evidence from the Qumran community (Rule of the Community, 1QS 2:19 and Rule of the Congregation, 1QSa 2:20–22), and from Philo (*Special Laws* 2.146). Cf. Pitre, *Jesus and the Last Supper*, 417–426.

nection with the bread and wine is to imply that they, too, will be repeated, and that they will have their place within the relationship between God and Israel going forward into the future. Furthermore, any explanation that severs the connection between the Last Supper and the eucharist will multiply historical problems: it requires scholars to specify the origins of the eucharist apart from the Last Supper, and then to account for the nonetheless pervasive appearance of this connection in the NT.

It seems much simpler to accept the assertions of the NT authors, not least Paul, that their ritual meal was traceable to Jesus, and that he intended its repetition in some form. We are not, of course, clear of all historical problems: there is still a need to explain how the meal came to be celebrated weekly or more-than-weekly rather than only on Passover, while yet retaining its Paschal associations. But this is a much easier problem to solve than those posed by the claim that the institution of the eucharist was an invention of Paul. Here, it is helpful to consider the proposal of Cullmann that the eucharist shows the influence of other meals than the Last Supper, namely the post-resurrection meals of Jesus.[8] The Jewish disciples of Jesus already grasped the intended use of the bread and wine as a means of sharing in his sacrificial death. They understood this partly because it was implicit already in the messianic bread-ritual that Jesus took up, but partly also because of the words of interpretation. From this understanding, coupled with the view that Jesus' death on the cross was an act of salvation, the desire of the early disciples to be united with the crucified Jesus would have been sufficient to motivate the repetition of the bread and wine rituals, whether Jesus intended such repetition or not.

The historical evidence of the following three centuries shows that the eucharist was by no means de-paschalized but was known by Christians and by Jews to be a Passover ritual transformed. This is exactly what we should expect if a Passover ritual were transformed into a weekly (or more frequent) meal. Awareness by both Jews and early Christians of the origins of the eucharist in Jesus' last Passover is manifested in a series of fingerprints that have been left on the pages of some of the earliest Rabbinic and Christian sources. These traces constitute a separate and supporting thread of evidence for Daube's thesis.

A HAGGADAH IN NT TIMES?

The word "Haggadah" means "narration." In the context of Passover, it denotes the scripted liturgy of prayers, stories, and ritual actions followed

---

[8] Cullmann, *Essays on the Lord's Supper*.

by Jews in the course of the meal.[9] The earliest manuscripts of the Passover Haggadah are all from the late medieval period, such as the Golden Haggadah (from Barcelona, around 1320) and the Sarajevo Haggadah (Bosnia, 1380 or so). It is possible that the prayers and recitations were not written down for centuries. Partly because of this paucity of written evidence, some scholars have doubted whether there was any set liturgy for the Passover in the first century CE.[10] Yet Petuchowski is actually erring on the side of caution when he says that the haggadah is "largely composed of tannaitic material,"[11] that is, material from before 250 CE. When material within the Haggadah is attributed to named rabbis, the names are those of Gamaliel and Hillel. The Gamaliel in question is either the contemporary of Jesus and Paul (Acts 5:34) or his grandson who headed the Sanhedrin after the first revolt (c. 80).[12] Daube, Jeremias, and Casey prefer to identify him as the grandfather; Kulp and Bokser prefer the grandson. But about Hillel, there is no question, since he is even earlier (traditionally 110 BCE to 10 BCE). There is thus no reason to doubt that much of the material of the Haggadah is old, and that Jews in the second Temple period were very much engaged in the same sorts of rituals and ceremonies as we find in the later medieval Haggadah. The New Testament's casual use of technical terms such as "the cup after supper" (τὸ ποτήριον μετὰ τὸ δειπνῆσαι, 1 Cor. 11:25), or "the cup of blessing" (τὸ ποτήριον τῆς εὐλογίας, 1 Cor. 10:16) shows that the Passover in Jesus' day had a set order and liturgy composed of elements and parts that could be referred to by name. And the New Testament is in fact evidence for Jewish praxis in the first century, even if some scholars have, out of theological *parti pris*, refused to use that evidence.[13]

---

[9]Haggadah is not to be confused with the Aramaic term Aggadah. The latter denotes the portions of Rabbinic literature that are devoted to anecdotes and folklore rather than to discussion of legal issues.

[10]Kulp speaks of "a near consensus among scholars that the Passover seder as described in rabbinic literature did not yet exist during the Second Temple period" but overreaches when he claims that "nearly all scholars agree that there was no seder or haggadah while the Temple still stood." Joshua Kulp, "The Origins of the Seder and Haggadah" in *Currents in Biblical Research* 4.1 (2005), 109–134. Instone-Brewer disagrees: "The relatively simple meal of the first century gradually grew into a long and fixed set of procedures and liturgy which are known as the Passover Seder (סֵדֶר, 'order') or Aggadah (אַגָּדָה, 'narrative'), much of which is present in embryonic form in the pre-70 traditions." David Instone Brewer, *Traditions of the Rabbis from the Era of the New Testament, vol. 2A: Feasts and Sabbaths: Passover and Atonement* (Grand Rapids, MI: Eerdmans, 2011), 116.

[11]Jakob Josef Petuchowski, "'Do this in remembrance of me' (1 Cor 11:24)," *Journal of Biblical Literature* 76.4 (Dec. 1957), 295.

[12]As Tabory points out, it is "quite probable that Rabban Gamliel is merely emphasizing the importance of an earlier tradition so that, even if we are dealing here with the younger Rabban Gamliel, the custom itself may go back to the time of the Temple." Joseph Tabory, "The Passover Eve Ceremony—An Historical Outline" *Immanuel* 12 (1981), 32–43 at 39.

[13]Astonishingly, some scholars have even attempted to describe Passover in the first century without taking into account the evidence of the New Testament. For instance, Tamara Prosic, *The Development and Symbolism of the Passover to 70 CE* (London: T&T Clark, 2004) contains no citations or references to the New Testament at all, and no references to the Last Supper accounts or to Paul. The words of Alan Segal are relevant: "Paul then becomes an extremely important person in the

BATTLE SCARS IN THE PASSOVER HAGGADAH: DAYENU AND IMPROPERIA

The text of the Passover Haggadah itself bears the marks of a fierce conflict between early Christianity and nascent Rabbinic Judaism.[14] Perhaps the most striking is the correspondence between a section of the Passover Haggadah called the Dayenu and an ancient Christian liturgy for Good Friday called the Improperia. Both of these have roughly the same form, which may be characterized as a "midrashic litany." The correspondence between them was first noted by the great Jewish scholar of the history of liturgy, Eric Werner.[15] The Dayenu's first appearance is either in the Seder of Rav Amram (ninth century) or else, if it is a later interpolation in that text, then in the siddur of Rav Saadiah Gaon (tenth century), while the Improperia is first attested in the pseudepigraphal Pontificale of Prudentius (846–891, though Prudentius himself lived 348–413). Both texts are probably much earlier than their first attestations, however.

The Improperia reads as a series of complaints by God against Israel, each pairing the benefits of the Exodus with the injustices of the Passion, using a catchword technique (e.g."I *led* you out of Egypt . . . but you have *led* your Savior, and nailed him to a cross"):

My people, what have I done to you? Or how have I injured you? Answer me.
Because I led you out of the land of Egypt: you prepared a cross for your Savior.
Ἅγιος ὁ Θεός.
Holy is God.
Ἅγιος ἰσχυρός.
Holy, strong.
Ἅγιος ἀθάνατος ἐλεῖσον ἡμᾶς.
Holy immortal one, have mercy upon us.

Because I led you through the desert for forty years and fed you with manna and led you into a land plentifully good: you prepared a cross for your Savior.
Ἅγιος ὁ Θεός.

---

study of Judaism. . . . But Jewish historians have been very wary about using him. Why should we believe what an apostate tells about Judaism? The answer is, of course, that we, as historians should never flatly believe anything in the historical record. But equally true methodologically is that if we want to be historians, we must also be responsible for weighing every piece of evidence, no matter how biased, and seeing what it does tell us about rabbinic Judaism. Under the circumstances it seems prudent for Jewish historians to look at Paul's witness to Pharisaism, skewed by conversion though it certainly is, to discover what he does tell us about it." Alan Segal, "Paul's Jewish Presuppositions" in *The Cambridge Companion to Paul* (Cambridge: Cambridge University Press, 2003), 162–163.

[14]Cf. especially Israel Yuval, "Easter and Passover as early Jewish Christian Dialogue," *Passover and Easter: Origin and History to Modern Times*, ed. Paul Bradshaw and Lawrence Hoffman (South Bend, IN: University of Notre Dame Press, 2000), 98–123.

[15]Eric Werner, *The Sacred Bridge*, vol. II (New York: Ktav, 1984). Chapter 6: "Two Hymns for Passover and Good Friday," 127–148.

Holy is God . . .
What more should I have done for you, that I did not do? I planted you as my own splendid vine; and you became very bitter to me, for you gave me vinegar for my thirst, and you pieced your Savior's side with a spear.
Holy is God . . .
For your sake I afflicted Egypt along with its first born; and you handed me over to be whipped.
My people, what have I done to you? Or how have I injured you? Answer me.
I led you up from Egypt and drowned Pharaoh in the Red Sea; and you handed me over to the chief Priests.
My people, what have I done to you? Or how have I injured you? Answer me.
I opened the sea before you, and you opened my side with a spear.
My people, what have I done to you? Or how have I injured you? Answer me.
I went before you in a column of cloud; and you led me to the praetorium of Pilate.
My people, what have I done to you? Or how have I injured you? Answer me.
I fed you with manna in the desert; and you struck me with blows and scourges.
My people, what have I done to you? Or how have I injured you? Answer me.
I gave you to drink of the water from the rock; and you gave me to drink of gall and vinegar.
My people, what have I done to you? Or how have I injured you? Answer me.
I struck the kings of the Canaanites for your sake; and you have struck my head with a cane.
My people, what have I done to you? Or how have I injured you? Answer me.
I gave you a royal scepter; and you gave me a crown of thorns for my head.
My people, what have I done to you? Or how have I injured you? Answer me.
I raised you up with great power; and you have hung me on the bar of the cross.
My people, what have I done to you? Or how have I injured you? Answer me.[16]

To this text, the Dayenu (Hebrew: "enough for us") reads as a rebuttal:

If he had brought us out from Egypt, but had not brought judgments upon them, *Dayenu*! ("It would have been enough for us!")
If he had brought judgments upon them, but had not brought [judgments] upon their gods, *Dayenu*!
If he had brought [judgments] upon their gods, but had not slain their firstborn children, *Dayenu*!
If he had slain their firstborn children, but not given their possessions to us, *Dayenu*!
If he had given us their possessions, but had not divided the sea for us, *Dayenu*!
If he had divided the sea for us, but had not brought us through the midst of it on dry ground, *Dayenu*!
If he had brought us through the sea on dry ground, but had not drowned our enemies in the midst of it, *Dayenu*!

---

[16]My translation from the Latin text of the Improperia in the *Gregorian Missal* (Solesmes: Les Editions des Solesmes, 1990), 311–317, which also offers another English translation.

If he had drowned our enemies in the midst of [the sea], but had not supplied our needs in the desert for forty years, *Dayenu*!
If he had supplied our needs in the desert for forty years, but had not fed us the manna, *Dayenu*!
If he had fed us the manna, but had not given us the Sabbath, *Dayenu*!
If he had given us the Sabbath, but had not brought us before Mount Sinai, *Dayenu*!
If he had brought us before Mount Sinai, but had not given us the Torah, *Dayenu*!
If he had given us the Torah, but had not gathered us to the Land of Israel, *Dayenu*!
If he had gathered us to the Land of Israel, but had not built for us the House of the Sanctuary, *Dayenu*![17]

The correspondence between the Dayenu and the Improperia and the inclusion of each in the liturgies for Passover and Good Friday, respectively, constitute historical evidence that the text of the Passover Haggadah was altered to respond to Christian interpretations and challenges. In form and content, the Dayenu appears to be a direct reply to the Improperia. Eric Werner originally noticed the correspondence between the Dayenu and the Improperia, but considered the Dayenu to be the first of the two, and the Improperia to be a response to it. Israel Yuval argued that since the Dayenu first appears in the tenth-century siddur of Rav Saadiah Gaon, and not as a mandatory text, it is unlikely to be earlier than the Improperia.[18] Alistair Stewart-Sykes points out that Melito of Sardis' (†180) similar list of benefits bestowed by God on Israel stops before the Dayenu's listing of the building of the Temple and switches instead to Christ as the true temple.[19] While it is possible that there may have been a common source for both litanies,[20] the consensus of scholarship dates the Haggadah to after 70 CE—*pace* Werner, who assumed that the Dayenu was earlier than the Improperia, relying on Finkelstein's controversial dating of the Haggadah. It is thus likely that the Dayenu's inclusion in the Seder is an answer to early Christian criticism of the sort evidenced in the later medieval Improperia and Melito's early second-century *Peri Pascha*. (The protomartyr Stephen's sermon in Acts 7 is of a similar genre, confronting his Jewish audience with a resumé of their past rejections of God's leaders.) In that case, the

---

[17]My translation from the Hebrew text of the Dayenu in N. Glatzer, ed. *The Passover Haggadah* (New York: Schocken, 1989), which also offers another English translation.

[18]On the debate over the relative dates of the Dayenu and Improperia, cf. Joseph Tabory, *The JPS Commentary on the Haggadah* (Philadelphia, PA: Jewish Publication Society, 2008), 46; Eric Werner, "Melito of Sardis, the First Poet of Deicide," *Hebrew Union College Annual* 37 (1966), 191–210, and "Two Hymns for Passover and Good Friday" in Eric Werner, *The Sacred Bridge, vol. 2* (Ktav, 1984), 127–148; Israel J. Yuval, "Easter and Passover as Early Jewish-Christian Dialogue" in *Passover and Easter: Origin and History to Modern Times,* ed. Paul F. Bradshaw and Lawrence A. Hoffman (South Bend, IN: University of Notre Dame Press, 2000), 98–123, especially 103–105; also, David Flusser, "Some Notes on Easter and the Passover Haggadah," *Immanuel* 7 (1977), 52–60.

[19]Alistair Stewart-Sykes, *The Lamb's High Feast* (Leiden: E.J. Brill, 1998), 195 and 63.

[20]Finkelstein's suggestion of a pre-Maccabean source has not met with scholarly acceptance. Louis Finkelstein, "Pre-Maccabean Documents in the Passover Haggadah" *HThR* 35 (1942) 291–332 and 36 (1943) 1–38.

Rabbis' answer to the church's accusation has become a permanent feature of the Passover Haggadah to this day, which suggests that Christians had been very successful in appealing to the Passover in their proselytizing of Jews. Alternatively, if we agree with Werner's claim that the Dayenu is earlier than Melito, then the Passover Haggadah would appear to be even earlier than, e.g., Kulp and Bokser would suggest, so that it is likely to be a first-century production. In general, the resemblance of Melito's *Peri Pascha* to the general shape of the later Passover Haggadah suggests that something like the seder was earlier than Melito.

THE DAMNATIO MEMORIAE OF MOSES

A second "battle scar" from the conflict between the early church and the synagogue lies in the rearrangement and expurgation of the Haggadah itself. Daube points out that the series of scripted questions by the "four sons" ("What does this service mean to you?" etc.) are placed nonsensically before the performance of the ritual meal to which they pertain. "Only the gravest reasons could have warranted so drastic a change, which ruins the whole structure of the celebration. It was done in order to forestall attempts to divert the exposition from its safe, recognized path into a heretical one—towards Christianity."[21]

Finally, there is the remarkable fact that the Haggadah contains no mention of Moses:[22]

> His name is not mentioned once in any of the prayers and recitals woven around the Biblical record, and, more than that, no biblical passage mentioning it is quoted. It is a fantastic tour de force. Think what it means. It is as if one were to spend annually a night commemorating Britain's rescue in the Second World War, rehearsing the main course of events as well as telling elaborate stories about them—without once mentioning Churchill. A fantastic tour de force: but there must be no human Mediator.[23]

---

[21]Daube, "He That Cometh," 437. Petuchowski adds, "This [omission of Moses] may have been accidental. But it is also possible that this omission was intentional. No person or hero was to be commemorated on this occasion. The real 'hero' of this drama, as it unfolds in the traditional account, was God himself! Indeed, there is a *midrash* incorporated in the Passover *haggadah* which may give us a clue to this omission. The following comments are made on Exodus 12:12: 'For I will go through the land of Egypt in that night'—*I, not an angel*: 'And I will smite all the first-born in the land of Egypt'—*I, not a seraph*: 'And against all the gods of Egypt will I execute judgment'—*I, not a messenger*. 'I am the Lord'—*I am he, and no other*." Then, in a footnote: "It is an interesting field for speculation to determine whether or not this *midrash* already represents a Jewish reaction to the role of Jesus in Christianity in general, and in the *seder* ritual in particular." Jakob Josef Petuchowski, "'Do this in remembrance of me' (1 Cor. 11:24)," *Journal of Biblical Literature* 76.4 (Dec. 1957), 293–298.

[22]Cf. Petuchowski, "'Do this in remembrance of me,'" 293–298.

[23]Daube, "He That Cometh," 438.

Similarly radical censorship can be adduced from outside the Passover in other aspects of Jewish history. The Septuagint, for instance, was once the pride of the Jews, their greatest literary production in Greek, and widely used in the Jews' proselytizing of Gentiles. But so successful were Christian interpretations and appeals to the Greek text that by the third century, the Rabbis rejected the Septuagint.[24]

These revisions of the Haggadah are all aimed, not against the eucharist as a new and heretical rite, but against the Christian use of the Passover as a way of identifying Jesus as Israel's Messiah. That is, they are aimed at preventing the very identification which, if Daube is correct, Jesus used the Passover bread to make.

THE CASE FROM PHILOLOGY

Despite these efforts to prevent Christological exegesis of the Seder, the Haggadah still retains a telling vestige of the ritual that Daube and Eisler conjectured: namely, in response to the "wise" son's demand to know the meaning of "all the testimonies, statutes, and regulations" commanded by God concerning the Passover, the leader of the Seder is to make the following scripted reply: ואין מפטירין אחר הפסח אפיקומן. "After the Passover lamb, we do not conclude with *afiqoman*."[25] Daube remarks how telling it is that this answer should be given to the "wise" son. How is it an adequate answer to his momentous question? It seems, on first glance, an utterly trivial detail. But the very fact that it is so poorly understood and seems so incongruous as an answer to the wise son's question suggests that there is more to this word than first appears.

The word *afiqoman* is manifestly Greek, not Hebrew or Aramaic. Daube and Eisler proposed that it is from ἀφικόμην or perhaps ἀφικόμενος, the aorist

---

[24]On the rejection of the LXX by Rabbinic authorities, see Emmanuel Tov, "The Septuagint between Judaism and Christianity," in *Textual Criticism of the Hebrew Bible, Qumran, Septuagint: Collected Essays* (Leiden: E.J. Brill, 2015), 449–470. Contrary to the 1871 theory of Heinrich Graetz that located the decisive moment of the LXX's rejection and the acceptance of the canonicity of the Kethuvim ("the writings"—the third portion of the Hebrew Bible after the Torah and the Prophets) at a posited council of Jamnia or Yavneh sometime between 70 and 90 CE, most modern scholars reject the idea of such a council, and simply conclude that the LXX fell out of favor in the first or second century: "Whether or not rabbinic Judaism officially rejected the LXX is unclear, but it was definitely disregarded since the rabbis did not quote from it." (Tov, "The Septuagint between Judaism and Christianity," 451.) Alfred Rahlfs' preface to his edition of the LXX says simply: "The Jews became alienated from the LXX a short time after its adoption by the Christian Church." Cf. Alfred Rahlfs, "History of the Septuagint Text," in *Septuaginta: Editio altera* (Stuttgart: Deutsche Bibelgesellschaft, 2006), XXXVI.

[25]*The Passover Haggadah*, ed. Goldschmidt, 39. The same words also occur in the Mishnah, m.Pes. 10.8. As Daube notes, they are contrary to Hebrew syntax and no translation of them can be considered successful.

and aorist participle of ἀφικνέομαι, the Greek verb "to come, to arrive"—thus, either "the coming one" or "I have come." For this *vorlage*, no changes of spelling are required; the transliteration into Hebrew follows the usual patterns of loanword orthography in the Talmud and Mishnah. It is the easiest of all solutions. Yet this "obvious, philologically easiest, naheliegendste derivation" was not only lost to the medieval Jewish commentators, who "give fanciful etymologies,"[26] but also has created a sort of desperation among modern scholars, who want to avoid its momentous consequences for the history of religion.

Our topic now requires some weighing of linguistic evidence and criteria. The matter is important, because the main objection that has been set against Daube's explanation for the meaning of *afiqoman* is to claim that the word is from some other Greek root. Those who reject Daube's and Eisler's derivation of *afiqoman* from ἀφίκομην[27] are not united on any alternative. All the competing proposals fall short philologically.[28]

Nahum Glatzer in his popular scholarly edition of the Passover Haggadah opts for ἐπικώμιος, "festival procession," saying that "the term covers the after-dinner revelry which was a customary sequel to the ancient banquet, especially for the young. The sages prohibited the afiqoman on the Passover night so that attention be not diverted from the paschal sacrifice."[29] But ἐπικώμιος occurs in only one Greek author in all of Greek literature: the archaic epinician poet Pindar, where it is an adjective, not a noun, meaning "related to a celebration." Even when it is a substantive (i.e., an adjective used as a noun), in Nemean Ode 6.32, it means, not "revelry," but the praise (= ἐγκωμίον, Lat. and Eng. encomium) appropriate to a victorious athlete in the Olympic games

---

[26]Daube, "He That Cometh," p 432.

[27]Either directly, or from the participial form ἀφικόμενος, since we have no way of knowing whether the Greek masculine ending was dropped, as happens frequently in transliterations of names from Greek into Hebrew and Aramaic (cf. Eleazar : Lazarus), or the aorist first person ἀφικόμην was transliterated whole and unaltered. On transliterations into Hebrew and Aramaic from Greek, see Richard Gottheil and Samuel Krauss, "Greek Language and the Jews," *Jewish Encyclopedia* (New York: Funk & Wagnalls, 1906) which gives a thorough discussion of the rules by which the rabbinic sources transliterated Greek.

[28]The topic of Greek loanwords in Rabbinic literature has always been a vexed one. Near the end of the nineteenth century, Samuel Krauss and Immanuel Löw published their *Griechische und Lateinische Lehnwörter im Talmud, Midrasch und Targum* (Berlin, 1898) in which they catalogued and discussed 2,370 words. This work was immediately criticized by linguists, who rejected 30–50% of its etymologies. Jastrow acerbically comments, "It is to be regretted that the proclivity to find Latin and Greek in words indisputably Semitic has led the author [sc. Krauss] into a labyrinth of fatal errors" (Jastrow, *Dictionary*, XII.) More recently, Daniel Sperber has critiqued Krauss and Löw's work and begun the task of compiling a more comprehensive dictionary of loanwords on a sounder linguistic foundation. Hitherto, however, the fruits of this effort have been published only as specialized dictionaries pertaining to circumscribed subjects: first legal loanwords in *A Dictionary of Greek and Latin Legal Terms in the Mishnah, Talmud and Midrashic Literature* (Ramat-Gan, Israel: Bar-Ilan University Press,1984), and then seafaring terminology in *Nautica Talmudica* (Ramat-Gan, Israel: Bar-Ilan University Press, 1986). Neither of these works includes the word '*afiqoman*.'

[29]N. Glatzer, ed. *The Passover Haggadah*, 33.

or other such Greek contests. There is thus no basis in Greek literature for connecting ἐπικώμιος with "after-dinner revelry."

A further difficulty arises from the pointing of the word in the Hebrew text: it is אֲפִיקוֹמָן (*afiqōman*), beginning with *hatuph-pathah* (a shortened "a"), not *hatuph-seghol* (a shortened "e"). While this deviation can be paralleled by at least one other Greek loan-word in Hebrew (i.e. *apikoros*, "atheist," from the name of the Greek philosopher Epicurus), there is a second vocalic transliteration that cannot be so easily explained: there is no second yodh (=i) in the spelling to account for the second iota of ἐπικώμιος; it is thus not an accurate representation of any form of that Greek word.

Like Glatzer, Baruch Bokser's edition of the Talmud Yerushalmi transliterates the word אֲפִיקוֹמָן as "*afiqomon*," thereby altering the last vowel to a *qames-hatuph* (short "o") in the manner of Ashkenazic pronunciation[30] to conform more closely to his preferred etymon, namely ἐπικώμιον. Yet it still is not a good match: one would expect אפיקומין (*afiqomiyon*) with a י for the Geeek ι, but there is none.[31] Then there is the qames under the penultimate mem: -מָ. This represents a quantitatively long a, which corresponds well to the Greek η. Taken together with the final nun, it gives the syllable מָן-, -μην, which is the first person aorist termination of the Greek verb ἀφικνέομαι. It is quite different from the final syllable of ἐπὶ κῶμον (*epi komon*), and even more different from the ending of ἐπικωμίον (*epikōmion*). This, despite the fact that "in the Talmud, Midrash, and Targum the Greek and Latin letters are transcribed according to purely phonetic principles."[32]

---

[30]Ashkenazic Hebrew pronounces qames as an open-mid back rounded vowel, so that the second king of Israel is *Dovid* or *Duvid* rather than *David*.

[31]Rarely do Greek loanwords elide the iota of the -ιον ending. I have been able to find only one example: συνεδρίον > Sanhedrin.

[32]R. Gottheil and S. Krauss, "Greek Language and the Jews" in *Encyclopedia Judaica* (New York: 1906), sv. The authors add that because of this straightforward method of transliterating Greek loanwords, "[the Talmud's] transcription [of Greek terms] may therefore assist in some measure the work of solving the probable original pronunciation of Greek, still a matter of dispute." In my analysis, I attempt to follow the principles laid out by Julia Krivoruchko:

"Good scholarly practice for suggesting a new *etymon* should include a proof that previously suggested *etyma* are worse matches (= that they violate more principles of loanword reconstruction). Like a jigsaw puzzle, loanword etymology demands fine matching, and if one aspect of the reconstruction is found unfit, it usually means that others were forced into their position too." This is precisely what has happened in the case of *afiqoman*: the transliterations are faulty, the cultural background is also a poor fit, the proposed loanwords are actually mistranslated, and there is no lexical support in Greek literature. Cf. Julia Krivoruchko, "Greek Loanwords in Rabbinic Literature: Reflections on Current Research Methodology," *Greek Scripture and the Rabbis*, ed. T.M. Law and A. Salvesen (Leuven: Peeters 2012), 193–216, ad 208. In the present case, Glatzer's choice of ἐπικώμιος violates Krivoruchko's criterion that "The phonetic sequence achieved through (a) and (b) should be a lexico-semantic variant *which existed in the given period or region, that is, occurs in the corpus of contemporaneous Greek texts.*" (emphasis mine)

The oldest of the modern proposals is that of Marcus Jastrow in his dictionary of the Talmud, later echoed by Saul Lieberman.[33] He gives two possibilities for אֲפִיקוֹמָן: "off to the *komos*" (a party with revelry and dancing) and "dessert." On this reading, the word is a transliteration of the Greek ἐπικώμοι, with the Greek masculine plural ending –οι replaced by the Hebrew plural –in, thus: *epikomin*. (The consonants are non-negotiable, since they, unlike the vowels, were actually written in the Amoraic and Tannaitic sources.) This is an improvement over Glatzer's *epikomios* in that it actually corresponds to the Hebrew letters of the Mishnah's transliterated word. Joseph Tabory adopts *epikomos* as the etymon behind *afiqoman,* glossing it as "revelry . . . that was a common after-dinner feature at Greco-Roman meals."[34] This etymology is thus attractive to scholars who attempt to understand the Passover (and eucharist) against the background of Greco-Roman symposia. The adoption of Jastrow's proposal has accordingly become the main basis for most modern rejections of Eisler's and Daube's explanation: there is no need to consider the idea of the bread representing the Messiah, because the name *afiqoman* can be explained as a rejected Greco-Roman custom of after-dinner revelry. Yet when we seek a basis in Greek literature for this proposal, we find nothing to support it. In all extant Greek literature, the word ἐπίκωμος means "a reveller." For instance, Dio Chrysostom, Oration 33.14.9:

> For these men come into life like some revellers or other (ἐπίκωμοί τινες), playing flutes and singing and getting drunk, under the impression that they have fallen in with some sort of festival or gathering of profligates. . . .[35]

Contrary to Jastrow, the word ἐπίκωμος does not mean "after-dinner entertainment" or "things belonging to the after-meal, dessert, sweet-meats," but rather the *participants* in a revel or wild party. It is special pleading to claim, as Baruch Bokser does in a parenthetical interpolation to his translation of *y.Pes.* 10.4,[36] that the Rabbis had such a practice in mind, since there is no

---

[33]Marcus Jastrow, *Dictionary of the Targumim, the Talmud Babli and Yerushalmi, and the Midrashic Literature* (New York: Judaica Press, 1903, repr. 1985), 104. Jastrow's proposal was later defended by Saul Lieberman, *Hayerushalmi Kifshuto* (Jerusalem: 1934), 521.

[34]Joseph Tabory, *The JPS Commentary on the Haggadah* (Philadelphia, PA: Jewish Publication Society, 2008), 15.

[35]Cf. other instances in Diogenes Laertius 4.62.1; Plutarch *Moralia* 128D9, 148B2, 357F6, 472D5, 784B9; Athenaeus, *Deipnosophistae* 5.8.24; Pindar *Pyth.* 10.6, *Nem.* 6.32, *Nem.* 8.50; Callimachus fr. 384.49; Apollodorus Gramm. fr. 70.40; Alciphron Rhet., Ep. 4.10.1.4; Triphiodorus Epic. Ἅλωσις Ἰλίου, 561; Cornelius Alexander Polyhist. fr. 144.1; Manetho Hist. fr. 13.17; Johannes Stobaeus 4.37.9.6; Priscus Hist. fr. 53.1–2; Georgius Syncellus *Eclog. Chron.* 115.22; Pseudo-Zonaras *Lexicon,* sv. ε, p. 792.18; and five Byzantine lexicons reproducing the word's usage by one or more of these authors. In every instance, the word means "partier" or "reveller." There is not a single instance of the word meaning what Lieberman and Jastrow want it to mean.

[36]Jacob Neusner and Baruch Bokser, *Yerushalmi Pesahim* vol. 13 (Chicago: University of Chicago Press, 1995), ad 10:4 and 10:7–8A, 495 and 503.

evidence in all of Greek literature for the use of the word ἐπίκωμος to mean an activity *after* a banquet. Instead, it denotes the *participants in* a banquet. Instone-Brewer claims that Plutarch's *Moralia* 148B "calls an ἐπίκωμος a time of 'drinking and enjoyment.'"[37] When we inspect the passage, however, we find no such thing. The word occurs in a scene of morbid humor: a human skeleton, brought to a symposium as a grim *memento mori* for the partiers, is called an ἄχαρις καὶ ἄωρος ἐπίκωμος—"a graceless and untimely party-guest" (i.e., not a revel, but a reveler). In the same note, Instone-Brewer says that Plutarch "in 784B mentions 'an ignorant man who comes by night' who is 'knocking unseasonably' in search of an ἐπίκωμος," implying that an ἐπίκωμος is an after-dinner party. But this is again a mistranslation of Plutarch's text, in which an older man trying to involve himself in affairs of state is said to be "knocking unseasonably at the door of the praetorium, like a rather artless *partygoer* who has arrived in the middle of the night (τις ἀτεχνότερος ὢν νύκτωρ ἐπίκωμος ἀφιγμένος)." Again, the word denotes a reveler, not a revel: it offers no support for Lieberman's and Jastrow's translation, nor for the rejection of Daube's and Eisler's. Unfortunately, Instone-Brewer makes this "after-dinner party" interpretation the basis for his conclusions about the date of the rule about *afiqoman* and thereby for the chronology of the seder's development. Century-old lexical mistakes thus continue to wreak havoc not only with the understanding of the term *afiqoman*, but also with the study of the origin of the seder, and the dating of its constituent elements. Daube's judgment must stand: "They do not even disdain formations for which there is no evidence whatever in the whole of Greek literature."[38]

R. Nathan Goldberg's translation of the Haggadah (1949, 1993) opts for an emended reading that fits better with the wise son's request to be informed of the meaning of all the ordinances of the Passover and prudently avoids the issue of the meaning of *afiqoman* entirely by not glossing the word, but simply leaving it untranslated: "And you shall explain to him all the laws of Passover, to the very last detail about the Afiqoman."

I could multiply further instances of mistaken explanations by modern rabbis.[39] The Amoraim who compiled the Talmud differ among themselves about the meaning of the word, which suggests that even they, in 450–550, no longer knew its meaning:

---

[37]David Instone-Brewer, *Traditions of the Rabbis from the Era of the New Testament*, vol. 2A. (Grand Rapids, MI: Eerdmans: 2011), 189–190.

[38]Daube, "He That Cometh," 432.

[39]For a few more, see here: http://www.balashon.com/2006/04/afikoman.html. For a wholesale denial of the word's Greek origin, and unpersuasive attempt to derive it from an Aramaic *vorlage* ("*afiku mina*"—"take it [the middle matzah] out from them [the other two]"), cf. http://joesettler.blogspot.com/2007/04/origin-of-afikomen.html.

R. Simon said in the name of R. Inainy bar R. Sisay, "Kinds of song." R. Yohanan said, "Kinds of sweet things." Samuel said, "For example, the mushrooms and pigeons of Hanania bar Shilat." (*y.Pes.* 10:7–8A)[40]

The Tosefta (*t.Pes.* 10:11) renders the Mishnah's injunction, "We must not offer dessert such as nuts, dates, and sweetmeats after eating the Paschal lamb." The Babylonian Talmud breaks this opinion down, attributing it to named rabbis: "Shemuel said: 'for example, truffles for me and young doves for Abba. And R. Hanina bar Shela and R. Jochanan: for example, dates, toasted cereals, and walnuts" (*b.Pes.* 119b). Lietzmann rightly rejects these attempts to identify *'afiqoman* with edible delicacies ". . . diese jüdischen Erklärer das Wort im Sinne von 'Nachtisch' fassen und gebrauchen, daß diese Bedeutung aber das griechische ἐπικώμιον nicht hat und auch nicht wohl haben kann."[41] The attempt to identify *'afiqoman* with "dessert" is transparently a guess at what might come "after the Passover meal" without any appeal to the Greek language. As Martin Sicker states, the "problem was that the Sages of the Talmud in Persian Mesopotamia and their later Rabbinic disciples, as opposed to the earlier Sages of the Mishnah in Roman Palestine, were no longer conversant with the Greek language."[42]

Lietzmann understands the explanation of R. Simeon in the name of R. Inainy bar Sisay as "types of song" (מִינֵי זֶמֶר, *y.Pes.* 10.8). We will see shortly that this is a mistake, but let us first examine whether there is any support for it in Greek. It has a slight possibility of matching some Greek *vorlage*, but it is a remote and extremely unlikely one: in Greek literature, the poet Pindar uses the word ἐπικώμιος both as an adjective with ὕμνος and as a substantive to designate the victory odes which he was in the business of composing for the celebration of athletes:

> . . . the sons of Aleuas, wishing to bring a song of praise (ἐπικωμίαν) to Hippocleas with excellent voice . . . (*Pyth.* 10.6)

> The Bassidae, a much-famed family, are not lacking [in good deeds], since their ships carry suitable praise-songs (ἴδια . . . ἐπικώμια). (*Nem.* 6.32)

> Surely the victory hymn (ἐπικώμιος ὕμνος) existed long before strife arose between Adrastus and the descendants of Cadmus. (*Nem.* 8.50)

If we ask what aspect or part of the Passover celebration this might be connected with, the answer is surely the Hallel psalms proclaiming the kingship

---

[40]trans. in B. Bokser, *Yerushalmi Talmud*, p. 503.
[41]Lietzmann, "Jüdische Passahsitten und der ἀφικόμενος," 301.
[42]Martin Sicker, *A Passover Seder Companion and Analytic Introduction to the Haggadah* (Lincoln: iUniverse, 2004), 15.

and victory of Israel's God. Unlike some other parts of the Rabbinic Seder, we can be reasonably confident that the Hallel psalms were already used in second temple times, since the singing of such psalms is mentioned in both m.Pes. 5.7 and in the gospels, Matthew 26:30 and Mark 14:26.[43] But the connection is made more difficult by the fact that the Hallel psalms were sung *after* the meal—precisely at the time when the Mishnaic prohibition appears to forbid *'afiqomen*. There is also the problem that all forms of ἐπικώμιος include the letter -ι- before the ending, and that this letter is omitted from the Hebrew transliteration.

But it matters little how slender the evidence for אפיקמן as "kinds of song" may be. The reality is that that explanation is not actually put forward by any ancient source at all. It arises from the confusion of two Hebrew homonyms, זֶמֶר, "fruits, dessert" and זֶמֶר, "music, song." These two nouns are from two distinct verbal roots: on the one hand זמר, "to nip, to prune," for example, a fruit tree;[44] and on the other hand זמר, "to make music, sing."[45] The former is the noun in R. Simeon's definition of *'afiqomen*. In support of the meaning "fruits" is the fact that זֶמֶר is appended to the construct מִינֵי, "types of"—used very frequently of biological vegetable species, and only later and metaphorically of abstract entities. Likewise, the immediate context in *y.Pes.* 10:7–8 supports the idea that זֶמֶר is "fruits, dessert": it is of a piece with the other more specific suggestions of edible delicacies by the other rabbis in the immediate context.[46] And in that case, R. Simeon's explanation should be lumped together with the other "dessert" guesses and dismissed for the same reasons: it is simply an attempt to conjecture what might normally come "after Pesaḥ" were it not for the cryptic Mishnaic prohibition.

Lietzmann accepts the etymology of R. Ḥiyyah in the Talmud Yerushalmi: "What does אפיקמן mean? That one does not leave one company (*ḥaburah*) and join another" (*y.Pes.* 10.4). He explains that the word should be read as *epi komon*, which he understands as "auf den Bummel!" ("off to a stroll!") or "von einer Kneiperei zur anderen" ("from one boozy party to another").[47] Here, at least, there is some lexical support in Greek literature. Theognis (1.940) declares, "I cannot sing sweet and clear like the nightingale, for last night I went to a revel (ἐπὶ κῶμον ἔβην)." Diogenes Laertius' life of Menedemus is similar: "When Antigonus consulted him as to whether he should go to a revel (εἰ ἐπὶ κῶμον ἀφίκοιτο), he sent a message to say no

---

[43]Cf. the discussion and references in Israel Yuval, *Two Nations in Your Womb* (Berkeley, CA: University of California Press, 2008), 63, n. 77.
[44]Lev. 25.3 and Is. 5.6 and, in Rabbinic literature, *b.Sabb.* 73b, *b.Sanh.* 26a.
[45]The word occurs dozens of times in the Psalter and, in Rabbinic literature, in *Genesis Rabbah* 91 and *Tosefta Ohol.* XVI.8. Cf. HALOT and Jastrow's *Dictionary*.
[46]Thus, rightly, M. Jastrow, *Dictionary*, s.v. זֶמֶר.
[47]H. Lietzmann, "Jüdische Passahsitten und der ἀφικόμενος," 301.

more than this, that he was the son of a king" (*Vitae Philosophorum* II.128; similarly, II.138). Likewise, Euripides, *Cyclops* 445: "He is so drunk and so happy now, that he wants to creep off to a party (ἐπὶ κῶμον ἕρπειν) with his cyclops relatives . . ." Other instances could be multiplied; the expression is common enough in Greek comedy and biographical literature. Is this, then, the true *vorlage*?

R. Hiyyah's etymology of אפיקמן relies upon a shift in the vowels, similar to *apikoros* for the Greek Ἐπικούρος. This is possible, if it could be shown that it fit the context. Modern commentators are swift to suggest that the Mishnaic injunction is intended to prohibit Jews from going to a Greek *komos* after dismissal from the Passover meal, on the grounds that the customs and practices prevailing at a *komos* are inappropriate for the pious atmosphere of Passover. For instance, Guggenheimer adds a footnote on the passage: "A (frequently drunken) revelry, characteristic of Greek celebrations and most objectionable to Jews."[48] This anti-Hellenizing interpretation has been defended by Saul Lieberman and more recently by Joshua Kulp.[49] It should not be accepted, for it is a projection onto the ancient Rabbis of a modern preoccupation with symposium customs. There is nothing in the context about drunkenness; nothing about symposia or *commissationes* or wild revelry. R. Hiyyah speaks not of leaving a Jewish gathering and going to a Greek *komos*, but rather, of moving from one *ḥaburah*—a Jewish company devoted to heightened piety and Torah-observance—to another, equally Jewish *ḥaburah*, presumably also engaged in the rites of Passover in all gravity and piety. R. Hiyyah's concern is not that "revelry" be avoided, but that the Passover be celebrated "under one roof" in accordance with the Torah's command (Ex. 12:46). The supposed concern with Hellenic debauchery is without any support in the text or context.

There is another controversy concerning m.Pes. 10.8's rule about the *afiqoman*: what action does it prohibit? The expression is ואין מפטירין אחר הפסח אפיקומן. It opens with אין, the usual impersonal formula for prohibition in the Mishnah, "one does not" or "one must not." There follows מפטירין, morphologically a hiphil participle. As with *'afiqomen,* the later rabbis cannot agree on what this word means. The fifteenth-century Italian commentator on the Mishnah, Obadiah ben Abraham of Bartenura, takes מפטירין to mean "to open [the mouth to consume food]" or "to begin [another course or dish],"[50] while Rashi (eleven-

---

[48]Heinrich Guggenheimer, *The Jerusalem Talmud. Second Order: Mo'ed Tractates Pesaḥim and Yoma* (Berlin: Walter de Gruyter, 2013), 370 n. 75.

[49]Joshua Kulp, "The Origins of the Seder and Haggadah," *Currents in Biblical Research* 4.1 (2005), 122–123 and S. Lieberman, *Hayerushalmi Kiphshuto* (New York: The Jewish Theological Seminary of America, 1995), 521.

[50]Eliyahu Dordek, ed, *Koren Mishna Sdura Bartenura* (Jerusalem: Koren Publishers, 2015), ad m.Pes. 10.8.

century) and his grandson the Rashbam (twelfth century) take it to mean almost the opposite, "to end" or "to conclude." Lietzmann follows them, claiming that the root פטר is "der technische Ausdruck für das 'entlassen' am Ende einer Kulthandlung."[51] "To dismiss" is the meaning of the root פטר in Mishnaic Hebrew and Jewish Aramaic, and likewise of the old Semitic root seen in the Akkadian cognate *pašaru* as well.[52] The Babylonian Talmud twice gives a similar instruction, using the same form complete with the same negative:

אין מפטירין במרכבה ורבי יהודה מתיר ר' אליעזר אומר אין מפטירין בהודע את ירושלם:
One may not conclude [the reading of the Torah] with [the passage about] the chariot [sc. the vision of God in Ezekiel 1]; but R. Judah allows it. R. Eliezer says, One may not conclude with [the passage that begins] "Make known to Jerusalem" [sc. Ezekiel 16:2]. (*b.Meg.* 25a)

The rabbis in this passage, R. Judah the Prince and R. Eliezer ben Hyrcanus, are from the second century. The considerations behind the prohibitions of the reading of these Scripture passages may be helpful as comparisons with the prohibition of *afiqoman*. The rabbis are concerned not to reveal the holy (the vision of the divine throne room in Ez. 1), and not to put Israel to shame by public denunciation (Ez. 16). These considerations should be kept in mind, for the meaning Daube and Eisler suggest for *afiqoman* would make it a prime target for similar prohibition, and for the same reason. There are, however, differences: these passages from Ezekiel are prohibited from being used as *haftarot*, the readings from the prophets that formed the last portion of the synagogue liturgy, read by the last lector, or *maftir*.[53] By contrast, the *'afiqomen* is prohibited within the Passover liturgy, not in a synagogue. Also, the Talmud uses the preposition ‑ב before the "titles" of the prohibited passages, but this preposition is not used in the Mishnah's instruction concerning *'afiqomen*. It is reasonable to suppose that the prohibition of *'afiqomen* was motivated by similar concerns.

Thus, the Mishnah's injunction may mean "One must not dismiss after the Passover lamb *'afiqomen*" or "One must not begin *'afiqomen* after the Passover Passover lamb"—taking *happesah* to mean the lamb rather than the feast as an event, though this is disputed. It may be a prohibition of any *'afiqomen* ritual, in which case it has long been disobeyed; or it may be a prohibition of connecting the *'afiqomen* with the Passover lamb, in which case, it may have been targeted precisely at Christian typological interpretation of the Passover.

---

[51] H. Lietzmann, "Jüdische Passahsitten und der ἀφικόμενος," 303.
[52] Cf. the passages cited in the articles for פטר in Hayim Tawil, *An Akkadian Lexical Companion for Biblical Hebrew* and in HALOT.
[53] On the *haftarot*, cf. Michael Fishbane, *The JPS Bible Commentary: Haftarot* (Philadelphia: Jewish Publication Society, 2002), xix–xxi.

As we shall now see, however, we are not reliant solely on a vestigial line of the Passover Haggadah. The ritual in question—whatever it was—has left its traces in several Christian texts as well.

PASSOVER BREAD AND THE MESSIAH IN 1 CORINTHIANS 5 AND 10

Eisler and Daube posit that the origin of the Messiah-bread ritual may have been an already existing custom of symbolizing the nation of Israel with a piece of bread, so that the Messiah was represented as a hidden part of the people of God, whose revelation completes Israel. Certainly, the imagery of Israel as bread appears to be at work in 1 Corinthians 5:7: "Therefore purge out the old leaven, that you may be a new lump, since you truly are unleavened. For indeed Christ, our Passover, was sacrificed for us . . ." Note that the people of God is symbolized, not just by any bread, but specifically by the unleavened bread of Passover. Note, too, the quick move from the bread to Christ as the Passover lamb—perhaps the very hermeneutical maneuver which the Mishnah's injunction against *'afiqoman* after the Passover Lamb was designed to preclude.

We find similar symbolism again in 1 Corinthians 10:16–17: "The bread which we break, is it not the communion of the body of the Messiah? For we, though many, are one bread and one body; for we all partake of that one bread." Here, the people of God is identified with the bread, which is also designated as the body of the Messiah. It is likely that this sort of symbolism was also available to Jesus, a few years before Paul. Eisler was faulted by Lietzmann and Marmorstein for making too much of the later Jewish identification of the three piece of unleavened bread with three classes of Israelites (Israel, Levites, priests), but he actually grants that this may well be regarded only as a later development. His central contention is not about the three pieces of bread, but about the symbolism of the bread itself, before such elaborations. He traces the ceremony as a whole—the sharing of bread that somehow represented the people of Israel—to "the very oldest aspect of the celebration of the Exodus from Egypt" and notes that Hosea 7:8 speaks of "Ephraim" as "a flatbread not turned over." Likewise, Psalm 14:4 and 53:4 speak of the "workers of iniquity" as "those who devour my people as men eat bread." Bread as a symbol for Israel is well established already, but Daube's and Eisler's explanation makes it likely that 1 Corinthians 10:16–17 is not some innovative Pauline midrash on the Last Supper account, but an unpacking of meaning that was already understood by all to be operative in the Last Supper and subsequent eucharists.

THE LORD'S PRAYER AND ESCHATOLOGY

Another passage worth commenting on in this connection is the Lord's Prayer, the fourth petition of which is usually rendered "Give us this day our daily bread." Yet the word rendered "daily" by Tyndale in 1525 and "täglich" by Luther in 1522 is the Greek ἐπιούσιος, which is so far from meaning "daily" that St. Jerome famously translated it as "supersubstantialem" instead.[54] Foerster's article on ἐπιούσιος in *TDNT* has an aporetic conclusion: "we cannot say with precision what is the exact derivation of ἐπιούσιος" before plumping for the meaning "the bread which we need."[55] It is unfortunate that some scholars continue to support the translation "daily," which ought really to be eliminated from consideration. There are perfectly good and common Greek expressions for "daily": καθ' ἡμέραν, which does not appear in the Prayer, though it is used often enough in the gospels (Mt. 26:55, Mk. 14:49, Lk. 19:47 and 22:53); and the derivative adjective καθημερινός (Acts 6:1; a frequent enough word in Hellenistic Greek). In contrast to these common expressions, ἐπιούσιον is a very rare word. Origen famously discusses it in *De Oratione* 27.7:

> But one must first understand what "ἐπιούσιον" means. And the first thing one must recognize is that the word "ἐπιούσιον" does not occur in even one of the Greek authors, not the wise ones, nor does it appear in the usage of the unlearned, but it seems likely to have been coined (literally "molded") by the gospel-writers.

What was it coined from? There are two verbs spelled εἰμί in Greek. One has a participle ὤν, οὖσα, ὄν and the other has a participle ἰών, ἰοῦσα, ἰόν. The former means "to be"; the latter means "to go or come." The verb of motion has an ι- at the beginning of all its verbals (participles, infinitive, etc). The verb of being does not. Thus, ἐπ-ιούσιον, having the ι- at the beginning of its stem,[56] must be from the verb meaning "to go or come": τὸν ἄρτον τὸν ἐπιούσιον is thus "the coming bread," the eschatological bread—essentially the same meaning as "*afiqoman*," and a meaning which Jesus plays upon

---

[54]In this connection, cf. Brant Pitre, *Jesus and the Jewish Roots of the Eucharist* (New York, NY: Crown, 2016), 95. Pitre attempts to defend the translation of ἐπιούσιος as *supersubstantialem*, but his pronouncements about the Greek are mistaken. He dismisses the correct translation with the remark that it is "not what the Greek text says," but advances no philological evidence to prove that claim. See below.

[55]Werner Foerster, "ἐπιούσιος" in G. Kittel, ed., *TDNT* 2 (Grand Rapids, MI: Eerdmans, 1964), 599.

[56]It would be improper Greek formation to preserve the -ι from the end of ἐπι- when prefixing it to a vowel-initial verb root like -οὐσ-. Thus, for Jerome's rendering "supersubstantialem" to be correct, the word would need to be spelled ἐπούσιος rather than ἐπιούσιος. Foerster, *TDNT* 2.593–594, grants the linguistic point.

in John 6:32–33: "My Father gives you the true bread from heaven. For the bread of God is he who comes down (καταβαίνων) from heaven and gives life to the world."

Werner Foerster's article on ἐπιούσιος in Kittel's *TDNT* gives a further piece of evidence concerning the meaning of this word, from Jerome's *Commentary on Matthew* on 6:11 and his *Tract on Psalm 135*.[57] In these passages, Jerome reports that the lost Gospel of the Nazarenes renders the word ἐπιούσιον by the Aramaic term מחר, meaning "tomorrow."[58] Joachim Jeremias points out that even though this gospel is later than the canonical ones, the Aramaic version of the Lord's Prayer found in it should probably be presumed to be earlier than our Greek gospels, since any Aramaic-speaker translating from the Greek would simply have "plugged in" the memorized Aramaic form of the Lord's Prayer known by every Aramaic-speaking Christian from the liturgy, not from the text of the gospels. The word מחר is therefore likely to be earlier than the Greek ἐπιουσίον, and is probably the original word in the memorized prayer which Jesus' disciples learned from him. Thus, the force of the word is to make the petition a request for "the bread of tomorrow" or the eschatological bread. Maurice Casey agrees that "this is very likely to be right, a preservation of the Lord's prayer from the Aramaic-speaking church."[59]

Maurice Casey and Joachim Jeremias have separately made convincing cases that the Lord's Prayer was originally Aramaic: besides the otherwise insoluble Greek ἐπιούσιον, readily clarified as a rendering of Aramaic למחר, there is also the use of τὰ ὀφειλήματα ἡμῶν (Mt. 6:12), "our debts" as a metaphor for "our sins" is a literal translation of the Aramaic חובינא. Again, we are to forgive τοῖς ὀφειλέταις ἡμῶν, "our debtors," a literal translation of חיבינא.[60]

As confirmation of Jeremias' interpretation of ἐπιούσιον, note how the word order of the Greek prayer's petition—"the bread of ours in the coming day, give us today"—is carefully arranged in order to stress the contrast between "impending, coming" and "today." To wit, Matthew's Jesus has used a reiterated article to keep his adjective attributive rather than predicative: τὸν ἄρτον ἡμῶν τὸν ἐπιούσιον. This is not the simplest way to make an attributive position. For instance, he could have said τὸν ἐπιούσιον ἄρτον. But he chose not to. Why? Because he wanted to place ἐπιούσιον in a position of emphasis,

---

[57]Foerster, "ἐπιούσιος," 590–599 and Joachim Jeremias, *The Lord's Prayer* (Minneapolis, MN: Fortress, 1969), 37.

[58]"In evangelio, quod appellatur secundum Hebraeos, pro *supersubstantiali pane* reperi *mahar,* quod dicitur crastinum, ut sit sensus: panem nostrum crastinum (i.e., futurum, da nobis hodie)."

[59]Maurice Casey, *Aramaic Sources of Mark's Gospel*, 1.

[60]Casey, *Aramaic Sources of Mark's Gospel*, 85 and *An Aramaic Approach to Q*, 55. Jeremias, *The Prayers of Jesus* (ET London: SCM, 1967), 94.

and thus of contrast. It comes at the end of its phrase, and thus invites comparison with the other time-word at the end of the predicate, σήμερον. "The bread of ours that is to come, give to us today." Jeremias, noting the division of the petition into two halves, printed it with a line dividing the cola: *lahmán d^elimhár / habh lán yoma dhén*,[61] so that the positions of the temporal words למחר and ימא דן are preserved, contrasting the two words.

The result is that this is an eschatological petition. The Aramaic מחר or למחר has a pre-Aramaic etymology, which is disputed,[62] but it is likely a cognate of the Akkadian *mahāru* in the sense "to approach" or "to meet" or "face" an event or a person,[63] thus "the approaching" or "coming" day. It is similar to the other great eschatological refrain "Maranatha!"—"Come, Lord!"—an expression of the Christian longing for Christ's appearance as judge, used as the conclusion of the eucharistic liturgy in the Didache.[64] It is also of a piece with the rest of the Lord's Prayer, which is preeminently concerned with bringing together the present age and the age to come, the two ages of Jewish eschatology. It is a prayer that beseeches God to make the obedience of the eschaton, the obedience of heaven, present on earth now; that asks him to forgive our debts (then) as we forgive (now) our debtors; that asks for deliverance from eschatological tribulation (that is what is meant by "temptation" here, not petty lack of self-control). It closes with reference to the Kingdom, that eschatological reality. Indeed, if we do not translate ἄρτον ἐπιούσιον as "coming bread," then 6:11 becomes the only petition that lacks an eschatological aspect to it. It is much better to be consistent, even at the cost of losing a much-loved and comforting translation of the verse.

Brant Pitre breaks down the possible meanings for ἐπιούσιος into four options: "daily bread," "natural bread," "supernatural bread," and "coming bread."[65] It is curious that although the Greek and Latin church fathers incline to the first three options, the Coptic versions of the Lord's Prayer (both the late second-century Sahidic and the early third-century Bohairic) read "bread for the morrow" (*penoeik etnēu taaf nan mpoou / penōik ǝnte rasti mēif nan ǝmphoou*). As a matter of textual criticism, it is difficult to imagine how the idea of "tomorrow's bread today," intelligible only by recourse to an implied timeline of Jewish eschatology, could have arisen from the simpler concept of *panem necessarium*, which requires no such eschatology. Given the ready availability of more common Greek words for "daily" and "necessary," it is more likely that the gospels' apparent coinage of the Greek ἐπιούσιος was an attempt to capture a Semitic expression; and since

---

[61] J. Jeremias, *The Prayers of Jesus* (ET London, 1967), 94.
[62] See the references in HALOT, "מחר."
[63] CAD sv. *mahāru*.
[64] *Didache* 10.14.
[65] Pitre, *Jesus and the Last Supper*, 171–178.

the Coptic versions and the lost Gospel to the Nazarenes give translations that are chronological in denotation and are freighted with Jewish eschatology, we should conclude that this was the intended meaning of the Greek word. It is far easier to see the Greek and Latin fathers, increasingly ignorant of Jewish eschatology, missing these overtones than it is to see Sahidic and Aramaic versions inventing such eschatological meaning and imposing it on an original that lacked them.

A further confirmation, noted by Eisler in 1925 and more recently by Brant Pitre, is the fact that the "coming bread" was associated by the Rabbis of the *Mekhilta* with the manna of the wilderness wanderings after the original Exodus.[66] According to Exodus 16:22, God provided enough manna for two days on Friday evening, so that the Israelites did not need to collect any on the Sabbath. This manna did not spoil, so that it is the type of the "bread which remains unto eternal life" in contrast to the "bread which perishes" and breeds worms. Thus, the OT typology also confirms the eschatological reference of the word ἐπιούσιος. And this eschatological reference has found acceptance even among scholars who refuse the etymology here offered: although Pitre inclines to Jerome's (in my view, impossible) translation "*supersubstantialem*" and rejects Jeremias' and Daube's *vorlage* of ἐπὶ + ἴουσα, he nonetheless agrees that "we can be confident that the petition for bread in the Lord's Prayer is tied to the Jewish eschatological hope for the return of the manna from heaven."[67]

Thus the etymology, the word order, and the context of the fourth petition all combine to prove that ἐπιούσιος is a term of eschatological significance, applied to bread with a meaning quite similar to *afiqoman* = ἀφικόμενος/ἀφίκομην.

MELITO OF SARDIS

Daube was unaware of a further confirmation of his claim: namely, the evidence of a spectacular document from the period before the Church had reciprocated the Jewish expurgation of their own liturgy, a time when "Jewish and Christian religious practices were not yet disentangled."[68] It remained for one of his students, Deborah Bleicher Carmichael, to discover it.

---

[66] Eisler (1925), 189–191 and Pitre *Jesus and the Last Supper*, 158–159, citing Josephus, *Antiq.* 2.315–17.
[67] Brant Pitre, *Jesus and the Last Supper* (Grand Rapids, MI: Eerdmans, 2017), 178.
[68] Bleicher Carmichael, "David Daube on the Eucharist and the Passover Seder," 59.

A second-century bishop of Sardis, Melito, composed a work entitled *Peri Pascha* ("on the Passover").[69] He was a member of a Christian sect called the Quartodecimans ("fourteenthers," after the 14th day of the Jewish month Nisan, the date of the Passover). These Christians, many of them probably Jewish by birth,[70] continued to celebrate Passover alongside the Jews, fasting while the Jews ate their Passover meal, and praying for the salvation of unbelieving Israel. The *Peri Pascha* itself is an astonishing piece of writing, exhibiting a thoroughgoing application of typological exegesis in its handling of the Exodus events, and—what is still more impressive—providing a sophisticated theoretical warrant for that typological exegesis by its abstract consideration of covenant history and the relation of Christ to Israel. Nothing in the later church fathers compares to it, not even Justin's *Dialogue with Trypho*. It is a product of deep reflection from a leader of a community whose members were connected with Judaism in a way that Christians would never be again. The council of Nicaea (325 CE) suppressed Quartodecimanism and banned, with one of its canons, the calculation of the date of Easter according to the Jewish calendar. The decree of the council was circulated by Constantine throughout the Empire with a letter which read, in part:

> It was declared improper to follow the custom of the Jews in the celebration of this holy festival, because, their hands having been stained with crime, the minds of these wretched men are necessarily blinded. . . . Let us, then, have nothing in common with the Jews, who are our adversaries . . . studiously avoiding all contact with that evil way. . . . Therefore, this irregularity must be corrected, in order that we may no more have any thing in common with those parricides and the murderers of our Lord.[71]

The apostle Paul fiercely defended the right of Gentiles to become members of Christ without becoming Jewish. What would he have thought of this requirement that Jewish Christians should be made to follow a Gentile calendar, and that the celebration of Christ's passion and resurrection should be forcibly divorced from calendrical and ritual connection with the Passover on which those events had historically occurred? With this attitude prevailing in the church, it is no wonder that the Jewish background and context of

---

[69] The chief works on Melito are S.G. Hall, *On Pascha and fragments* (Oxford: Clarendon Press, 1979) and Alistair Stewart-Sykes, *The Lamb's High Feast: Melito, Peri Pascha and the Quartodeciman Paschal Liturgy at Sardis* (Supplements to Vigiliae Christianae xlii) (Leiden: E.J. Brill, 1998).

[70] A. Stewart-Sykes has suggested that Melito himself was Jewish by birth. Cf. Alistair Stewart-Sykes, "Melito's Anti-Judaism" in *Journal of Early Christian Studies* Volume 5, Number 2 (1997), 271–283 and *The Lamb's High Feast: Melito, Peri Pascha, and the Quartodeciman Paschal Liturgy at Sardis* (Leiden: E. J. Brill, 1998), 1–6.

[71] Quoted in Theodoret, *Ecclesiastical History*, 1.9, trans. Schaff.

the New Testament was largely lost from view for centuries. Fortunately, a manuscript of Melito's *Peri Pascha* was discovered in the 1930s.

Jeremias describes the celebration of Passover among the Quartodecimans as it is evidenced in the *Peri Pascha*:

> The primary concern was neither with the remembrance of the passion or with the remembrance of the resurrection, but with the expectation of the Parousia! That the messiah would come on the night of passover was both a Jewish and a Christian hope. Each year, therefore, during the passover night the primitive community awaited until midnight, in prayer and fasting, for the return of the Lord. They prolonged the waiting into the hours after midnight. If he had not come bodily by cockcrow, then they united themselves with him in the celebration of table fellowship.[72]

Bleicher Carmichael remarks on this last sentence: "we might note how close he comes to describing a ritual reminiscent of the one suggested by Daube":[73] a celebration of the eucharist highlighting the aspect of it—anticipation of the Messiah—most similar to the Passover bread ritual from which it had been born.

But this is not the only evidence. The *Peri Pascha* is divided into two parts. In the first, Melito gives a typological exegesis of the narrative of Exodus 12 (§1–33). There follows an interpretation of the symbolic meaning of the lamb (§71), the unleavened bread (§80), and the bitter herbs (§93), in obedience to Rabban Gamaliel's rule—thereby proving that Jewish celebration of Passover was structured in this manner by the time of Melito. Says Israel Yuval, "The structure of Melito's sermon is congruent with the Haggadah as a whole. It opens with a 'Midrash,' clarifies the symbolic meaning of the symbols (*pesach, matsah, maror*), and ends with an 'anti-Hallel,' attacking Israel's ingratitude"[74] in much the same manner as the later Improperia. The entire production is "nothing less than a Christian Passover Haggadah."[75] Stuart Hall agrees, at least in part. He would divide the *Peri Pascha* into two parts, with sections 1–45 being an exposition of Exodus 12.1–20 ("a Christian version of the Jewish pre-Passover Sabbath exposition), while "sections 46–105 are recognizably a Christian Passover Haggadah."[76]

---

[72]Jeremias, *Eucharistic Words*, 123, following the evidence presented in Bernhard Lohse, *Das Passafest der Quartodecimaner* (Gütersloh: 1953) 63–70.

[73]Deborah Bleicher Carmichael, "David Daube on the Eucharist and the Passover Seder," 59.

[74]Yuval, "Early Jewish-Christian Dialogue," n. 58. By contrast, Eric Werner, "Melito of Sardis, the First Poet of Deicide" in *Hebrew Union College Annual* 37 (1966), p. 191–210 paints Melito as the "first poet of deicide" and lays against him a charge of anti-semitism. For a vindication of Melito from this charge, cf. Todd Hanneken, "A Completely Different Reading of Melito's Peri Pascha," *Meqorot: The University of Chicago Journal of Jewish Studies* 3 (1997), 26–33.

[75]F. L. Cross, *Early Christian Fathers* (London: Duckworth, 1960), 107.

[76]Stuart G. Hall, "Melito in Light of the Passover Haggadah," *Journal of Theological Studies* new series, XXII pt. 1 (April 1971), 29–46 at 37.

Evidence from Jews and Greeks   63

Within this Christian Passover Haggadah, we find further verbal confirmation of Daube's conjecture. Lietzmann had rejected Eisler's original identification of *'aphiqomen* with the Greek ὁ ἀφικόμενος as "ein Phantasiegebilde," claiming that there was no evidence for the use of ἀφικόμενος as a messianic term. Poor Eisler had no reply to this objection in 1925. In 1938, he was arrested by the Nazis and sent to the Buchenwald and Dachau concentration camps for fifteen months. His health never recovered. If not for this misfortune, he might have noticed Melito's *Peri Pascha*, published for the first time in 1940 by Campbell Bonner.[77] If he had, Eisler might have triumphantly pointed out to Lietzmann († 1942) that the word ἀφικόμενος is twice used as an epithet for Christ in Melito's *Peri Pascha*:[78]

> 65. Many other things have been proclaimed by many prophets regarding the mystery of the Passover, which is Christ, to whom be the glory unto the ages. Amen.
> 66. This one who came from heaven to earth (Οὗτος ἀφικόμενος ἐξ οὐρανῶν ἐπὶ τὴν γῆν) for the sake of the one who was suffering, having clothed himself with that very one through his virgin mother, and having come forth (προελθών) as man, received the sufferings of the one who was suffering through his body which was able to suffer....
> 86. This is the one who came to you (ὁ πρός σε ἀφικόμενος), the one who healed your suffering ones and who raised your dead. This is he against whom you dared; this is he against whom you acted impiously; this is he against whom you did wrong; this is he whom you killed ...[79]

Thus, we have the word ἀφικόμενος used as an epithet of Christ in his first advent, and so used in a Christian Passover Haggadah composed by the leader of a Judaeo-Christian sect within a century of Christ's death and resurrection. The verbal connection was first noticed by Eric Werner in 1985:

> The word "*aphikomenos*," which means "arrived," "to come to," has a similar sound as the "*aphikomon*" in the text of the Passover Haggadah. The word "ἀφικόμενος" comes from ἀφικνέομαι, and occurs mainly in poetic works.... Why did Melito use this rather recherché expression? It is my belief that he wanted to mimic the Passover *halachah* instead: "One does not dismiss after the Passover the *aphikomon*." This enigmatic passage was already formulated by Melito's time

---

[77]Campbell Bonner, ed. *The Homily on the Passion by Melito Bishop of Sardis and Some Fragments of the Apocryphal Ezekiel* (Philadelphia, PA: University of Pennsylvania Press, 1940).

[78]Hall points out that the same verb is used in *Peri Pascha* 16 and 18. These passages, however, contain the aorist 3rd person singular form ἀφίκετο, which does not correspond phonologically to the Hebrew אפיקמן; moreover, the subject of ἀφίκετο is not Christ. In 16 it is the angel of death; in 18 it is "all Egypt" that comes to mourn before Pharaoh for the death of the firstborn. It seems best, therefore, to leave the instances of ἀφίκετο 16 and 18 out of the reckoning of connections with אפיקמן in the Rabbinic sources. Stuart G. Hall, "Melito in Light of the Passover Haggadah," 31.

[79]My translation from the Greek text in S.G. Hall, *Melito of Sardis*, 34.

and, with or without the framework of the midrash of the "four sons," constituted an integral part of the Jewish ritual. It seems to me suspicious that at the end of Melito's midrash on the Exodus he uses that very expression which characterizes the reply to the faithful Jew, the *hacham*.[80]

I suspect that Werner may have experienced while reading Melito the same serendipitous flash of recognition that I did when hearing the Passover Haggadah. He notices the verbal connection with Melito, but he follows Jastrow's etymology of *'afiqoman*, and takes the word in the Passover Haggadah to refer to an arriving dinner guest rather than to the Messiah—despite the fact that in Melito, ὁ ἀφικόμενος is an epithet of Christ! Accordingly, he misses the Messianic and eschatological expectation that is confirmed by Melito's usage. The verbal echo he observed was only finally connected with Daube's thesis by Deborah Bleicher Carmichael in 1990.[81]

OTHER SIMILAR TITLES FOR THE MESSIAH

Melito's use of "coming" as an epithet for the Messiah is not original with him, though his choice of the specific verb that lies behind the word *afiqomen* is unusual. If we broaden our net to include other verbs of "coming," we find that such Messianic epithets reach back into second-Temple Judaism. John the Baptist sends his disciples to ask Jesus, "Are you the coming one (ὁ ἐρχόμενος) or do we wait for another?" (Mt. 11:3)[82] The Samaritans expected a messianic figure whom they designated with the name *Assaief* (from שוב, to return), connecting this idea with the expected Deuteronomic "prophet like Moses" or with Moses himself returning.[83] In the fourth gospel, we see a Samaritan woman professing belief that "Messiah is coming (ἔρχεται)." (Jn. 4:29)[84] At the feeding of the five thousand, "the people who saw the sign which he did said that 'This is truly the prophet who is coming into the world (ἐρχόμενος εἰς τὸν κόσμον)." (Jn. 6:14) Lacking access to Melito and the instances of ἀφικόμενος in the *Peri Pascha,* Eisler appealed to these other, similar verbs of coming. This apparent equivocation diminished the force of his argument in the eyes of Lietzmann and Marmorstein. But the fact that Werner (of all scholars!) discovered confirmation of ἀφικόμενος as an escha-

---

[80]Werner, *The Sacred Bridge* II (New York, 1984), 143.
[81]Deborah Bleicher Carmichael, "David Daube on the Eucharist and the Passover Seder," 45–67.
[82]Oddly, Casey claims that "ὁ ἐρχόμενος" was "not a known title, either in Judaism at the time of Jesus or in the early church. It must therefore be a reference to John the Baptist's own prediction [in Mark 1:7]." Casey, *An Aramaic Approach to Q*, 108.
[83]Cf. Frederic Godet, *Commentary on the Gospel of John* (London: T&T Clark, 1881), 118.
[84]This same pericope also uses ἔρχεται with ὥρα twice ("the hour is coming"), in what is unquestionably an eschatological phrase.

tological title for the Messiah is a strong confirmation of Eisler's etymology of the word. Werner considered Melito an anti-semitic supersessionist and accordingly titled his article on the *Peri Pascha* "The First Poet of Deicide." Critics rejected Eisler as a messianic-Jewish convert and characterized his argumentation as loose and fantastical. The same cannot be said about Werner.

ALISTAIR STEWART-SYKES AND MELITO

Alistair Stewart-Sykes' interpretation of Melito's *Peri Pascha* takes this term ἀφικόμενος as a reference to the Jewish Passover bread ritual: "What we are claiming is that Melito understood the messianic significance of the ἀφικόμενος, and that this ritual was part of his paschal tradition.... We can assume that the *aphikomen* is shared out among the company at the triumphant conclusion of Melito's rite as it was in the Jewish ritual. It is the bread of life, the messianic bread of which John 6 speaks; it is by virtue of the rite of *aphikomen* that the bread of life becomes a subject of pre-Passover teaching in the Johannine church [in Sardis]."[85] There are several difficulties with this proposal. The first, and largest, is the fact that Melito nowhere uses ἀφικόμενος as a label for any bread; second, that the Rabbinic evidence for the use of the term *afiqomen* post-dates Melito by nearly a century, and is *still* not clearly a label for a piece of bread. It would be safer not to read the name *afiqomen* as a label for bread in either the Rabbis or in Melito, but rather to see it as a Messianic title used by Melito in the early second century in a Jewish-Christian (Quartodeciman) context, and thereafter prohibited from connection with the Passover by the Rabbis in the early third century. Whether they were prohibiting the grafting onto the Passover of a Christian ritual or the typological, messianic exegesis of an existing Jewish ritual, we cannot be sure.

With this degree of uncertainty around both Melito's use of ἀφικόμενος and the Rabbis' use of *'afiqomen*, it would be rash to conclude too much. Stewart-Sykes' Anglo-Catholic presuppositions appear to be coloring his historical reconstruction when he concludes that "the *aphikomen* was the basis of the Quartodeciman paschal liturgy" and that "this came to be the case because the *aphikomen* was the means by which the Lord bestowed his presence to the believers."[86] But the very fact that *'afiqomen* is a Greek word means that it will not have been the name used for a Messiah-bread ritual at the Last Supper, for at that point, it is likely to have had an Aramaic name. The most likely sequence of development is that an equivalent Aramaic term

---

[85]Stewart-Sykes, *The Lamb's High Feast*, 198.
[86]Stewart-Sykes, *The Lamb's High Feast*, 199–200.

was used in the second Temple Passover ritual; this was then translated into Greek among Greek-speaking Jews such as Melito, presumably at an early period, probably during the Gentile mission of the apostle Paul; it was then prohibited as it became a tool of Christian proselytizing sometime between Paul and Melito, and this prohibition is recorded in the Haggadah, Mishnah, and other Rabbinic Sources. Something like this sequence of development is necessary to explain how the word came to be included in the Haggadah in Greek despite having originated in a Jewish milieu.[87]

APHIKOMEN IN EPHREM'S HYMNS ON THE UNLEAVENED BREAD

The conflict between church and synagogue reached a fiercer pitch in the century after the council of Nicea, especially in the regions where Jews and Christians shared a common language, Aramaic. The Peshitta, the translation of the Hebrew Bible into Syriac Aramaic, had been produced by the end of the second century, probably by Jews living in Syria, and the New Testament was duly added to it by Christians. The deacon Ephrem the Syrian (306–373), under Mar Jacob the first bishop of Nisibis, produced liturgical hymns (*madrāšê*), many of which draw pointed and polemical contrasts between Christianity and Judaism. The rhetoric, theology, and typological exegesis of these hymns stands in nearly perfect continuity with Melito's *Peri Pascha*. And just as Melito has been speculatively identified as a Jewish Christian on the evidence of his exegetical traditions and his Quartodeciman use of the Jewish calendar, so Ephrem also has been identified as possibly Jewish, on the evidence of his use of exegetical traditions that are found in the Jewish Targums.[88] His name and that of his bishop Jacob are both Jewish, though this is not necessarily dispositive. Regardless of his ethnicity and religion of birth, later authors identify Ephrem as an "interpreter" for the church in Nisibis, suggesting that he had knowledge of Jewish literature and used it in

---

[87]The inclusion of a Greek word in the Haggadah itself would have been uncontroversial. There is evidence of other Greek words in *haggadot* from the Cairo Genizah in documents from the twelfth century, reflecting a Byzantine milieu. Cf. Nicholas de Lange, "Jewish Use of Greek in the Middle Ages: Evidence from Passover *Haggadoth* from the Cairo Genizah" *The Jewish Quarterly Review* 96 (Fall 2006), 490–497.

[88]Elena Narinskaya, *Ephrem, a 'Jewish' sage: A Comparison of the Exegetical Writings of St. Ephrem the Syrian and Jewish Traditions* (Turnhout: Brepols, 2010). Narinskaya's attempts to mitigate Ephrem's anti-Judaism have not been persuasive to most scholars (e.g. Joseph Amar, "Book Review: Ephrem, a 'Jewish' Sage" *Theological Studies* 75.1 (2014), 209–210), but her arguments and evidence for the presence of Jewish exegetical traditions in Ephrem are strong, especially parallels between his hymns and the Targums on Exodus.

his exegetical works and hymns.[89] Ephrem thus represents a Christian community living in contentious rivalry with Jews in Syria, but at the same time able to access Jewish exegetical sources like the Targums.

In this connection, it is extremely interesting to find, first, that the Jewish Passover presented a pressing issue for the church in Syria in Ephrem's day. He wrote 21 Syriac hymns *On the Unleavened Bread* (*Azym.*), part of a larger collection of Paschal Hymns. These are concerned to warn Christians in Nisibis away from participation in the Jewish Passover, suggesting that the boundaries between the church and the synagogue in fourth-century Syria were "somewhat permeable."[90] The theology of these hymns is thoroughly supersessionist, praising Christ who has abolished the Passover and made "the people" (sc. of the Jews) and its rituals obsolete: "In this feast our Lord dismissed the symbols / that struggled in his proclamation. / In this feast the lamb of truth abolished/ the paschal lamb, which had run its course" (*H.Azym.* 12.3–4, trans. Walters). Ephrem blesses Christians "who have rejected the people [sc. the Jews] and their unleavened bread because their hands were stained with the precious blood!" (*H.Azym.* 17.2) and urges Christians not to "eat with the medicine of life the unleavened bread of the people as the poison of death" (*H.Azym.*19.22).[91]

Second, within the first two hymns *On the Unleavened Bread*, we find Ephrem repeatedly referring to Jesus as the one who "came" (*'atha'*) or who "came down" (*nḥt*) 6 times in the 19 tristichs of *H.Azym.* 1:

He who makes all wise came in his love to the foolish . . . (*H.Azym* 1.1)
The good one who came was judged. . . . (1.6)
But behold, the good one came in order to perfect the righteous ones . . . (1.9)
The conqueror came down to be defeated. . . . (1.11)
The wisdom of God came down to the foolish. (1.15)

In the rest of the *Hymns on the Unleavened Bread*, only *H.Azym.* 2 includes two further instances, again with Jesus (under different titles) as its subject:

Hope came to the people, but the people gave up its hope. . . . (2.13)
For this is the reason that he had come in their days / that if they received him, they might live. . . . (2.15)

---

[89]On Ephrem's relation to the Targums, cf. Christine Shepardson, *Anti-Judaism and Christian Orthodoxy: Ephrem's Hymns in Fourth-Century Syria* (Washington, DC: Catholic University of America Press, 2008), especially 13 n. 37, which gives bibliography on Ephrem and Jewish exegetical traditions.

[90]Shepardson, *Anti-Judaism*, 4.

[91]Translations of Ephrem from J. Edward Walters, *Ephrem the Syrian's Hymns on the Unleavened Bread* (Piscataway, NJ: Gorgias Press, 2012).

Obviously, these verses cannot be considered evidence for an Aramaic *Vorlage* behind *'afiqomen*, since the repeated use of these verbs in connection with the Messiah is later than the prohibition of *'afiqomen* in the Passover and Mishnah, and is Syriac rather than Galilean Aramaic. Nonetheless, these lines may well be instances in which Ephrem has preserved earlier Jewish-Christian, or even pre-Christian Aramaic language about the Messiah in relation to the bread of the Passover. Along with Melito's ἀφικόμενος, Ephrem's Syriac verbs may be traces of a time when the coming of the Messiah, whether considered in prospect or retrospect, was symbolized by the bread of Passover.

Ephrem's *H.Azym.* 2 also explains the Last Supper as a proleptic symbol of Christ's self-offering, in terms remarkably similar to Daube's and Eisler's understanding:

> He broke the bread with his hands as a symbol for the sacrifice of his body.
> He mixed the cup with his hands as a symbol for the sacrifice of his blood.
> He sacrificed and offered himself, the priest of our atonement. (*H.Azym.* 2.7)[92]

SUMMARY OF THE DEBATE

Let us now review the history of the controversy over Eisler's proposal. We have seen that the Rabbinic etymologies of *'afiqomen* in the Mishnah and the Passover Haggadah are without any basis in Greek literature. By contrast, Eisler's proposed etymology, from ἀφικόμενος or ἀφικόμην, is superior in its closeness to the Hebrew as written. Lietzmann dismissed Eisler's idea on the grounds that ἀφικόμενος was unattested as an epithet for the Messiah. That objection must now be considered to have been effectively countered by the discovery of the word ἀφικόμενος in Melito of Sardis (see below) and Ephrem the Syrian.

Marmorstein's criticism is different.[93] He objected that Eisler's thesis was constructed on an anachronism: the retrojection into the time of Jesus of the custom of using three matzot labeled "Kohen," "Levi" and "Israel." This custom, Marmorstein points out, cannot be found attested earlier than the seventeenth century. This objection is sound, but it tells only against Eisler's argument, not Daube's. Unlike Eisler, Daube does not insist upon such details, since he claims only that *some such ritual* must have existed as the necessary background of Jesus' words and actions in the Upper Room: "If we did not find such a ritual in the Jewish background, we should have to invent it. As it does occur, the reasonable course seems to be to accept it for what it

---

[92] Walters, trans. *Ephrem the Syrian's Hymns on the Unleavened Bread*, 20.
[93] A. Marmorstein, "Miscellen," *ZNW* 25 (1926), 249–258.

is."[94] The word *afiqomen* may or may not have been the name of the ritual in use at the time of Jesus. What seems more likely is that there was an existing Jewish ritual of anticipation for the Messiah observed during the course of the Passover meal; and that Jesus took this already-known ritual and used it to identify himself as the Messiah. This is the central point on which both Eisler and Daube are agreed: Jesus' action at the Last Supper requires some existing Messiah-bread ritual in the pre-rabbinic, pre-Seder Passover. This is a conclusion that stands independent of the use of the term *afiqomen* in the medieval Haggadah and Rabbinic sources.

Some time between the NT and 130 CE, the term ἀφικόμενος came to be used as an eschatological label for Christ. Melito's *Peri Pascha* exhibits this usage. This may or may not have been connected with the eucharistic bread (it is not clear in Melito), but in either case, this is the *afiqomen* that the Rabbis, in good chronological order *after* Melito,[95] are concerned to prohibit. This might be either an attempt to stamp out a pre-Christian messianic bread ritual that had become a liability because it was interpreted by Christians as a symbol of Christ; or else it could be an attempt to prevent Jews from adopting a Christian custom, perhaps one that developed in connection with Christian observance of Passover in such communities as that of Melito's Quartodecimans. The evidence for all these claims is suggestive, but not conclusive, and it would be rash to attempt to overthrow received chronologies of the development of the Passover on the basis of them.

THE RESULT: MAIMED RITUAL MEALS

The evidence presented in this chapter should leave us in no doubt that there was a bread ritual concerning the Messiah, anticipating his coming in keeping with Jewish eschatological expectation. The *fortuna* of this ritual and the references to it in the extant sources reflect the strife between the early Christians and early Rabbinic Judaism over the question that the ritual was used to answer: namely, whether or not Jesus was the Messiah. The Jews who ate with Jesus in the Upper Room would have known and recognized the ritual breaking of bread that he performed. Those who believed that he was the Messiah linked the bread inextricably with Jesus from that time forward (e.g. the disciples on the road to Emmaus in Lk. 24). For those who did not believe, there was a tremendous motive to sever that connection, remove the Messiah from the Passover, and prohibit Messianic interpretation of its rituals. This proved a costly surgery, and it provoked a counter-amputation

---

[94]Daube, "He That Cometh," 439.
[95]*Pace* Alistair Stewart, *The Lamb's High Feast*, 198.

by the Church that removed from its collective consciousness all sense of its Jewish roots, leaving a void in its understanding of how the eucharist operates. Rather than considering biblical models such as the Passover itself, or the sprinkling of blood in Exodus 24, the Church Fathers turn to other ways of thinking about the Lord's Supper, using new concepts derived from other sources. Thus, rather than situating Jesus the Messiah and the bread within the context of Israel's story, the Church and the Synagogue each made a tragic separation within their respective narrative rituals. The Church divorced the eucharist from the story of Israel while the Rabbis divorced the Passover from the Messiah.

Chapter Four

Layers of Meaning

Bread and wine had multiple layers of symbolic meaning for Jesus' audience. We can distinguish three levels with progressively narrow specificity: (1) general biblical symbolism of bread and wine; (2) meanings arising from the narrower context of Israel's covenant with YHWH; and (3) meanings dictated by the most specific context of the Passover celebrated in the Upper Room.

PRE-EXISTING GENERAL MEANINGS

The most basic meanings are seen in the Old Testament. The first instance of bread as human flesh or body in the Bible occurs in the dream of Pharaoh's baker:

> I also was in my dream, and there were three white baskets on my head. In the uppermost basket were all kinds of baked goods for Pharaoh, and the birds ate them out of the basket on my head. So Joseph answered and said, "This is the interpretation of it: The three baskets are three days. Within three days Pharaoh will lift off your head from you and hang you on a tree; and the birds will eat your flesh from you." (Gen. 40:16–19)

Likewise, we can find metaphorical use of "blood" in the story of David's mighty men breaking through the Philistine lines to bring him water from the well of Bethlehem:

> And David longed, and said, Oh that one would give me drink of the water of the well of Bethlehem, which is by the gate! And the three mighty men brake through the host of the Philistines, and drew water out of the well of Bethlehem, that was by the gate, and took it, and brought it to David: nevertheless he would

not drink thereof, but poured it out unto the LORD. And he said, Be it far from me, O LORD, that I should do this: is not this the blood of the men that went in jeopardy of their lives? therefore he would not drink it. (2 Sam. 23:16–20)

In this passage, the use of the term "blood" is metaphorical: the drink of water has become too precious a thing for David to dare to drink himself because it has been obtained at the *risk of death* on a mission that his men undertook out of loyalty to him. (The water did not actually turn into blood.)

Wine is also designated as the "blood of the grape" (Dt. 32:14 and Gen. 49:11), and is used as a symbol of suffering, usually suffering inflicted by the wrath of God. This imagery is most familiar to many American Christians via Julia Ward Howe's line from the Battle Hymn of the Republic taken from Revelation 14:17–20 ("He is trampling out the vintage where the grapes of wrath are stored"), but it is actually first introduced in Psalm 75:

> For a cup is in the hand of the LORD, and the wine foams;
> It is well mixed, and he pours out of this;
> Surely all the wicked of the earth must drain and drink down its dregs. (Ps. 75:8)

Jeremiah presents the cup as God's judgment on the nations (Jer. 49:12 and 51:7 and Lam. 4:21), and this usage is taken up also by Habakkuk (Hab. 2:16). The imagery appears to be the rather appalling one of getting an enemy drunk in order to abuse her in her senseless stupor. The result is that the drinker "goes mad" (Jer. 51:7), "makes herself naked" (Lam. 4:21), and suffers "utter disgrace" (Hab. 2:16). These uses are the antecedents of Jesus' imagery in His words to the sons of Zebedee ("Can you drink the cup that I am going to drink?," Mt. 20:22 and Mk. 10:38) and in his prayer in Gethsemane ("Father, if you are willing, take this cup from me . . . ," Mt. 26:39, Mk. 14:36, Lk. 22:42).

These meanings are derived from certain physical characteristics of bread and wine. Bread is solid, yet soft and able to be torn, like flesh. Wine is red like blood, and can produce drunkenness, leading to vulnerability and humiliation. This simplest level of symbolic meaning is certainly at work in Jesus' words at the Last Supper, but it would be a mistake to stop at this point. The fuller meaning of his words and of the bread and wine must be sought, first, within a biblical understanding of Israel as a corporate entity within time, and finally, in a more specific and elaborated ritual context within the Passover itself, and specifically within the proximate historical context of the Passion week, which we will find borne out in details of the gospel narratives.

THE CORPORATE DIMENSION

A second level of meaning ties the elements to the covenant between Israel and YHWH. Daube and Eisler suggested that the bread ritual grew out of a symbolism whereby Israel, the people of God, was itself represented by bread, with the Messiah then symbolized as a hidden piece broken off from this bread. Certainly, the symbolism of Israel as a piece of bread was available in the time of Jesus. We find it in 1 Corinthians 5:6–8:

> Your glorying is not good. Do you not know that a little leaven leavens the whole lump? Therefore purge out the old leaven, that you may be a new lump, since you truly are unleavened. For indeed Christ, our Passover, was sacrificed for us. Therefore let us keep the feast, not with old leaven, nor with the leaven of malice and wickedness, but with the unleavened bread of sincerity and truth.

Paul's metaphor represents the people of God as bread, and places that bread within the context of Passover. The "purging out" that he urges here is the expulsion of the sexually immoral man from the Corinthian congregation—an expulsion that was to be accomplished ultimately by barring him from the eucharist. Of particular interest here is the move Paul makes from the fact of Christ's sacrifice to the need for "unleavened" conduct and moral purity of the congregation, especially in connection with the eucharist. The phrase "Christ, our Passover" is τὸ πάσχα ἡμῶν Χριστός, and the word τὸ πάσχα can also mean "the Passover lamb." Since it is the subject of the verb ἐτύθη ("has been sacrificed/slaughtered"), τὸ πάσχα must refer to the sacrificial animal rather than to the entire feast. Thus, Paul's argument assumes a causal connection between the sacrifice of Christ (as the "Passover lamb") and the obligation to "keep" the church and the eucharist free from the contamination of sexual immorality.

Within 1 Corinthians 5–6, this causal connection is supported by the corporateness of the Christian community, expressed through the metaphor of the "body" of Christ. Members of the Christian community are considered as "members" of that body, so that a sexual union between a member and a harlot is uniting the body of Christ to a harlot.

The understanding of the bread as a symbol of the Christian community's corporateness persisted in early church liturgies. The *Didache* uses the symbolism of the bread as the people of God: "As this broken bread was scattered upon the mountains and being gathered together became one, so may Thy Church be gathered together from the ends of the earth into Thy kingdom." (*Didache* 9.8, tr. Lightfoot.)

UNION WITH THE MESSIAH

This union of believers with Christ is also expressed in another passage about the eucharist, 1 Corinthians 10:16–17:

> The cup of blessing which we bless, is it not the communion of the blood of Christ? The bread which we break, is it not the communion of the body of

Christ? For we, though many, are one bread and one body; for we all partake of that one bread.

Here we see again the people of God represented as bread. But there is more to be learned here, for Paul relates the bread and wine to the body and blood of Jesus. This is the verse most often cited by advocates of "real presence," that is, of a realist view of the relation between Jesus' historical body ("the body born of Mary") and the sacramental body (the eucharistic elements of bread and wine). Yet strictly speaking, Paul uses stronger language concerning the *ecclesial* body's—the church's—identification with the bread than concerning the historical body's identification with it. For Paul actually uses the verb ἔσμεν in 10:17: "we [sc. the church] *are* one bread." Yet, as Ratramnus once pointed out, the advocates of "real presence" do not take this verb as literally as the one in 1 Corinthians 11:24 ("this *is* my body"). Further, 10:16 equates the bread, not with Christ's historical body or flesh, but with our *sharing* (κοινωνία) in that body. Paul means that by eating and drinking in obedience to Jesus' command, participants share in the events that are designated by the terms "body" and "blood"—namely, the events of Jesus' sacrificial death and resurrection.

I say "share in the events" rather than "the bread becomes the body of Jesus" because despite the attempts of several scholars to find "real presence" in second Temple Judaism,[1] there is no warrant for thinking that first-century Jews had any conceptual precedent for the idea of transubstantiation or a local presence of God (or the Messiah, or anyone else) in bread. In this connection, Bruce Malina's study of the Palestinian Targums' teachings about manna is helpful. His survey of Jewish exegetical traditions reveals no instance in which the presence of Israel's God or of the Messiah was thought to be found in manna or bread. Instead, the Targums are concerned with "the saving events which the community experienced in cult as 'a living present reality related to their own lives.'"[2] Malina suggests that in Paul's statements in 1 Corinthians 10:3–4 about Israel "eating spiritual food" and "drinking spiritual drink," the adjective πνευματικός should be understood to mean "pre-existent, in heaven." Pointing to the Damascus Document and the Mekhilta, Malina finds that early Judaism taught that "the well was the Law [sc. The Torah] or imparted the Law," so that when Paul identifies the Rock with the Messiah, he is employing an available Jewish procedure, however difficult it might seem to us: "What Paul does here is employ the exegetic traditions current in his day. That both the well and the manna were created at the beginning in

---

[1] For advocacy of "real presence" in the elements and an attempt to ground this concept in first-century Jewish ideas, see Brant Pitre, *Jesus and the Last Supper*, 143–147 and *passim*.

[2] Bruce Malina, *The Palestinian Manna Tradition* (Leiden: E.J. Brill, 1997) 35, quoting Weiser, *The Psalms*, 673–674.

heaven, and there reserved for the Israelites of the desert wanderings is well known from the [Palestinian Targums] and other sources contemporary with Paul."[3] Malina then turns to Revelations 2:17, where Christ promises "to him who overcomes, I will give some of the hidden manna (τοῦ μάννα τοῦ κεκρυμμένου)." This idea is consistent with the exegetical tradition that God has hidden away manna as a reward for the righteous, and that it will be bestowed on the righteous at the end. Malina cites R. Eliezer b. Ḥasama (ca. 110 CE): "In this world (בעולם הזה) you are not going to find [the manna], but in the world to come (לעולם הבא), you are going to find it" (Mekhilta on 16.25).

We thus find in the Targums good reasons to think that Palestinian Jews thought about their own sacred meals in terms of the Exodus as the paradigmatic instance of God's saving action in history. In this exegetical tradition, God's action is to make the past salvation effective again in the present. That is the force of saying that the manna is "from heaven." There is no implication that the manna has become God, or that God is locally present in it. We see this same tradition at work in the statements of Jesus and Paul concerning bread.[4] There was ample precedent for the idea that by sharing in a ritual meal, the people of God were sharing in an event, even if that event was not present, but past or future. This was how the Passover worked. It is also how Paul construes the operation of the Rock from which Israel drank during the wilderness wanderings: "they drank from the spiritual rock that followed them, and the rock was the Messiah." This statement has often provoked puzzled commentary about Paul's alleged allegorizing: How could the rock be the Messiah? The Messiah was not to be born for another 1500 years. Was the pre-incarnate Son present in the rock? How, by what metaphysical transformation, was this possible? But in light of the exegetical tradition of the Palestinian Targums, it seems more likely that Paul has a different idea in mind: namely, that by drinking, the Israelites shared in a future event of salvation proleptically.

This raises two problems: one is how we ought to understand participation in a distant event such as the crucifixion of Christ or his resurrection. Is it a sort of time travel? Second, there is the problem of what it means to "have a share in" the Messiah. I want to approach the first question via the second.

SHARING IN CHRIST

We need to submit our sacramental theorizing to Paul's actual language rather than pressing his words into the service of our theories. That means

---

[3] Bruce Malina, *The Palestinian Manna Tradition*, 99.
[4] Bruce Malina, *The Palestinian Manna Tradition*, 99.

taking seriously the full import of his rhetorical questions, "Is it not the sharing in the blood of Christ?" and "Is it not the sharing in the body of Christ?"

First, the opening word of both these questions: οὐχί, "Is it not . . . ?" This is a word used to introduce the strongest sort of rhetorical question that expects the answer "Yes, of course." It is not the way one introduces a surprising conclusion (such as a doctrine of localized "real presence" or transubstantiation would have been). It is, rather, the phrasing of an uncontroversial premise, part of an argument leading to the conclusion of 10:21: "You cannot drink the cup of the Lord and the cup of demons; you cannot partake of the Lord's table and the table of demons." Paul starts from what is, for us, a very non-obvious and non-intuitive premise ("How can I 'share in' Christ's body by eating a piece of bread?"), and argues to what is, for us, a more obvious conclusion ("Of course a Christian can't share in idol sacrifices!"). Yet in Paul's day, and for his readers, the premise was obvious. The fact that he introduces it with οὐχί is proof of that.

Paul's rhetorical question was only possible because he and his original audience shared certain assumptions that modern readers lack. For moderns, it is not at all clear that eating a ritual meal *can be*—let alone obviously *is*—a means of sharing in Jesus and the events of his death and resurrection. But for Paul and his readers, it was obvious.

The reason was a shared assumption between Paul and his readers concerning the Messiah, an assumption which is bound up with the word κοινωνία. Too often, the word has been emptied of its force by being made too general, without any realization of how vividly Paul's phrasing denotes what it speaks of. The idea of κοινωνία has precedent in the OT, especially in passages speaking of the king of Israel. In 2 Samuel 20:1, Sheba the son of Bichri initiates a rebellion against David with the words, "We have no *share* (Heb. חֵלֶק) in David, nor is there an inheritance for us in the son of Jesse." Or again, the men of Israel protest their greater "share in" King David after his restoration:

> And the men of Israel answered the men of Judah, and said, "We have ten *shares* in the king" (LXX: δέκα χεῖρές ἐν τῷ βασιλεῖ, "ten hands in the king," literally translating the Heb. עֶשֶׂר־יָדוֹת בַּמֶּלֶךְ), therefore we also have more right to David than you." (2 Sam. 19:44)

This notion of "having a share in" the king is probably also at work in the fourth gospel's account of Jesus telling Peter, "Unless I wash your feet, you do not have a part with me (οὐκ ἔχεις μέρος μετ' ἐμοῦ)" (Jn. 13:8). Peter's response to this trades upon the logic of μέρος, hoping to increase his share in Jesus by submitting more of his body to washing. Modern commentators cite a few instances of Greek and Roman deities giving human beings a μέρος of themselves (Epictetus *Diatr.* 1.12 and Marcus Aurelius 4.14, 7.13), but these are remote from our context.[5] More relevant is the eschatological and messianic sense seen also in Matthew 24:51 and Luke 12:46, in which "the lord of that servant shall appoint him his portion with (τὸ μέρος αὐτοῦ θήσει μετὰ) the hypocrites/unfaithful (τῶν ὑποκριτῶν/ἀπίστων)." Neither these synoptic passages nor John 13:8 contrasts "a portion with the Messiah" directly with "a portion with the hypocrites," but both use the peculiar construction μέρος μετὰ, which may be a Semitism corresponding to חֵלֶק ב־.

A similar idea is at work in the famous opening line of *Pirkei Avot*,[6] which speaks of the Jewish hope for the restoration of all things, and the belief that every Jew would "have a share" in it:

All Israel has a share (חֵלֶק) in the age to come (or "the world to come"—הָעוֹלָם בָא). (*m.Sanh.* 10.1, cf. *b.Sanh.* 90a)

There was later debate about whether the age to come was for Jews only, or whether righteous gentiles would also "share in" it (*t.Sanh.* 13.2), with R. Joshua's opinion prevailing that the righteous gentiles would also "have a portion in the world to come."[7]

The case of David presents special similarities with the case of Jesus. 1 Samuel's narrative of David's heroism and rise to the kingship shows that David, by fighting Israel's battle against Goliath by himself, so that the fate of the nation was bound up in his fate, was behaving in a kingly manner—and that Saul and all Israel recognized it.[8] As the men of Israel in 2 Samuel 19 hope to share (and Sheba son of Bichri in 2 Samuel 20 disclaims any share) in the benefits bestowed by king David; and as the rabbis of the Mishnah and Tosefta hoped to share in the age to come (which was the age of the Messiah), so Paul expresses his belief that by participating in the eucharist, Christians

---

[5] J. Ramsey Michaels, *The Gospel of John* (Grand Rapids, MI: Eerdmans, 1971), 231 and Craig Keener, *The Gospel of John: A Commentary* (Grand Rapids, MI: Baker Academic, 2003), 909 n. 19.

[6] This verse is not part of tractate *m.Avot* in the Mishnah, but is included as a preface to its liturgical form as *Pirkei Avot*, and indeed is traditionally recited before each chapter. Cf. Martin Sicker, *The Moral Maxims of the Sages of Israel: Pirkei Avot* (New York: iUniverse, 2004).

[7] Tosefta Sanh. 13.2: "R. Eliezer says all nations have no portion in the world to come because it is written: 'The wicked shall be turned into hell, even all the nations that forget God' (Ps. 9:18). The wicked shall be turned into hell: these are the wicked of the Israelites. R. Joshua said unto him: if it had said all the wicked shall be turned into hell, all nations, and nothing further, I would have agreed with your words. Seeing that the Scriptures say: 'that forget God' (you can infer from this) that there are righteous (*tsadiqim*) among nations who have a portion in the world to come." Translation quoted in Julius Newman, "The Righteous of the Nations of the World" in *De Fructu Oris Sui: Essays in Honour of Adrianus van Selms* (Leiden: E.J. Brill, 1971), 130–144.

[8] As N.T. Wright states, "His fate becomes theirs, his inheritance becomes theirs, his life becomes theirs. To be 'in the king,' or now, for Paul, 'in the anointed one,' the Messiah, is to be part of the people over which he rules, but also part of the people who are defined by him, by what has happened to him, by what the one God has promised him." N.T. Wright, *Paul and the Faithfulness of God*, 830.

will be sharing in the crucified-and-resurrected Messiah Jesus, and thereby in the age to come.

RITUAL SHARING IN PAST EVENTS

The Pauline sacramentology is simply Paul's incorporative soteriology brought into relation to a ritual meal. Since salvation involves Jesus' death and resurrection, the *koinonia* of 1 Corinthians 10:16–18 is participation in those events. This is the *koinonia* of which Paul speaks in Philippians 3:10: "... that I may know him and the power of his resurrection, and the *koinonia* of his sufferings, being conformed to his death. . . ."

There is Jewish precedent for this idea of sharing in the events of Jesus' sufferings, death, and resurrection: subsequent Passover meals after the original one in Egypt were thought to make their participants share in the original Passover event. The Mishnah cites Rabban Gamaliel urging that

> "In every generation a man must so regard himself as if (לִרְאוֹת אֶת עַצְמוֹ כְּאִלּוּ) he came forth himself out of Egypt, for so it is written, 'And thou shalt tell thy son in that day, saying, It is because of that which the Lord did for me when I came forth out of Egypt.'" (Ex. 13:8) (*m.Pes.* 10.5)

To speak with strict historical accuracy, it is of course not the case that subsequent Jews "in every generation" actually "came forth out of Egypt"[9]; they were in fact born in the land of Israel (or Brooklyn, or eastern Europe, etc.). Yet Gamaliel wants each individual to think of himself as personally having experienced this event—and it appears that participation in the Passover, especially with its recitation and "edible reenactment" of the narrative of the historical Exodus, is the means by which the event is experienced by each individual. It is a distinction that makes a difference on the subjective level of the individual: a life of freedom enjoyed in the land would be experienced quite differently by Israelites who celebrated Passover as a way of contextualizing this liberty.

Gamaliel's use of the verb "regard" or "look upon" (לִרְאוֹת) is similar to Paul's use of the Greek οἶδα when urging Christians to see each other as a new creation (καινὴ κτίσις) because of their sharing in Christ's resurrection (2 Cor. 5:15–16), or his command to "consider (λογίζεσθε) yourselves dead to sin, but alive to God in Christ Jesus" (Rom. 6:11). Paul corrects his readers' imagination, urging them to see themselves as involved in, sharing in, the events of Christ. That his near-contemporary Gamaliel (whether Gamaliel I

---

[9]The Jesus of Matthew 2:15 is an exception.

or II) used similar language about Passover participants sharing in the events of the Exodus is evidence that this was an available first-century Jewish way of thinking.

A similar diachronic thought appears in the later rabbinic explanation of Exodus 24:8: the rabbis held that Moses' words, "This is the blood of the covenant" was intended to identify this blood with the blood of the Passover lambs from Exodus 12,[10] so that Moses' sprinkling of the people was thought of as a reiteration of the earlier marking of the doorposts and lintels.

When we turn to Jesus' words over the cup, there is the close similarity of expression, which makes us suspect a verbal echo. Mark's version has "my blood of the covenant"; others, only "the blood of the covenant" without the possessive "my"; but whichever expression was the original, the genitive expression "blood of the covenant" is distinctive enough. Both sentences begin with a deictic expression ("This is . . ."). Such closeness of phrasing is a strong reason to believe that Jesus has Moses' words in mind. Since the Jews had an understanding of how Moses' utterance related the sprinkled blood to the blood of the original Passover lambs, we are entitled to ask whether Jesus (and Paul, and the NT authors generally) intended the same understanding when thinking about how the cup of wine related to His coming death on the cross.[11] Henceforward, the blood of the covenant is no longer that of the Passover lamb, but the blood of Jesus. The author of the epistle to the Hebrews makes the same move when he writes of "trampling the son of God underfoot and counting the *blood of the covenant* by which he was sanctified a common thing" (Heb. 10:29).

---

[10]Scot McKnight, *Jesus and His Death*, 288, cites Pirqe de Rabbi Eliezer 28–29 and Exod. Rab. 19:2 as sources where the Jews connected the idea of the covenant ceremony with the lamb's blood from Egypt, and also with the blood of circumcision:

The Israelites took the blood of the covenant of circumcision, and they put (it)—upon the lintel of their houses, and when the Holy One, blessed be he, passed over to plague the Egyptians, he saw the blood of the covenant of circumcision upon the lintel of their houses and the blood of the Paschal lamb. He was filled with compassion for Israel, as it is said, "And when I passed by thee, and saw thee weltering in thy (twofold) blood, I said unto thee. In thy (twofold) blood, live; yea, I said unto thee. In thy (twofold) blood, live" (Ezek. xvi. 6). "In thy blood" is not written here, but "in thy (twofold) blood," with twofold blood, the blood of the covenant of circumcision and the blood of the Paschal lamb; therefore it is said, "I said unto thee, In thy (twofold) blood, live; yea, I said unto thee. In thy (twofold) blood, live."

Rabbi Eliezer said: Why did the text say twice, "I said unto thee. In thy blood, live; yea, I said unto thee, In thy blood, live"? But the Holy One, blessed be He, said: By the merit of the blood of the covenant of circumcision and the blood of the Paschal lamb ye shall be redeemed from Egypt, and by the merit of the covenant of circumcision and by the merit of the covenant of the Passover in the future ye shall be redeemed at the end of the fourth kingdom; therefore it is said, "I said unto thee, In thy blood, live; yea, I said unto thee, In thy blood, live." (Pirqe de Rabbi Eliezer 28–29)

[11]As Richard Hays puts it in *Echoes of Scripture in the Gospels*, the words of institution over the cup in Mark's gospel affirm "that Jesus' death stands in direct continuity with God's covenant with Israel, first enacted by Moses (Exod 24:8)." Richard Hays, *Echoes of Scripture in the Gospels* (Waco, TX: Baylor University Press, 2016), ch. 1, §2.

In both Christian and pre-Christian sources, second temple Judaism exhibits a strong conception of participation in events of other times, both past and future. Whether second temple Jews entertained the "real presence" or time-travel of past *objects,* however, is more doubtful. David Daube notes that the unleavened bread used in subsequent Passovers was thought by some rabbis—and denied by others—to be a reiteration of the original bread in Egypt:

> An old Aramaic proclamation over the unleavened bread begins: "This is the poor, afflicted bread that our fathers ate in the land of Egypt." Some medieval Rabbis felt that the phrasing might encourage the notion of transformation, the notion that the bread on the table was actually the same as had figured during the exodus. (Whether the phrasing was in fact chosen with a view to this interpretation I leave undecided. It will be noticed that we find here the personified bread of the *Jer. Targum Deut.* 16:3.) They introduced a slight change, so slight as in the Aramaic to consist in one additional letter, *ke,* "like," and thereby obtained, "Like this was the poor, afflicted bread that our fathers ate. . . ." Their innovation, however, did not prevail; the common reading is still "This is."[12]

Daube declined to decide whether the composers of the Passover Haggadah thought that "This is the poor, afflicted bread" meant that the bread of the subsequent Passovers in the land was actually transformed into the original bread eaten by Moses and the Israelites on the night of the Exodus. No metaphysical explanation is given in the Targum. At any rate, it was the re-presentation of the experience of the Exodus via the ritual meal that generated the possibility of the original bread being somehow present; the ritual reenactment and personal experience did not arise from or depend upon a miraculous transformation of the bread.

Bruce Malina adduces another early Jewish instance of "time-travel" applied to ritual food: the Palestinian Targums and the school of Hillel held that both the water from the rock and the manna were "created at the beginning in heaven and there reserved for the Israelites of the desert wanderings."[13] Malina suggests that this explains Paul's language in 1 Corinthians 10.3–4, according to which Israel ate "spiritual food" and drank from the rock "which was the Messiah." Paul was, after all, a student of Gamaliel in Beth Hillel, and would have been familiar with these ideas. This same idea of pre-existent manna appears again in Revelations 2.17, where the ascended Christ, located in heaven, promises to give to "him who overcomes" to eat from "the hidden manna." Provocatively, Malina cites a saying of R. Eliezer b. Hasama (c. 110 CE) from the Mekhilta on Exodus 16.25, concerning the manna: "You will not find it in this world (*ba'olam hazzeh*) but you will find it in the world to come (*la'olam*

---

[12]Daube, "He That Cometh" in CWDD vol. II, p. 438, n. 46.
[13]Bruce Malina, *The Palestinian Manna Tradition* (Leiden: E.J. Brill, 1968), 94–99.

habba')."¹⁴ Heaven is conceived of as the place where the manna, symbol of God's salvation, is reserved, and from which it "comes down" both at the time of the Exodus and at the eschatological time of salvation and the beginning of the age to come.

How did this experience work upon the consciousness of the participants? Jonathan Brumberg-Kraus discusses the way the early Rabbinic seder worked by the connection of the Torah's stories (*legomena* in Jane Harrison's terms¹⁵) with actions (*dromena*) and symbolic foods (*deiknumena*) in the course of the entire ritual meal: "[I]t is not either a 'reenactment' or a 'recollection' of rabbinic [or Scriptural] myths—it is both/and. The separate awareness of the 'past-ness' and 'present-ness' is fused into single experience, prompted especially by specific visual cues provided by the food, drink, activities, and company at the table."¹⁶ The unity of the experience is crucial: "The single setting of the table provides a dream-like experience of 'condensed, symbolic, immediately visual' images, and I would add gustatory, olfactory, auditory, and palpable "images" as well."¹⁷ Brumberg-Kraus aptly labels this mode of experience a "*ke-ilu* (as if) experience," after the expression used in Gamaliel's famous dictum: "In every generation a person should view himself as if (*ke-ilu*) he himself went out of Egypt" (*m.Pes.* 10.4).

In a similar vein, Alan Zemel suggests that a written text such as the narrative of the Exodus, or even the Haggadah itself, inevitably opens up a chronological gap between the past and present that needs to be bridged if the events of the past are to be applied to the participants in the present.

> According to Bell, "The fixing of the past in writing" [as with the Haggadah] "can open a gap between the present and the past that appears to demand different forms of mediating authority—perhaps an authority that represents 'sanctified tradition' not through a convincing evocation of the continuity of the past with the present but through privileged access to the 'sources' of the past." The source of the past, in this context, is the Haggadah itself. Access is accomplished through the process of recitative reconstruction, which authorizes and constitutes the textual links that bridge the gaps between past, present and future. In other words, by reconstructing the argument text of the Haggadah, access to the Jewish past, present and future becomes a matter of efficacious performance, authorized and authenticated by the participants themselves, the text and the roles that they fill.¹⁸

---

¹⁴Bruce Malina, *The Palestinian Manna Tradition* (Leiden: E.J. Brill, 1997), 101.

¹⁵Jane Ellen Harrison, *Themis: A Study of the Social Origins of Greek Religion* (New York: Cambridge University Press, 2010).

¹⁶Jonathan Brumberg-Kraus, "Performing Myth, Performing Midrash," *Meals in Early Judaism: Social Formation at the Table* (New York: Palgrave MacMillan, 2014), 109.

¹⁷Brumberg-Kraus, "Performing Myth," 111.

¹⁸Alan Zemel, "Haggadah as Argument" in *Argumentation* 12 (1998), 57–77.

In other words, the performance of the Passover seder—the recitation of its narrative texts and the consumption and handling of the ritual foods—is a means of making the events of the Exodus that the seder celebrates real and vivid to the participants in a subjective sense. I have in mind not only eating, but also such rituals as making a sort of sandwich out of unleavened bread and bitter herbs together ("thus did Hillel"[19]), setting out a "cup for Elijah," using a finger to put ten drops of wine on a plate for each of the plagues, or hiding a piece of unleavened bread and recovering it. (I make no claim that all these ritual actions were done in the Second Temple period, though perhaps some of them were. Even though some are much later, they are no less typical of Jewish ritual practice in the context of Passover.) Such "efficacious performance" would include the dialogue of the leader with the "four sons" and also—to name only those that we have examined earlier in this book—such things as the Dayenu and the Christian *Improperia* (both framed as dialogue with God himself), or even, to take a Jewish-Christian example, Melito's *Peri Pascha* as an acted performance. In sum, it is the especial job of a ritual meal to make past and future events present to the members of the community that participates in the meal, to involve them in the events, to make the events true of them personally, so that they "regard themselves" as having personally shared in them. And ritual meals do this by a performance that involves the senses and body and mind—in short, the whole person—of every participant to a greater degree than, say, mere reading and exposition of a narrative without accompanying ritual.

Alastair Roberts, drawing on the work of Jeremy Begbie, suggests that it is helpful to think of sacraments and time in a musical way. He quotes Begbie: "[E]very eucharistic celebration can be seen as a repeated opportunity for time-laden creatures to be incorporated into a temporal environment, established in Christ, in which past, present and future coinhere, in such a way that our identities can be healed, recast and reformed."[20] Roberts elaborates:

> Much as in the case of Passover meal, a memorial of a past deliverance anticipates future salvation and each repetition re-establishes us within musical cycles of memory and hope. It repeatedly stabilizes us by restoring us to Christ's decisive, once-for-all, action in the past, and destabilizes us by exposing us to the fecundity of the future that this action opened. It ties together founding action with the anticipation of final judgment.[21]

---

[19]Hillel's originally sectarian custom of eating matzah and maror (bitter herbs) together became standard practice, and is unpacked by the Haggadah's narration: "Together they shall be: the matzah of freedom, the maror of slavery. For in the time of freedom, there is knowledge of servitude. And in the time of bondage, there is hope of redemption." N. Glatzer, ed. *The Passover Haggadah* (New York: Schocken, 1989).

[20]Jeremy Begbie, *Theology, Music, and Time* (Cambridge: Cambridge University Press, 2000), 166, quoted in Alastair Roberts. *A Musical Case For Typological Realism* (Birmingham, AL: Theopolis, 2016), 24.

[21]Roberts. *A Musical Case For Typological Realism,* 24.

For Roberts, music is more than a metaphor; it is a familiar phenomenon in which the relationship of various elements is obvious and real despite their temporal discreteness: a theme once propounded is then reiterated or inverted or resolved, and each instance is thereby connected to other instances within the same musical work. Any given passage within a musical work may be much more closely connected to a more distant passage than it is to passages that are closer in time to it. Roberts primarily uses this to argue for "typological realism," that is, to "resist regarding typology as only formal analogies between discrete events, persons, or objects in time, a conclusion to which our spatialization of time tempts us. Instead, we are trained to perceive a living unity through it."

Roberts and Begbie are attempting to explain precisely the phenomenon which Gamaliel taught concerning the Passover: namely, that participants in a ritual meal in the present are thereby participating in the saving events of the past and the future. This is not a peculiar sectarian belief of one party of Pharisees. It is, rather, the common sacramentology of ancient Judaism, traceable to the institution narrative of the Passover in Exodus 12:24–27:

> And you shall observe this thing as an ordinance for you and your sons forever. It will come to pass when you come to the land which the Lord will give you, just as he promised, that you shall keep this service. And it shall be, when your children say to you, "What do you mean by this service?" that you shall say, "It is the Passover sacrifice of the Lord, who passed over the houses of the children of Israel in Egypt when he struck the Egyptians and delivered our households." (Ex. 12:24–27)

We see in this passage that the Passover, like the eucharist, was instituted in advance of the saving event that subsequent celebrations would retrospectively commemorate. Yet it also points beyond that to a future in which God has kept his promises: "when you come to the land which the Lord will give you, just as he promised. . . ." It looks forward to future generations, and points back to "when [the Lord] struck the Egyptians and delivered our households." Both Passover and the eucharist thus stretch backward to the past and forward to the future, marking their participants as belonging to the people of God that had its origins in that past saving event, and sealing them as the proper recipients to whom the promised future events belong. As N.T. Wright puts it, "Paul sees the eucharistic action as part of inaugurated eschatology, looking both back and forwards."[22] "Jesus Christ is the one who comes to us from God's future. His words at the Last Supper mean what they mean within the Passover experience, where bread and wine looked back to the rescue from Egypt and on to the time when Israel would be free at last."[23] Both ritual meals are thus grounded in the covenantal relationship of Israel

---

[22] N.T. Wright, *Paul and the Faithfulness of God*, 1347.
[23] N.T. Wright, *The Meal Jesus Gave Us* (London: SPCK, 2014), ch. 12.

and Israel's God that arches over history, embracing past, present, and future. That is why they work as they do.

Maurice Casey, though he does not claim to find Jesus' *ipsissima verba*, nonetheless argues persuasively that the Aramaic utterance that generated the Greek τοῦτο ἐστιν τὸ αἷμά μου τῆς διαθήκης in Mark 14:24 was something like הוא דקימא, דן דמי, so that "Jesus must have said הוא after קימא: 'This is my blood, it is of the covenant.' This is exegetically interesting, because it puts the emphasis of the sentence all the more clearly on the existing framework of God's covenant with Israel."[24] Casey thus solves the problem that a personal possessive suffix cannot be attached to a noun in the construct state, and a noun with such a suffix cannot precede ד or די ("of"). Jeremias had proposed דן אדם קימי, but this would have resulted in τοῦτο (ἐστιν) τὸ αἷμα (τῆς) διαθήκης μου, "This is the blood of my covenant," and if that had been the Aramaic original, a translator would never have changed the position of μου to follow αἷμα as it does in Mark 14:24. As Casey notes, "the giving of this interpretation *after* the wine was drunk will also have helped to make the symbolism dramatic rather than revolting. . . . Following the interpretation of the unleavened bread as Jesus' body, the interpretation of a cup of wine as his blood intensifies the presentation of the sacrificial death which he had predicted. . . . With the words דקימא הוא ('it (is) of the covenant'), Jesus asserted that his death would be significant in the redemption of Israel."[25] The words over the wine are a telling indicator of both the historicity of Mark's account and of the theology within which Jesus understood his own actions during and after the Passover meal with his disciples.

THE SPECIFIC PASSOVER CONTEXT OF THE WINE

The final layer of meaning results from Second Temple Jews articulating the covenantal and diachronic sacramentology of the second layer *in particular ceremonies*. We must move from the general to specific. Accordingly, our conclusions at this level will of necessity be more tentative, since it is difficult to pin down with certainty the specific ceremonies of the Last Supper beyond what is described for us in the New Testament texts. For this reason, most modern scholarly treatments of the Last Supper interpret its meaning in terms of the "general symbolism" of wine and bread in the Bible which is discussed above. This is an entirely appropriate thing to do, and bears good, but limited fruit.

There are, however, dangers of misinterpretation, of which the greatest are the projection onto the Second Temple period of the concerns and dogmas of

---

[24] Maurice Casey, "The Original Aramaic Form of Jesus' Words Over the Cup," 10.
[25] Maurice Casey, "The Original Aramaic Form of Jesus' Words Over the Cup," 8.

later Christian theology, and the insufficiently controlled "free association" of Old Testament rituals that are not, in fact, closely connected with the Last Supper. We could survey the Old Testament for antecedents and prototypes of the bread and wine: manna, unleavened Passover bread (matzah), the showbread, and so forth. All these things have sometimes been thought to have constituted the background by which Jesus' disciples understood the Last Supper, and it is true that they were available to Jesus and the disciples. Availability is not enough, however. We must also determine the volume of these echoes in the mental chorus of Jesus' disciples.

As an example of the dangers of not distinguishing the comparative "volume" of possible echoes, consider the proposal of Brant Pitre that "Jesus' words over the bread and wine at the Last Supper are not just evocative of the covenant sacrifices at Mount Sinai, but also of the bread (and wine) of the presence that is instituted by Moses in the Pentateuch [sc. Ex. 25:23–30] as the symbolic and sacrificial memorial of the covenant sacrifices and a kind of earthly participation in the heavenly theophanic banquet."[26] Since Jesus was holding bread, it is possible that this bread could have reminded his disciples of the showbread. But is it likely? A child might think he knew what a wedding cake meant, because, after all, he had a cake at his last birthday party, but no one with an adult's cultural knowledge would make that mistake. What features of the scene in the Upper Room spoke of showbread? This interpretation is weak because it fails to confirm the alleged allusions by appeal to details of the NT and related texts. Pitre attempts to retroject a doctrine of "real presence" into the showbread, by translating its name (*lehem panîm*) as "bread of the presence [of God]." But Exodus 25:30 makes clear that the showbread (literally, "face bread") is called by that name because it is set "before the face" (*lep'ney*) of the LORD, and not because of any "real presence" of God *in* the bread. The showbread, that is, is placed in the tabernacle in the presence of God, but there is no suggestion that God is present in the bread.

We must resist the temptation to read our own doctrines back into the text. (Daube, being a Jew and not a Christian, had an advantage on this point. They were not his doctrines, not his text, and not his ritual.) Daube's theory finds confirmation in its ability to make sense of the details of the NT texts and of the traces of the Messiah-bread ritual in rabbinic sources and Melito of Sardis, while remaining unaffected by the doctrinal developments of later Christian theology.

The same is true of Daube's explanation of the wine. It is one thing to connect the wine of the eucharist with the wine used in the Passover. It is another thing to show from the details of the NT's narrative and diction that specific Passover rituals are actually presupposed by the gospels' narratives

---

[26]Brant Pitre, *Jesus and the Last Supper*, 129.

of the Last Supper, and that Jesus' understanding of his coming death and the Kingdom of God shaped his use of the wine on that occasion. For beyond the general connotations of cups and wine, there was a more specific sequence and significance to the cups used in the celebration of the Passover. Without this context, the elements would have been mere static symbols of body and suffering—as indeed, they are often taken by many Christians. Within the Passover meal, however, they are placed within Israel's story, and it is in that narrative context that Jesus took them up and used them to insert himself into that same story, with astonishing results.

Although wine does not appear in Exodus 12's commands concerning Passover, we should probably assume that it was used as an expected drink at any normal festival.[27] At any rate, wine is first mentioned in connection with Passover in the Book of Jubilees (second century BCE):

> They should eat it . . . from the time of the setting of the sun. For on this night—the beginning of the festival and the beginning of the joy—ye were eating of the passover in Egypt, when all the powers of Mastema had been let loose to slay all the firstborn in the land of Egypt. . . . And all Israel was eating the flesh of the paschal lamb, and *drinking the wine, and was lauding and blessing and giving thanks to the LORD* God of their fathers, and was ready to go forth under the yoke of Egypt, and from evil bondage. . . . And the man who . . . does not come to observe it . . . and *to eat and to drink* before the LORD on the day of its festival . . . (*Jubilees* 49, trans. B. Bokser)[28]

In the medieval seder, the wine was consumed at four appointed moments in the course of the celebration and *ad libitum* between these moments (with one exception, which we will see shortly). The four prescribed moments for drinking are designated as the "four cups," and are present already in the Mishnah:

> On the eve of Passover, close to [the time of] *minchah* [sc. the grain offering], a person should not eat until it gets dark. Even a poor person in Israel should not eat until he reclines. [Those who serve] should not give him fewer than four cups of wine even if [the funds come] from the charity plate. (m.Pesahim, 10:1, trans. Bokser)[29]

According to the medieval Haggadah and modern usage, there are four cups served in the course of the Passover Seder, each linked with a particular verb of Exodus 6:6, considered as the summary of God's actions toward Israel in the

---

[27]Consider the social scandal that Jesus' mother Mary attempts to avert from the wedding hosts in John 3: "They have no more wine." If wine was expected at a wedding feast, we should assume its consumption also at major festivals of the Jewish calendar.
[28]Bokser, *The Origins of the Seder*, 19.
[29]Bokser, *The Origins of the Seder*, 45.

Exodus ("I will take you. . . . I will bring you out. . . . I will redeem you. . . . I will bring you into the land"). It is unclear whether this precise sequence of cups was already standardized in NT times. It is likely, however, that there was some such sequence, for already in the Mishnah the rabbis decreed that no drinking was permitted between the third and fourth cups:

> [They] poured for him the third cup [of wine]—[he] says the blessing over his food. [At] the fourth [cup]—he finishes the Hallel, and says over it the blessing of song (*birkat hashir*). Between the former cups, if [he] wants to drink [further] he may drink. Between the third and fourth, [he] should not drink. (m.Pesahim, 10:7, trans. Bokser)

This is from the third century, but as we shall see, the rule it cites is earlier, and is at work in the NT. Joseph Tabory notes that the Hallel psalms were prescribed in the Second Temple period, and that there was debate between the schools of Hillel and Shammai concerning whether Psalm 114 needed to be included.[30] The connection between the Psalms and the Hallel suggests that the sequence of cups was also part of the Second Temple Passover. Instone-Brewer believes that the first three cups were a Second Temple practice, but claims to detect that the fourth is a post-70 addition.[31] Casey finds no reason not to accept that a sequence of four was already in use.[32]

Despite Lietzmann's demurral, the consensus of scholarship is that the unusual phrase "cup of blessing" in 1 Corinthians 10:16 is in fact the technical designation of this cup.[33] Further evidence is Luke's designation of it as "the cup after supper" (Lk. 22:20, and cf. 1 Cor. 11:25). Both these labels, "the cup of blessing" and "the cup after supper," require a context of other cups in order to make sense. Without such a context, we would expect "a cup" or

---

[30] Joseph Tabory, "The Passover Eve Ceremony—An Historical Outline," *Immanuel* 12 (1981), 42.
[31] David Instone-Brewer, *Traditions of the Rabbis from the Era of the New Testament vol. 2A: Feasts and Sabbaths: Passover and Atonement* (Grand Rapids, MI: Eerdmans, 2011), 186–188.
[32] Maurice Casey, "The Original Aramaic Form of Jesus' Words Over the Cup."
[33] The phrase is mentioned twice in b.Ber. 51b, but not clearly in the context of Passover: "Ulla was once at the house of R. Nahman. They had a meal and he said grace, and he handed the cup of benediction to R. Nahman. R. Nahman said to him: Please send the cup of benediction to Yaltha" and "R. Assi said: One should not speak over the cup of benediction." Baruch Bokser (1986) agrees with Lietzmann, but Jeremias, Daube, Hägerland, Casey, and the majority of scholarship sees *some* sequence of cups as already part of the meal in the time of Jesus. Cf. the bibliographical citations in Anthony Thiselton, *The First Epistle to the Corinthians: A Commentary on the Greek Text* (Eerdman's, 2000), 759. Lietzmann's theory that the "cup of blessing" was part of *ḥaburoth* meals has been decisively refuted by J. Jeremias, R. D. Richardson, and I. Howard Marshall, the last of whom concludes, "There is no evidence whatever that the Jewish *ḥaburoth* held meals that were in any way different from ordinary Jewish meals" (I. H. Marshall, *Last Supper and Lord's Supper*, p. 20.) Mary Marshall's observation is the clincher: "The fact that there was a dispute between the houses of Shammai and Hillel about the order in which these blessings [over the cups] should be said, demonstrates that wine was being used liturgically in the first century." Mary J. Marshall, "Re-examining the Last Supper Sayings in Light of the Hebrew Scriptues," *Jesus and the Scriptures: Problems, Passages, and Patterns*, ed. T. Hägerland (London: T&T Clark, 2016), 201.

some other anarthrous construction. Luke, moreover, explicitly depicts more than one cup.[34] We are thus within our rights as interpreters to supply *some* sequence of specified cups or liturgical drinkings at the Last Supper. I say "some sequence" because it would be presumptuous to see the full sequence of cups from the medieval Haggadah at work in the Second Temple period. As always when using rabbinic sources, we face the challenge of dating the material. And as always, the proof is in the pudding: if the details of the gospels' narrative are made more satisfyingly vivid and coherent; if otherwise mysterious words and behavior become clear; if there is an economy of explanation—then we should feel some confidence that a rabbinic custom was already at work in the time of Jesus, even if that custom is otherwise attested only in sources from the later Tannaitic period.

I believe that David Daube provides us with a secure and satisfying explanation. He does it by focusing, not on the cup over which Jesus spoke his words, but on the fourth cup:

> There is, however, in Matthew and Mark a reference also to the fourth and last cup of the Passover liturgy. It is contained in the words: "I will not drink henceforth of this fruit of the vine until I drink it new in my father's kingdom" or "in the kingdom of God." The meaning is that the fourth cup will not be taken, as would be the normal thing, at a subsequent stage of this service; it will be postponed till the kingdom is fully established.[35]

Several reasons may be adduced in support of this interpretation. The phrase "fruit of the vine" is a verbal echo of the usual Jewish prayer over wine, "Blessed art thou, O Lord our God, who creates the fruit of the vine," and this prayer would have been said before the fourth cup. Then, too, the Mishnah (*m. Pes.* 10.7) contains strict rules about informal drinking between the formal cups of the seder: it is permissible to drink *ad libitum* between the first and second cups and between the second and third. Between the third and fourth cups, however, non-liturgical drinking was not permitted. Since the fourth cup was associated with the eschatological kingdom of God, this abstention symbolically enacted the patience of Israel awaiting the fulfillment of the promised kingdom.

---

[34]Cf. Darrel Bock, *Luke* (Downer's Grove, IL: Intervarsity Press, 1994), 348, note on 22:7–20. "If the meal followed the normal pattern, it would have had a preliminary course with a blessing, a cup of wine, green and bitter herbs, a meal serving and then preparation of the second cup. With the second cup of wine came the Passover liturgy. The main meal followed with a prayer said over the bread. Here is where Jesus would have spoken of his broken body. The main meal consisted of lamb, unleavened bread, and herbs. Then came the third cup of wine, known as the cup of blessing. Here is where Jesus would have discussed his shed blood. Finally, the meal closed with the singing of the Hallel psalms (Ps. 114–18), another prayer and a fourth cup of wine, which on this occasion Jesus refused. The first of Luke's two cups of wine would have been either the first or second cup."

[35]Daube, "Two Incidents After the Last Supper," 441–442.

There is further confirmation of Daube's interpretation from Mark's statement that "when they had sung a hymn, they went out to the Mount of Olives" (Mk. 14:26). The fourth cup was drunk with the recitation of the *birkat hashshir*, the "blessing of the song," which is consistent either of Psalm 145 ("All thy works shall praise thee . . .") or else the prayer beginning "The breath of every living thing shall bless thy name . . ." Either one works for Daube's argument, since both, he notes, contain the clause, "and they shall assign kingship to thy name, our King." The theme of the fourth cup was thus the kingship of Israel's God; for Jesus to abstain from this cup was thus to put aside the anticipatory drinking in favor of his impending action to bring about the kingdom for which it stood.

This fits with Jesus' announcement that "I will certainly not drink of this fruit of the vine from now on until that day when I drink it new with you in my Father's kingdom" (Mt. 26:29), words which take on a new significance in light of this context. Daube is correct to say that it "is in accordance with the Rabbinic rules" concerning drinking between the third and fourth cups. Joachim Jeremias saw Jesus' words (and also "with desire I have desired to eat the Passover") as a vow of abstention for the sake of Israel,[36] but this proposal has not met with acceptance by other scholars. Against Jeremias' theory, the words appear to be spoken in the course of drinking the third cup, and there is no other evidence that Jesus violated the Torah by abstaining from the Passover meal. But these objections do not tell against Daube's proposal that Jesus abstained only from the fourth cup. Since that cup stood for the kingdom of God, Jesus' vow means that he intended to substitute the actual coming of the kingdom for the anticipatory ritual that pointed to it.

And in light of this meaning, we may also reread the gospels' accounts of Jesus on the cross. Mark 15:23 records that Jesus refused to drink of the wine mingled with myrrh (ἐσμυρνισμένον οἶνον) that was offered to him as a partial anesthetic to relieve his pain: "But he did not take it." The results of Daube's interpretation are striking: Jesus associated the fourth cup with the coming Kingdom of God, and his intentions were focused on that Kingdom and his coming death. With this realization, we gain a more vivid and distinct impression of his thoughts on the cross: his refusal of sour wine there was a reiterated affirmation of his trust in God to bring about the Kingdom through his suffering and death.[37] Even wracked with pain as he was, he remained focused on his mission—and not on his mission in the abstract, but on his mission framed and defined by the Passover meal he had just interpreted for his disciples! (Now, too, we can appreciate Daube's interpretation of Jesus' request for his disciples to stay awake and preserve intact the Passover *ḥaburah*

---

[36] Jeremias, *Eucharistic Words*, 207–218.
[37] Daube, "Wine in the Bible," *CWDD* II, 461.

while he prayed in Gethsemane![38]) Now we see how false it is to suppose that Mark's account of the Last Supper is an unhistorical retrojection of utterances from later developed eucharistic liturgy. Quite the contrary, it is such a faithful transcript of historical testimony that it preserves unexplained and unglossed details which in turn disclose further meaning when unfolded against the Passover background.

THE CONTEXT IN JESUS' SELF-UNDERSTANDING AND THE PASSION WEEK

N.T. Wright links the Passover to the Jewish expectation of the "end of the exile" as the "forgiveness of sins." This is surely correct in the case of the Last Supper, even if other Passover meals celebrated by other Jews might exhibit a different eschatology and a different understanding of Israel's plight at the time. Sadducees, for instance, would have observed Passover, but they would likely not have seen the political situation of contemporary Israel as a "plight" crying out for a divine solution on the model of the original Exodus. Jesus' disciples, however, were drawn primarily from those persuasions of Judaism that were especially "looking for the redemption of Israel" (Lk. 2:38): namely, "zealots," Pharisees, and disciples of John the Baptist. Like Cleopas on the road to Emmaus, they believed both that Israel was in need of redemption and that Jesus "was the one who was going to redeem Israel." Wright points to Zechariah 9:9–11, which uses the phrase "blood of the covenant" (αἵματι διαθήκης):

> Rejoice greatly, O daughter of Zion!
> Shout, O daughter of Jerusalem!
> Behold, your King is coming to you;
> He is just and having salvation,
> Lowly and riding on a donkey,
> A colt, the foal of a donkey.
> I will cut off the chariot from Ephraim
> And the horse from Jerusalem;
> The battle bow shall be cut off.
> He shall speak peace to the nations;
> His dominion shall be from sea to sea,
> And from the River to the ends of the earth.
> As for you also, because of the *blood of your covenant*,
> I will set your prisoners free from the waterless pit.
> Return to the stronghold, you prisoners of hope.
> Even today I declare that I will restore double to you. (Zec. 9:9–11)

---

[38] cf. chapter 1 above, p. 8.

Layers of Meaning 91

Wright's suggestion coheres well with the historical situation of Jesus' utterance: Jesus used the phrase "blood of the covenant" just four days after having personally enacted the scene described in Zechariah 9:9, riding a donkey into Jerusalem to the acclamation of the crowds—a symbolic action that could not be misunderstood by his Jewish contemporaries. With this action, Jesus declared that the events of Israel's long-await redemption were taking place in and through himself. Matthew's account of the cup adds the phrase "for the forgiveness of sins." This is not to be understood as a timeless promise of individual forgiveness, but as the visible action of Israel's God in history to rescue his people from the political and social plight that had come upon her because of her sins.[39] This is a still more specific historical context than the general connotations of blood and wine in the Old Testament. Wright argues that "the forgiveness of sins" was not "an abstract atonement," but that Jesus' death would "be the means of rescuing YHWH's people from their exilic plight."

The peculiar expression "poured out for many" (περί πολλῶν ἐκχυννόμενον Mt. 26:28, ἐκχυννόμενον ὑπὲρ πολλῶν, Mk. 14:24) also echoes OT prophecy. Isaiah 53:12, where the suffering "servant of YHWH" has "poured out his soul unto death . . . and bore the sin of many." The word is unusual enough that it is fair to see the use of it in the gospels of Matthew and Mark as a deliberate echo of Isaiah 53. It might be objected that in the gospels, Jesus speaks of his "blood" being poured out, while in Isaiah 53:12, the servant pours out his "soul." But this difficulty disappears when we consider that Isaiah uses the Hebrew *nephesh*, which means equally "life," and it was a dictum in the Torah that "the *nephesh* is in the blood (*baddam*)" (Lev 17:11). Thus, to use "blood" with the participle "poured out" was to evoke this same principle: "It is the blood that makes atonement, with the life." This is an important chapter for Jesus' own self-understanding, since he saw Isaiah's words about the suffering Servant of YHWH as thematic for his own vocation.[40] Not only his synagogue sermon in Nazareth (Lk. 4:16–21), but also this use of

---

[39]In a similar way, Andrew Perriman makes the point that when "Paul speaks of the 'righteousness of God,' what he has in mind is not an abstract ethical quality which might, for example, be imputed or transferred to the unrighteous, but divine action at critical moments in the history of his people, in keeping with contextually appropriate commitments, interpreted with reference to paradigmatic biblical narratives, by which the God of Israel is publicly vindicated, shown to be in the right." Andrew Perriman, *The Future of the People of God: Reading Romans Before and After Western Christendom*. (Eugene, OR: Cascade Books, 2010), ch. 7. The historical-political nature of both God's righteousness and the forgiveness of sins is essential to an understanding of the Last Supper and the eucharist.

[40]On Jesus and Isaiah 52–53, cf. R.T. France, "The Servant of the Lord in the Teaching of Jesus" *Tyndale Bulletin* 19 (1968), 26–52; Morna Hooker, *Jesus and the Servant* (London: SPCK, 1959); and N.T. Wright, *Jesus and the Victory of God*, 584–593, and especially 601–604, where Wright summarizes the correct approach well: "I am not suggesting that Jesus 'regarded himself as "the servant"' . . . [Rather,] it is a matter of understanding Jesus' whole kingdom-announcement in the light of several major themes from the Jewish scriptures, and showing that it is absurd, granted the whole picture, to disallow reference, allusion and echo to Isaiah 40–55 in general, and to 52.13–53.12 in particular."

"poured out" indicates that the latter chapters of Isaiah loomed large in Jesus' understanding of Israel and of his own vocation and mission. Bruce Chilton suggests that in his preaching, Jesus "took up the actual vocabulary of the Aramaic translation of the book of Isaiah (the Targum) which was current in an oral form within the synagogues of his time."[41] Similarly, Maurice Casey notes that the Tosefta, the Mekhilta, and Exodus Rabbah evince the presence of a complex of Jewish tradition regarding the redemptive power of blood. The Tosefta applies the phrase "blood of the covenant" to the blood shed at circumcision (*t.Shab.* 15.9). These Rabbinic sources represent a later stage of a tradition of Jewish thought about the significance of blood within the covenant between God and Israel. It is credible that Jesus drew upon an earlier stage of this tradition in order to assert that his own impending death would be significant in the redemption of Israel.

Thus, as we also found in the case of the words over the bread, we discover that Jesus' words about the wine are more concerned with using the Passover to speak to his disciples about his own impending death and its significance within Israel's story than they were about explaining the metaphysical relation of the bread and wine to his body and blood. His words over the bread identify himself as Israel's Messiah; his words over the cup are a way of indicating that he will offer himself as a sacrifice, a new Passover lamb to accomplish a new Exodus; and that this will bring about the coming Kingdom of God. Messiah, new Exodus, and coming Kingdom: this is a deeply Jewish set of meanings for these rituals, full of the themes that were on every mind and heart at Passover. Jesus in the Last Supper is doing what we should expect for a Jewish Messiah's last meal with his disciples; he is doing exactly what Jews have always done with the food and drink of the Passover: make them tell the story of God and Israel—past, present, and future—and by ritual participation inscribe themselves in that story, in those events.

---

[41]Bruce Chilton, *Types of Authority in Formative Christianity and Judaism* (New York: Routledge, 1999), xi.

Chapter Five

Mechanics and Misinterpretations

For Jesus to take up Messiah-bread and identify himself with it; for him to take up a cup anticipating the kingdom of God and to declare that the kingdom would be brought about by his own impending death—to approach the Passover rituals this way was to transform them, no doubt. But because meaning arises from limited, not unlimited difference, Jesus' changes to the ritual meal's meaning meant that there could be no drastic change in its mode of operation. In whatever manner the Passover was thought to "work," that is how Jesus and his disciples also understood what they were doing with bread and wine. To change the referents of the symbolic foods, all that was necessary was to hold them up and speak words tying them to Jesus and his coming death. And this is precisely what Jesus did. But to change the *way the Passover worked*, Jesus would have needed to engage in a far lengthier explanation than the gospels show him giving. He would especially have needed to do this if he had wanted to set up the eucharist as a means for himself to be *locally present* in the elements of the bread and wine, for this was not the way any Jew understood the operation of the Passover meal and its connection with the Messiah: it was, rather, a way of sharing in the past events of the Exodus and the future life and events of the Messiah. The effect of Jesus' words was to change the referents of the ritual, but not to introduce a new *mode of reference*. The eucharist now inscribes its participants into a transformed body and a different saving event than the Passover did. It does not, however, relate to that body or that event *in a different way* than Passover related to the body of the slaughtered lamb and the event of the Exodus.

If this account of the Last Supper is correct—not about every detail, but only about the general idea that Jesus worked with pre-existent rituals to reshape the Passover with his impending sacrificial death at the center of it—then it provides a potentially ecumenical understanding compatible with the vast majority of modern second-order explanations in Christian sacramentology. For if Daube is correct, then the effect of Jesus' words over the bread and cup was precisely to tie these rituals to himself and to his impending death. Naturally, their original situation in the context of the Passover was quickly overshadowed by the greater salvation wrought by the cross. The semiotic connection to Passover itself was loosened, so that the bread ritual became self-contained. Even within the pages of the New Testament, we find the disciples of Jesus apparently sharing in the bread ritual outside of Passover, and as early as Acts 20:7 it appears to have become a weekly or more-than-weekly observance, connected with the church's *agape* meal rather than an annual one celebrated only at Passover. These changes also made the eucharist more accessible to Gentile converts, who could be included in it without being fully informed about the Passover.

Yet in another sense, the loss of the eucharist's paschal roots was deeply problematic. When Jesus chose to identify himself as the Messiah using a Passover meal, he thereby pointed back to the Old Testament scriptures that had shaped the description of his messianic office.[1] Thus, to say that the Lord's Supper is a transformed Passover meal is to say that it can never be understood rightly apart from the story of Israel. It also implies that if Jesus intended it to be repeated as a continuing ritual after his death, then he will have intended it to work in the same way that Passover was thought to work. And the apostle Paul will have done the same. The thesis has implications for both the meaning and operation of the eucharist.

The hypothesis I am defending, especially concerning the bread, is not new. It has been advanced by Eisler, Daube, Bleicher Carmichael, and David Stacey. Some of its advocates have been reluctant to admit that the theory of an already existing bread-ritual poses such a challenge to the Church's developed views. David Stacey, for instance, after defending something very close to Daube's view, writes:

> I have recognized that there are many other interpretations of the Lord's Supper than the one I have argued for here, interpretations that were worked out by the early church in those first creative decades and in the centuries since. None of these has to be surrendered.[2]

Stacey means that second-order theological explanations operate on a different level from Daube's and Eisler's first-order account of the meaning of the Last Supper in its original context. He perceives the threat posed to received

---

[1] N.T. Wright would no doubt add, more controversially but still correctly, that the OT scriptures had also shaped the self-understanding of Jesus.

[2] David Stacey, "The Lord's Supper as Prophetic Drama," in Morna Hooker, *The Signs of a Prophet* (Eugene, OR: Wipf and Stock, 1997), 95.

Christian sacramentologies by such a thoroughgoing reinterpretation of the Last Supper. Daube himself realized that "the principal motivation for the fierceness of the assault [on Eisler's original article] (whatever its merits in substance), I am sure, lay far deeper."[3] The hypothesis calls into question modern Jewish scholars' assurance that Christianity, especially in the eucharist, represents a heretical deviation from Judaism "too monstrous even to debate" rather than an expression of deeply Jewish ideas. At the same time, it calls into question the historical foundations of prevailing Christian sacramentologies: by specifying the historical picture, it does not leave adequate "blank canvas" to accomodate the second-order language of Christian sacramentologies that have been devised over centuries of tradition.

In this chapter, I want to explore how Daube and Eisler's hypothesis fits with, or conflicts with, some prominent Christian explanations of the eucharist.

CONTAINERS OF MEDICINE?

The first difference we find in medieval Christian sacramentology is a focus on the elements of bread and wine removed from the narrative which they were designed to inscribe ritually. The elements are separated from their proper connotations and resonances. The result is a semiotic vacuum. Yet because the eucharist is an evocative ritual act that begs to be explained, the semiotic vacuum cries out to be filled. The eucharist's connections with Israel's story had to be replaced with alternative, metaphysical theories.

The twelfth-century Saxon theologian Hugh of St. Victor taught that sacraments work like containers so that there is an invisible grace contained in the visible elements:

> God is the doctor, man is the sick person, the priest is the assistant or messenger, grace is the medicine, and the sacrament is a container. The doctor gives, the assistant dispenses, the container preserves that which cures the sick man who perceives the spiritual grace. Therefore, if *sacraments are containers of spiritual grace,* they do not heal of themselves, since *containers do not cure a sick man, but medicine does* . . . In order to display his skill, the doctor has concocted his cure from that very thing, by which a sluggish man received the cause of his disease. For since a man had become corrupt by longing for visible things, it was fitting for him to be cured in a symmetrical way, and receive the cause of his health in the same visible things, so that he might rise up whole through the same things through which he had fallen sick.[4]

---

[3]Daube, "He That Cometh," 432, n. 21.
[4]Hugh of St. Victor, *De Sacramentis* 1.9.4 in *Patrologia Latina* 176, 323. Cited in Peter Leithart, *The Priesthood of the Plebs* (Eugene, OR: Wipf & Stock, 2003), 12, n. 17.

In Hugh's account, Man is corrupted by loving the visible world—a view quite at odds with Judaism, according to which the visible world was created by God and approved as good. The elements of bread and wine in the eucharist therefore must have their efficacy by *containing invisible grace*. Man's "disease," his "sluggishness," his "corruption by longing for visible things" are universal human problems, and their solution is conceived of in universal terms. There is no "scandal of particularity" here. The framing of the problem by analogy to the situation of a doctor and his assistant administering medicine to a patient makes it equidistant from every culture and every time. The "medicine" is abstracted from any connection to Israel and its history: it is simply "spiritual grace," considered as something that can be contained, administered, and consumed.

The efficacy of medicine is both *inherent* in the medicine itself and at odds with its outward ordinariness: small pills or potions have great power, and that power is *contained inside* them. Thus, the consumption of a mouthful of medicine produces effects far greater than the swallowing of a mouthful of ordinary food or drink. In default of any overt connection with the story of Israel, the power of the eucharist is left to be located within the elements themselves. The result is the late-medieval conception of grace as a substance able to be transferred into various "containers," as seen in an untechnical, popular sense in Christopher Marlowe's 1593 play *Doctor Faustus:*

> Ah, stay, good Faustus, stay thy desperate steps!
> I see an angel hovers o'er thy head,
> And, with a vial full of precious grace,
> Offers to pour the same into thy soul:
> Then call for mercy and avoid despair. (V.i)

Here, the angel's "vial full of precious grace" is wholly invisible and imaginary. The soul is a "leaky vessel" needing to be refilled with grace from time to time. Grace as a substance is a metaphysical replacement for the Jewish narrative substructure of the eucharist.

If the bread and wine either contain grace or are transformed into the body and blood of Jesus, then it follows that the grace or the body and blood is available and present in a way that does not require or entail *the story*. They can be encountered the way any object is encountered, that is, merely thrown up against (Lat. *ob-jectum*) us, as a raindrop falls on a man's head or a stone is kicked up from a roadway by a tire to strike another car's windshield. Thus the elements of the eucharist no longer depend upon the nexus of Paschal, Israelite, narrative meaning for their efficacy or significance. Rather than being a means by which participants share in the past and future events concerning Israel and Israel's long-expected king, the bread and wine become *objects present* and able to be worshipped, quite apart from connection to the narrative of Israel. This is not merely an academic distinction. It shapes not only the objective meaning of the eucharist, but also Christians' subjective experience of it and the practices they engage in around it.

PARTICIPATION, NOT PRESENCE

The Roman Catholic theological tradition since Paschasius and many Anglicans (especially since the Oxford movement) have spoken of the eucharist's efficacy as consisting in the "real presence" of Christ in the elements. The idea of "presence" requires examination, for it applies differently to objects and persons than it does to events or experiences. On Daube's and Eisler's hypothesis, Jesus' words in the Upper Room carry no suggestion that the bread and wine will be a remedy for his impending personal absence from the disciples.

The etymological sense of "presence" (Lat. *prae* + *esse*) is "being in front of [a person],"[5] and it is a characteristic of presence of every sort that it can happen without any narrative context at all. In a "real presence" theory, the body and blood (the *res* of the Augustinian *sacramentum/res* dichotomy) are thought to be "there," to "be in front of" us. I may see a man on the bus and have no idea who he is. A bird lands on the fence outside my window, and I don't know where it came from. Such story-less, low-context, bare presence is, in fact, how we are usually confronted[6] with things and persons in everyday life: because things can be present to us without our understanding them, we face the continual task of getting to know the things and persons in front of us. We are confronted with things and persons that are *not we*, and we learn their stories and our own possible or actual relation to them only via inquiry and further experience. "Presence" is not the same as relationship, let alone "participation." (It may of course be a preliminary step toward participation.)

Jesus' Last Supper with his disciples on Passover, far from culminating in a sacramental "real presence," begins with presence and moves from presence to something higher. The disciples have Jesus "present"—sitting in front of their eyes—but they still do not understand who he is or how they are to relate to him. Likewise, the disciples on the road to Emmaus "come to know him in the breaking of bread" (Lk. 24:35). They move from "not know[ing] how to

---

[5]Augustine's erroneous etymology in *City of God* XI.3 gets half the word right. He correctly explains *prae*, but gives a wrong etymology for the rest: "Things which are within reach of our senses, whether interior or exterior . . . are said to be 'present,' because, as we say, they are 'before our senses' (*prae sensibus*), as things accessible to sight are 'before our eyes.'"

[6]Like "presence," "confront" denotes existence in a spatial sense relative to a person: Latin *con* + *frons* = "before your forehead," "face to face."

locate" Jesus' resurrection "within Israel's story" to recognizing, understanding, and worshipping him.[7] This transition from ignorance to knowledge and from despair to hope is wrought, not by "real presence" but by their "eyes" being "opened." And when, thereafter, they narrate these events to the eleven in Jerusalem, they do not see the bread as a "presence" of Jesus that persisted after he "vanished from their sight" (Lk. 24:31). Rather, they understood that he was absent from them until he suddenly became present again in their room (Lk. 24:36–37). The narrative of Luke 24 is concerned not with the institution of the eucharist as a means of Christ's continued "presence" but with the bread ritual as the means by which the disciples on the road to Emmaus were at last caught up into the climax of Israel's story so that they understood both Christ's role in that story and their own role. That is why the story is narrated with a consistent focalization through the eyes of the disciples, who were no doubt the eyewitness source for Luke's written version. Luke bends all his descriptive detail to highlight the disciples' subjective experiences: their incomprehension, their encounter with Jesus, their eating of bread and ensuing realization, their misapprehension of him as a "spirit." All this works together and builds to the climax that is summed up in Luke 24:45: "He opened their understanding, that they might comprehend the Scriptures." By this is meant, not merely the unpacking of some "prooftexts," but the realization that "the whole story of Israel builds to its narrative climax in Jesus. That is what Jesus tries to teach them on the road."[8]

This is not mere knowledge of facts. It involves what Richard Hays calls "the conversion of the imagination" and results in worship of Jesus and of Israel's God. The great irony is that the disciples on the road to Emmaus were in a state of confused incomprehension, not understanding the story or Jesus or themselves, and consequently gloomy and depressed (σκυθρωποί, 24:17)—and all *while Jesus was present.* No sooner did they recognize him than he absented himself from them again (24:31–32). This pattern is repeated at the end of the chapter for the gathered disciples in Jerusalem: Christ appears bodily to them and blesses them (presence), then is "parted from them and carried up into heaven" (absence), whereupon they "worshiped him, and returned to Jerusalem with great joy" (Lk. 24:52). In this narrative, the presence of Christ is not effected by the eating of the bread (still less by "consecration" of it); indeed, the resurrected Jesus appeared and was bodily present to his disciples on the road to Emmaus only *in order to* bring about the disciples' participation in his new life, which is the life of the renewed Israel, the climax and fulfillment of Israel's story. *The goal is participation, not "presence."*

---

[7] R. Hays. *Reading Backward,* ch. 1.
[8] R. Hays. *Reading Backward,* ch. 1.

AGAINST EDIBLE FLASHCARDS

The other main answer that the Christian tradition has given to explain how the eucharist works is to locate the efficacy of the ritual not in a "real presence" but only in the mental acts which accompany it. The actual eating and drinking are, on this view, of no great moment; what matters is rather the thoughts of the participants, since it is by thinking that they "exercise faith." The sacrament becomes a sort of edible flashcard to prompt pious thoughts or reflection. Such a view is actually very old; we can find a similar denial of any reality applied to the laws about cleanness in the Tannaitic period: Johanan ben Zaccai explained that a person "did not become really unclean by a corpse nor did he become really clean by the 'water of separation,' but that the relevant provisions must be observed because it was the will of God."[9]

With some important exceptions, the Reformed and Presbyterian churches have been especially insistent on this, at times reifying faith and treating it as a faculty by which Christians receive the benefits conveyed in the sacrament. The Belgic Confession's Article 35 is one example:

> God has sent a living bread that came down from heaven: namely Jesus Christ, who nourishes and maintains the spiritual life of believers when eaten—*that is, when appropriated and received spiritually by faith*. To represent to us this spiritual and heavenly bread Christ has instituted an earthly and visible bread as the sacrament of his body and wine as the sacrament of his blood. He did this to testify to us that just as truly as we take and hold the sacrament in our hands and eat and drink it with our mouths, by which our life is then sustained, so truly we receive into our souls, for our spiritual life, the true body and true blood of Christ, our only Savior. *We receive these by faith, which is the hand and mouth of our souls.* Now it is certain that Jesus Christ did not prescribe his sacraments for us in vain, since he works in us all he represents by these holy signs, although the manner in which he does it goes *beyond our understanding and is incomprehensible to us*, just as the operation of God's Spirit is hidden and incomprehensible.

It is worth asking whether we ordinarily speak of "appropriating" things spiritually. How does faith do this? The mechanics of faith's action in receiving the body and blood of Christ are by de Brés' own admission "beyond our understanding" and "incomprehensible." As we shall see, however, later Reformed theologians, especially the Puritans, were not shy about supplying an explanation of how this incomprehensible action took place.

---

[9] Num. Rab. on 19.2; P. de R. K. 40a f., cited in David Daube, "A Baptismal Catechism" in *Collected Works of David Daube vol. II: New Testament Judaism* (Berkeley, CA: the Robbins Collection, 2000), 501–502.

What stands out above all else in the Belgic Confession's explanation is that these saving benefits are received *in parallel* to the eating and drinking, and not *by means* of the meal considered as a meal. The consumption of the bread and wine with the mouth is carefully distinguished from the reception of Christ's body and blood into the soul. There are two different, but simultaneous actions going on: Hands and mouths consume bread and wine, but Christ's body and blood are received "by faith, which is the hand and mouth of the soul." The function of the bread and wine is to "represent" Christ's body and blood, and thereby to serve as an analogy for our minds to consider: "*just as truly* as we take and hold . . . in our hands and eat and drink it with our mouths, . . . *so truly* we receive into our souls. . . ." What matters is what happens in the mind and on the spiritual plane.

In a similar manner, the Westminster Larger Catechism's question 170 says that Christ is "spiritually present to the faith of the receiver, no less truly and really than the elements themselves are to their outward senses." Faith is here considered as a faculty to be used by the believer to "receive and apply unto themselves Christ crucified, and all the benefits of his death." Question 174 lists the actions which ought to be performed by a recipient of the Lord's Supper "in the time of the administration of it." Among those actions is "feeding on Christ by faith," an expression with a long pedigree in English Protestant piety also. It is part of Cranmer's 1552 edition of the Book of Common Prayer, in which the words spoken when the priest hands the bread to a recipient are, "Take and eat this in remembrance that Christ died for thee, and feed on him in thy heart by faith, with thanksgiving."[10]

The idea of "eating by faith" is rather tricky and hard to understand. Most Christians, when told that they need to exercise faith, will start thinking about God and the Bible and the Creeds, and try hard to believe and love him. But when told to eat Jesus with their faith, most Christians don't know where to start. It is rather like wizarding students at Hogwarts trying to learn how to cast non-verbal spells or apparate: a matter of trying to channel and use an as-yet untried power or faculty inside them, the workings of which they are unable to explain or articulate. Faced with this daunting task,[11] Christians do what they know how to do: think about Jesus.

---

[10] This formula replaced the earlier words, "The Body of our Lord Jesus Christ, which was given for thee, preserve thy body and soul unto everlasting life." The later 1662 BCP uses both sentences together.

[11] According to the Westminster Larger Catechism's formulations, it is a positively daunting feat of reverence and emotions, requiring 14 different mental acts beforehand, another 13 during the Supper, and another 7 if they judge themselves to have partaken successfully, or 5 if unsuccessfully! Astonishingly, the Westminster Divines do not actually state that those "that receive the sacrament" must eat and drink the bread and wine. Every action specified in Q. 174 (as well as those in Q. 171 and 175) is something Christians do with their minds. By contrast, all of the commands of Jesus concerning the Supper—"take, eat, drink, do this"—are things that Christians do with their bodies.

E. Brooks Holifield, writing in his history of Puritan sacramental theology, notes precisely this connection among the early Puritans: "Corresponding to suspicion of the outward and material was a conviction that conceptual understanding was essential to sacramental worship . . . Thus in the Lord's Supper the Puritan reformers insisted that every outward action of the ceremony ought to produce an inward comprehension of doctrinal truths."[12] This tendency is borne out in the Puritans. William Perkins (1558–1602) writes:

> The signes and visible elements affect the sense outward and inward: the senses convey their object to the minde: the minde directed by the holy Ghost reasoneth on this manner, out of the promise annexed to the Sacrament: He that useth the elements aright, shall receive grace thereby: but I use the elements aright in faith and repentance, saith the minde of the believer: therefore shall I receive from God increase of grace. Thus, then, faith is confirmed not by the work done, but by *a kinde of reasoning caused in the mind*, the argument or proofe whereof is borrowed from the elements, being signes and pledges of God's mercie.[13] (emphasis in the original)

The Cambridge Puritan divine William Bradshaw (1571–1618) similarly explains what it means to eat the flesh of Christ in the Lord's Supper:

> Hence also it appears, that we specially eate the flesh of Christ, and drink his bloud, when with a beleeving heart and mind, we effectually remember and in our remembrance, we seriously meditate of, and in our meditations are religiously affected, and in our affections thoroughly inflamed with the love of Christ, grounded upon that which Christ has done for us, and which is represented and sealed unto us in this Sacrament.[14]

Thus, the working of the Supper is explained as mental remembrance leading to the stirring up of religious affections. In the Bible, however, the efficacy of the Lord's Supper is not located in any accompanying mental acts. Paul's instructions to the Corinthians make clear that the Supper is vitiated by their obvious failure to love each other and to eat together, and that this, not a failure to think the right thoughts, is the reason why "many of you are sick and many have fallen asleep" (1 Cor. 11:30).

To be fair, there are other theologians in the Reformed tradition—John Williamson Nevin and John Calvin himself—who viewed the Supper as more than a mental exercise. It is an open question, however, whether the

---

[12] E. Brooks Holifield, *The Covenant Sealed: The Development of Puritan Sacramental Theology in Old and New England, 1570–1720* (Eugene, OR: Wipf and Stock, 2002), 38. I am indebted to John Barach for calling these passages to my attention.
[13] William Perkins, *Reformed Catholike*, 590, cited in Holifield 2002, 58.
[14] William Bradshaw, *Preparation*, 18, 30, 37, cited in Holifield 2002, 59.

explanation of Perkins and Bradshaw is not the dominant one in Reformed and Presbyterian churches today.

VISIBLE SIGNS OF INVISIBLE GRACE?

The Reformed confessions employ the medieval scholastic conception of the sacraments as visible signs of invisible grace in their explanations of the way the sacraments work. Consider the Heidelberg Catechism:

> Q 75. How does the Lord's supper signify and seal to you that you share in Christ's one sacrifice on the cross and in all his gifts?
> A. Christ has commanded me and all believers to eat of this broken bread and drink of this cup in remembrance of him.
>   With this command he gave these promises: First, as surely as I see with my eyes the bread of the Lord broken for me and the cup given to me, so surely was his body offered for me and his blood poured out for me on the cross.
>   Second, as surely as I receive from the hand of the minister and taste with my mouth the bread and the cup of the Lord as sure signs of Christ's body and blood, so surely does he himself nourish and refresh my soul to everlasting life with his crucified body and shed blood.[15]

As in the Belgic Confession, the observable actions are not instrumental, but pledges by which the believer may trust that a simultaneous action is being accomplished invisibly. The confession adds a footnote to the words "gave these promises" adducing Matthew 26:26–28, Mark 14:22–24, Luke 22:19, 20, and 1 Corinthians 11:23–25 as evidence. But these narratives of the Last Supper do not contain any "as surely . . . so surely" logic, nor do they indicate that the Supper operates as a visible and edible sign of a promise. In fact, the instructions that Jesus gives are commands to participate in a feast: "eat," "drink," and "do this." He does not say anything about "seeing with the eyes" or even about "tasting"; there is nothing about perception at all, because the Supper was not designed to address itself to passive persons as a collection of signs working upon their senses. Rather, it was intended to involve persons through their participatory actions. If a participant were blind and incapable of tasting food because of an injury or disease, such a person would not for those reasons be any less a full participant.

Inclusion in a meal is not reckoned by one's ability to perceive the food. That simply is not how a ritual meal worked in second temple Judaism. Only by forgetting that it is a ritual meal would Christian theologians ever have felt

---

[15]Heidelberg Catechism from *The Book of Praise: Anglo-Genevan Psalter* (Hamilton: Canadian Reformed Churches, 1984), 506–507.

the need to theorize the eucharist as a visible analogy for transactions occurring on a parallel, invisible plane or in the minds of the participants.

EPICYCLES AND PUZZLES I: THE NINTH CENTURY

It is characteristic of mistaken explanations that they generate puzzles, absurdities, and false questions. As the Ptolemaic astronomers' geocentric model of the planets' orbits required epicycles to save the phenomena, so these de-Judaized sacramentologies, both "real presence" and "eating by means of faith," provoke questions requiring forced answers—questions that simply do not arise if we treat the eucharist as a ritual meal.

Some puzzles concern the logical consequences of "real presence": if Christ is locally present in the elements of bread and wine, what happens when these elements are not consumed by the faithful, but are spilled, dropped, or eaten by animals? The concern is an old one. As early as the third century, Origen can appeal to his audience's habitual care not to drop any pieces of the bread.[16] Thirteen centuries later, the following story is told of Luther by Johann Hachenburg:

> [In 1542, in Wittenberg] a woman wanted to go to the Lord's Supper, and then as she was about to kneel on the bench before the altar and drink, she made a misstep and jostled the chalice of the Lord violently with her mouth, so that some of the Blood of Christ was spilled from it onto her lined jacket and coat and onto the rail of the bench on which she was kneeling. So then when the reverend Doctor Luther, who was standing at a bench opposite, saw this, he quickly ran to the altar (as did also the reverend Doctor Bugenhagen), and together with the curate, with all reverence licked up [the Blood of Christ from the rail] and helped wipe off this spilled Blood of Christ from the woman's coat, and so on, as well as they could. And Doctor Luther took this catastrophe so seriously that he groaned over it and said, "O, God, help!" and his eyes were full of water.[17]

On this view, spilled wine is "a catastrophe" and a cause for weeping. A similar realism underlies the common practice of filling the empty chalice with

---

[16]"You who are accustomed to take part in divine mysteries know, when you receive the body of the Lord, how you protect it with all caution and veneration lest any small part fall from it, lest anything of the consecrated gift be lost. For you believe, and correctly, that you are answerable if anything falls from there by neglect. But if you are so careful to preserve his body, and rightly so, how do you think that there is less guilt to have neglected God's word than to have neglected his body?" Origen, *Homily on Exodus* 13:3, in *Homilies on Genesis and Exodus*, trans. Ronald D. Heine (Washington, DC: Catholic University, 1982) 380–381, cited in Chauvet, *The Sacraments*, 44.

[17]Johann Hachenburg, quoted in E.F. Peters, *The Origin and Meaning of the Axiom: "Nothing Has the Character of a Sacrament Outside of the Use"* (Fort Wayne: Concordia Theological Seminary Press, 1993), 191. I owe this quotation to Michael Keith Templin.

water and drinking the water, lest any drops be wasted. (Later Lutheranism departed from the founder on this point and embraced a form of receptionism, while still maintaining "real presence."[18])

Seven hundred years earlier, the illuminators of the Book of Kells (early ninth century) devoted their artistic talents to the depiction of mice struggling over the host of the eucharist, or a cat chasing a mouse as it makes off with a host. These details are tucked unobtrusively in between lines of the text or in corners of the larger decorative pages.[19] The consumption of eucharistic hosts by mice was, no doubt, a common enough occurrence in medieval church buildings, but their inclusion in the book's decorations is a sign that such consumption was not merely occurring, but was noted and remarked upon by Christians. Judaism, by contrast, has never had such concerns about animals eating Passover matzah; the rabbis permit the feeding of matzah and other Passover food to pets; there are even businesses that sell kosher pet food certified ḥametz-free by rabbis.[20] What matters is that the household or business establishment be free of leaven. But because of the Christian identification of the elements of the eucharist with the body and blood of Christ, the eating of them by animals was a more remarkable matter. Such decorations indicate a sense of humor on the part of Kells' illuminators, but they also are indicative of a peculiar conception of the eucharistic elements and an incipient belief in "real presence."

The mice in the Book of Kells are symptoms of a change in sacramentology in the ninth century. Around the same time, we find the Frankish liturgical scholar Amalarius of Metz (*c*.775–*c*.850) practicing a bizarre custom: he would spit after he had received the sacrament. In answer to critics who found this practice irreverent, he justified himself as follows:

> When the body of the Lord has been received with good intention, I must not discuss whether it is invisibly taken up into heaven, or is kept in our bodies till the day of burial, or is breathed out into the air, or passes from the body with the blood, or goes out through the passages, as the Lord says, "Everything which goeth into the mouth passeth into the belly, and is cast out into the draught." This alone must be my care that I take it not with the heart of Judas, and that it is not despised but most healthfully discerned from common food.[21]

---

[18]For instance, Loehe's Catechism, Q. 863: "Why is there no danger of spilling any of Christ's blood? Answer: Because the Almighty Lord unites his Blood with the wine that is drunk, but not with the drops of wine that are spilled. The error of the Romanists is a consequence of their wrong teaching that there is only Blood, and merely the appearance of wine, in the Holy Supper." (174) Loehe does not elaborate on the mechanics of this union with wine as it is drunk rather than before. Wilhelm Loehe, *Questions and Answers to the Six Parts of the Small Catechism of Dr. Martin Luther* (Columbia: W.J. Duffie, 1893).

[19]Cf. the details of pages 48 recto and 34 recto in the Book of Kells. See also the cover of this book, which reproduces the cat and mouse from 48 recto.

[20]See, for instance, Ruth Schuster, "Israel's Safari Animals Are Keeping Kosher for Passover, and Loving It," *HaAretz*, April 10, 2017, complete with video of chimpanzees eating matzah; and Niv Elis, "Why Israeli Dairy Cows Eat Kosher for Passover," *Jerusalem Post*, April 6, 2014.

[21]Amalarius, Ep. VI (*Patrologia Latina* vol. CV, 1338).

Despite his refusal to choose any of these theories, Amalarius' commitment to the real presence of Christ in the elements compels him to admit the necessity of some such explanation. In keeping with ancient and medieval scientific method, he is concerned only to "save the appearances" and thus gladly allows that there may be multiple possible explanations. While not insisting dogmatically on any of these over the others, he implies that for his own part, he prefers not to take any chance that the body of the Lord might "go out through the passages"; spitting it out is the safer method. Yet we may note how very remarkable a solution this is. Those of a scholastic or rabbinic bent would be justified in asking whether Amalarius could truly be considered to have received the bread at all. Amalarius' contemporary Florus of Lyon accused him of the error of "stercorianism," or "stercorism," the idea that the body of Christ becomes excrement after digestion.[22]

Another voice from the same period is Paschasius Radbertus (785–865), the Abbot of Corbie and champion of transubstantiation.[23] What is unique about Paschasius' view is his claim that the bread and wine cease to be bread and wine and become body and blood *instead*. Indeed, for Paschasius, after consecration they can no longer be rightly called "bread" and "wine" except improperly, by metonymy or a sort of *communicatio idiomatum*:

> That this mystery, although it is real flesh, can be called bread the Apostle proves, when he says, "Let a man examine himself, and so let him eat of that bread and drink of the cup"; for it is the flesh of Christ and real flesh, and yet it is rightly called the living Bread which came down from heaven, flesh indeed by grace but bread by effect, because, as this earthly bread supplies temporal life, so that heavenly Bread affords eternal and heavenly life, because it is life eternal.[24]

Paschasius is aware of the absurdity of his view and of the fact that it requires the faithful to discount entirely the evidence of their senses. Yet for him, this is actually a positive argument in its favor:

> God is truth; and if God is truth, whatever Christ promised in this mystery, that certainly is true; and therefore it is the real flesh and blood of Christ, which he who eats and drinks worthily has eternal life abiding in him; but to bodily sight and taste they are not changed for this reason that faith may be exercised to righteousness, and that because of the merit of faith the reward of righteousness may ensue.

---

[22]On Amalarius and stercorianism, cf. Rainer Warning, *The Ambivalences of Medieval Religious Drama* (Stanford: Stanford University Press, 2001), 35. ". . . Amalarius belongs to the so-called realistic-metabolic trend in pre-Scholastic eucharistic doctrine, from which the doctrine of transubstantiation emerged, and his contemporaries even already accused him of stercorianism."

[23]This is the most widespread understanding of Paschasius' eucharistic doctrine. But see now Timothy R. LeCroy, "The Role of Corpus in the Eucharistic Theology of Paschasius Radbertus" (Ph.D. diss., Saint Louis University, 2012).

[24]Paschasius Radbertus, *De corpore et sanguine Domini* xv–xvi, cited in Darwall Stone, *A History of the Doctrine of the Holy Eucharist*, vol. I. (London: Longmans, 1909), 219–220.

It is, then, a good thing that the evidence of our senses is opposed to the reality of Christ's body and blood present in the elements: we therefore have a chance to exercise faith in God's promise and show that we believe the words of Scripture rather than our own senses:

> Learn, O man, that you taste something else than that which is perceived by the fleshly mouth, that you behold something else than that which is shown to the eyes of the flesh.[25]

But how does Paschasius understand the words of Scripture? According to a remarkable hermeneutic:

> When he brake and gave to them the bread, he did not say, This is, or there is in this mystery, a kind of virtue or figure of my body, but he said plainly, "This is my body." And therefore it is what he said, and not what any one pretends . . . Wherefore I marvel that there are some now who want to say that in the Sacrament there is not in fact the reality of the flesh and blood of Christ, but a kind of virtue of the flesh and not the flesh itself, a virtue of the blood and not the blood itself, a figure not a reality, a shadow not a body.[26]

Yet Paschasius' reading of Jesus' words over the bread is manifestly not the natural one. If it were, the apostle Paul could never have asked, "The bread which we break, is it not a participation of the body of Christ?" (1 Cor 10:28) If Paul had thought that the Supper had been instituted as a sort of test of whether Christians could believe in an invisible and unobservable miracle against the evidence of their senses, he would never have asked, "Is it not . . . ?" On Paschasius' reading, such a rhetorical question could have quite plausibly been answered, "No, it isn't." No other miracle ever worked this way, for an unobservable miracle is not a miracle at all in the biblical sense of the word ("signs," "wonders," "mighty works"). A miracle that cannot be observed is itself in need of attestation. Accordingly, medieval legends claimed that the unobservable miracle of transubstantiation was in turn authenticated by observable miracles.[27] It was said that persons did not age while in the presence of the consecrated host; miraculous cessations of bleeding and various healing miracles were also claimed; the transubstantiated host was alleged to bleed with real blood. From Buenos Aires in 1996 (under the episcopacy of then-cardinal Bergoglio, now Pope Francis), there were reports of a eu-

---

[25]Paschasius Radbertus, *De Corpore et Sanguine Domini*, viii.1–2, cited in D. Stone, *A History of the Doctrine of the Holy Eucharist*, vol. I. (Longmans: London, 1909), 219–220.
[26]Paschasius Radbertus, *Ep. ad Frudegardum* in Migne, ed. *Patrologia Latina* vol. CXX, 1357.
[27]Cf. Peter Browe, *Die Eucharistischen Wunder des Mittelalters* (Breslau: Müller and Seiffert, 1938) and Gary Macy, "Medieval Theology of the Eucharist and the Chapel of the Miracle Corporal," *Vivens homo* 18 (2007), 59–77. As Macy notes, by 1230 AD, stories of such miracles abruptly ceased to be used as proofs in theological arguments.

charistic host that had been dropped on the floor during a Mass, stored away in holy water, and several weeks later was discovered to have flowered into "flesh"—which credulous scientists authenticated as heart tissue, but which skeptics would say was a reddish mold.[28]

Paschasius' new and stronger conception of real presence was actually opposed as an innovation by three of his contemporaries: Rabanus Maurus (780–856), Ratramnus (d. 870), and Walafrid Strabo (808–849). Walafrid's words on the eucharist are in marked contrast to Paschasius:

> In the Last Supper, which he held with his disciples before his betrayal, after the rites of the ancient Passover, Christ gave to the same disciples the Sacraments of his body and blood in the substance of bread and wine, and taught them to celebrate these for the commemoration of his most sacred passion. . . . We must so understand that the same mysteries of our redemption are really the body and blood of the Lord that we ought to believe them to be pledges of that complete unity which we now have with our Head by hope and shall have hereafter in fact. . . . He who eats and drinks the body and blood of the Lord worthily shows that he is in God and that God is in him.[29]

Walafrid represents a position which, though still operating without a Passover-based diachronic view of the eucharist's operation, nonetheless approaches closer to the view we are arguing for: participation and union with Christ as the controlling principle of the sacrament. He has nothing to do with Paschasius' idea of the local real presence of Christ's historical body and blood ("the same which was born of the virgin Mary"); he accordingly feels no need to delve into questions of what happens to the elements after consumption. His focus is rather on the celebration of the ritual, which is to say, on the congregation, their actions, and their relation to the Lord. It is especially remarkable that he explains the identification of the elements with the body and blood in an eschatological manner: "pledges of that complete unity which we now have . . . by hope and shall have hereafter in fact." As we have seen, this is a very Pauline interpretation.

Rabanus Maurus seems to have had Paschasius especially in mind when he wrote:

> Certain people lately, having wrong ideas about the Sacrament of the body and blood of the Lord, have said that this [sc. the eucharistic elements] is the body itself and blood of the Lord which was born of the Virgin Mary, and in which the Lord himself suffered on the cross and rose from the tomb, in reply to which

---

[28]Mieczysław Pietrowski, "Eucharistic Miracle in Buenos Aires," *Love One Another* 17, 2010, http://www.loamagazine.org/nr/the_main_topic/eucharistic_miracle_in_buenos.html.

[29]Walafrid Strabo, *De ecclesiasticarum rerum exordiis et incrementis*, 16, in Migne, ed. *Patrologia Latina* cxiv. 936.

error, writing as fully as we could to Egilus the abbot, we have explained what is rightly to be believed about the body itself.[30]

Rabanus Maurus' statement is noteworthy for its explicit denial of the presence of the historical body of Christ, "the body itself and blood of the Lord which was born of the Virgin Mary." This locution seems to have been Paschasius' own preferred way of stipulating which "body" he meant, and is one reason why most scholars have seen Paschasius as the target of Rabanus' (unfortunately lost) refutation.[31] It appears that part of his objection to Paschasius' doctrine was grounded in the idea that if the "body born of the Virgin Mary" were digested, it would be subjected to the chemical changes involved in digestion, and would end up as excrement. "Stercorism" is the label now applied to this idea. Like concern about mice eating hosts, stercorism is a problem that does not arise without a doctrine of "real presence."

The fourth of our ninth-century monks, Ratramnus, is most famous for having advocated a symbolic understanding of the eucharist which influenced Berengar of Tours in the eleventh century and Thomas Cranmer in the sixteenth. Without delving into the particulars of Ratramnus' views,[32] I simply note him as further evidence that Paschasius' strong views of "real presence" and transubstantiation did not represent settled orthodoxy in the ninth century, still less a "plain meaning" of the words of institution. He pushes back against the immoderate realism of Paschasius, but is no less a prisoner of the limited sources available in his day.

DULY USE THEM

Thomas Cranmer's protest against accumulated medieval abuses of the Holy Communion strikes the correct note:

> The Sacraments were not ordained of Christ to be gazed upon, or to be carried about, but that we should duly use them . . . The Sacrament of the Lord's Supper was not by Christ's ordinance reserved, carried about, lifted up, or worshiped.[33]

---

[30]Rabanus Maurus, *Poenitentiale*, 33. *Patrologia Latina* ex. 492, 493. Cited in Darwall Stone, *A History of the Doctrine of the Holy Eucharist* (London: Longmans, Green, and Co. 1909), vol. 1, 223.

[31]cf. Hans Boersma and Matthew Levering, ed. *The Oxford Handbook of Sacramental Theology* (Oxford: 2015), 191, tracing Rabanus Maurus' objections to stercorism, and James O'Connor, *The Hidden Manna: A Theology of the Eucharist* (San Francisco, CA: Ignatius Press, 2005), 90, on Rabanus Maurus' objections to Paschasius' attempt to father his doctrine on Ambrose of Milan.

[32]See the discussion and extensive quotations in D. Stone, vol. 1, 226–233, and the original texts in Migne, ed. *Patrologia Latina* vol. CXXI.

[33]The text of the 39 Articles can be found in most editions of the Book of Common Prayer, e.g. *The Book of Common Prayer 1662* (Oxford: Oxford University Press, 1989).

The 39 Articles lay stress upon proper use of the eucharist and obedience to Christ's ordinance because Cranmer believed that the eucharist was instituted by Jesus and worked according to that institution. In this, the eucharist is unlike, for example, the Eleusinian Mysteries, in which new initiates were invited to gaze upon sacred objects called δεικνύμενα, "displayed objects" or "things pointed-to."[34] The eucharist is a meal, not an object for display. Thus, the only way in which the eucharist can actually function and be of benefit for the participants is if they *use* the elements as Christ intended:[35] "take . . . eat . . . drink . . . do this." These are the verbs of a ritual meal, not of worship or obeisance before a presence.

Although Cranmer wrote in an age when Protestant eucharistic practice was defined in contrast to Roman Catholic practices such as Corpus Christi processions and adoration of the sacrament, modern Catholicism reflects an appreciation for the point Cranmer made. Louis-Marie Chauvet, a modern Roman Catholic theologian, urges that the eucharist is a ritual meal to be rightly used:

> Sacramental theology is the theory of a practice. Its object is the church's celebration itself. It has nothing relevant to say that does not stem from the way the church confers the sacraments. If one had always obeyed this golden rule many deviations would have been avoided. One example of these deviations pertains to the eucharistic presence of the Lord, which has been understood in isolation independently of its purpose as nourishment for its partakers, demonstrated by the gestures, the words, and even the material elements used in the narrative of the institution.[36]

It is encouraging that Chauvet's understanding of the purposes of the eucharist is shaped by consideration of the Last Supper ("the narrative of the institution"), and of the fact that the eucharist is a practice, not an object. Chauvet even quotes Gamaliel's dictum about "regarding oneself" as though he had

---

[34] cf. Luc Brisson, *How Philosophers Saved Myths: Allegorical Interpretation and Classical Mythology*, trans. Catherine Tihanyi (Chicago, IL: University of Chicago Press, 2004), 60. "The most important priest of the Eleusinian mysteries was the Hierophant, 'the one who shows the sacred objects.'"

[35] It is ironic, in this connection, to find some of my fellow Anglican ministers defending the practices of elevation, reservation, and adoration of the eucharist by taking the words of the Articles *au pied de la lettre* and missing their clear sense: "Yes, it is true that Christ did not command us to do these things with the elements of the Holy Communion, but the Articles mean no more than that. No prohibition of these actions is expressed, only a historical concession that these actions were not commanded." The historical context of the Articles and the fierce strife over eucharistic piety in sixteenth-century Europe makes such a construal impossible. Cf. Christopher Elwood, *The Body Broken: The Calvinist Doctrine of the Eucharist and the Symbolization of Power in Sixteenth-Century France* (Oxford: Oxford University Press, 1999). On this interpretation of the Articles, Purgatory is also perfectly permissible for Anglicans to believe, though it is "a fond thing, vainly invented."

[36] Louis-Marie Chauvet, *The Sacraments: The Word of God at the Mercy of the Body* (Collegeville: Liturgical Press, 2001), 48.

"personally passed out of Egypt."[37] It would be fair to consider Chauvet as an example of Roman sacramentology tempered by historical research into the Jewish background of the NT.

Medieval debates about "body" and "substance"; discussion of invisible "miracles" that pit the senses against invisible grace; concern about spilling the wine; fears of mice eating the host; worries about passing the body of Christ into the latrine—these epicycles and puzzles are symptomatic of a system orbiting the wrong center. But Daube's thesis about the Last Supper and eucharist fits perfectly with the extant texts and the historical context, relies upon ideas that were available in the first century, yields a clearly intended meaning that is deeply rooted in Israel's scriptures, and eliminates many interpretive difficulties. In the next two chapters, we will follow the hermeneutical spiral back to the text to test our ideas. We have attempted to reshape our ideas about the eucharist in light of history. Will this revised understanding of the eucharist ring true in the gospel of John and Paul's first epistle to the Corinthians?

---

[37]Chauvet, *The Sacraments*, 55.

Chapter Six

Rereading John 6

We have seen that consideration of Jesus' words at the Last Supper in their historical context leads us to see them as messianic self-identification and a declaration of Jesus' intended and impending sacrificial death. Does this thesis comport also with Jesus' discourse in John 6?

FAILURE TO RECOGNIZE THE BREAD FROM HEAVEN

Not without reason has modern research on the historical Jesus focused on the synoptic Gospels as the primary evidence for his teachings and life. The Fourth Gospel is comparatively late, appears to be theologically rather than diachronically organized, and bears few of the Aramaisms that characterize the synoptics.[1] Maurice Casey holds that John's Gospel is a falsification of the historical Jesus;[2] Richard Bauckham, by contrast, argues that it alone of the four Gospels was actually written by an eyewitness.[3] The identity of the author is also controverted, with candidates ranging from John the son of Zebedee to John the Elder, to Lazarus(!). To resolve the controversies that surround John's Gospel would take us beyond our present scope. Without

---

[1] But see now the impressive correspondences between the fourth Gospel and Aramaic traditions concerning the Exodus detailed in Craig Evans, "Feeding the Five Thousand and the Eucharist," *John, Jesus, and History volume 2: Aspects of Historicity in the Fourth Gospel*, ed. Paul N. Anderson, Felix Just, and Tom Thatcher (Atlanta, GA: Society of Biblical Literature, 2009), 131–138. "We may wonder if the association of the feeding of the five thousand with Moses typology originated with Jesus himself, on analogy with the Moses/Joshua typology that probably underlay the public actions and teachings of men such as John the Baptist, Theudas, and the Jew from Egypt."
[2] Maurice Casey, *Is John's Gospel True?* (London: Routledge, 1996).
[3] Bauckham, *Jesus and the Eyewitnesses*, ch. 14.

committing myself to any particular view of the historicity of John's Gospel, I propose to examine John 6 and see how it fits with what I have argued so far concerning the Last Supper and eucharist.

The discourse of John 6 is prompted by a question which Jesus asks to his disciples. Specifically, Jesus asks Philip, in John 6:5,

> πόθεν ἀγοράσωμεν ἄρτους ἵνα φάγωσιν οὗτοι;
> Where shall we buy loaves, that these may eat?

The question is highlighted in the memory of the witness (John's memory or the memory of his source) because it sets up the problem that Jesus will go on to solve by his teaching. On the surface, this is a straightforward question about providing food for a large number of people. But really it is a bit of *eironeia* worthy of Socrates: Jesus knows full well that when answered, the question will turn out to be loaded with messianic significance.

This significance is immediately understood by the multitude. What conclusion do they draw? Surprisingly enough, not a practical one about how to feed people bread. Rather, they draw a conclusion about Jesus' identity and his role in the story of Israel; and thus also a conclusion about where or at what point in the narrative of Israel's eschatology they therefore find themselves:

> οἱ οὖν ἄνθρωποι ἰδόντες ὃ ἐποίησεν σημεῖον ἔλεγον ὅτι οὗτός ἐστιν ἀληθῶς ὁ προφήτης ὁ ἐρχόμενος εἰς τὸν κόσμον.
> So the people, seeing the sign which he had done, started saying, "This is truly the prophet, the one Coming into the world."

I capitalize "Coming" to indicate that this was a word denoting a figure from Jewish eschatological expectations—expectations that are equally at work in the Passover and the Lord's Prayer's petition concerning "the coming bread." Jesus has deftly moved his disciples from the practical question of how to feed a crowd to the idea of the dawn of the Messianic Age. Jesus is also aware that the crowd has drawn a second conclusion:

> ... Ἰησοῦς οὖν γνοὺς ὅτι μέλλουσιν ἔρχεσθαι καὶ ἁρπάζειν αὐτὸν ἵνα ποιήσωσιν βασιλέα ...
> ... so Jesus, knowing that they were about to come and snatch him to make him king ...

All this, simply from the sign: the eschatological Prophet like Moses has arrived to bring about the new Exodus accompanied by miraculous food, and the time has arrived, the crowd thinks, to restore the kingdom to Israel (cf. Acts 1:6). Thus, the narrative revolves around the central question: Is Jesus the eschatological king? And the crowd appears to believe that he is. And yet, when Jesus finds them again on the other side of the sea (6.25), he accuses them of not understanding, and of treating the miraculous feeding in a crassly greedy manner:

> ζητεῖτε με οὐχ ὅτι εἴδετε σημεῖα, ἀλλ' ὅτι ἐφάγετε ἐκ τῶν ἄρτων καὶ ἐχορτάσθητε . . .
> You seek me not because you see the signs, but because you ate of the loaves and were satisfied . . .

It is a commonplace among advocates of "real presence" to treat this sentence as an indictment of the Jews' failure to look beyond their senses. But that is not actually the force of Jesus' statement. Rather, he is alluding to an OT narrative of the miraculous feedings during the Exodus. Since the manna and quail were both given in response to Israel's ungrateful complaining, the OT tends to emphasize the "satisfaction" or "fullness" of the Israelites after their eating. We see this detail in Psalm 78, first with regard to the bread:

> [He] had rained down manna on them to eat
> And given them of the bread of heaven Men ate angels' food;
> He sent them food *to the full* (LXX εἰς πλησμονήν) (78.24–25)

And again, with the miraculous quail:

> So they ate and were *well filled* (LXX ἐνεπλήσθησαν σφόδρα),
> For he gave them their own desire. (78.29)

In both these passages, the "fullness" comes after God responds to the complaining of the congregation of Israel. The same sequence—complaint, provision by an indignant God, and resulting fullness—is first found in Exodus 16.8 (LXX), where Moses responds to complaints:

> When the Lord gives you *flesh to eat* (κρέα φαγεῖν) in the evening and bread early in the morning, *to fullness* (εἰς πλησμονην), for the Lord hears your complaints which you make against him. And what are we? Your complaints are not against us but against the Lord. (Ex. 16:8 LXX)

The phrase "flesh to eat" is also echoed by John's narrative in 6:52, when the crowd asks, "How can this man give us his flesh to eat (σάρκα φαγεῖν)?"[4] These echoes of Exodus 16 and Psalm 78 are the narrator's way

---

[4] The Greek uses σάρξ in John 6:52, not the κρέα of Exodus 16:8 LXX, but in context, the two words mean the same thing. (By contrast, the word σάρξ does not here mean what it means in, e.g., Rom. 8:5–13.)

of framing the conflict between Jesus and his first century Jewish hearers as a reprise of an episode familiar to the readers of the Gospel: to wit, the miraculous manna and quail constitute *the* Jewish paradigm of ingratitude committed even while God is bringing about the hoped-for salvation. That is the overtone that would have been immediately obvious to any Jewish audience hearing the story.

Sadly, the result of these two miraculous feedings is not faith and loyalty:

> In spite of this they still sinned
> And did not believe in his wondrous works.
> (LXX: οὐκ ἐπίστευσαν ἐν τοῖς θαυμασίοις αὐτοῦ).
> (Ps. 77.32 LXX, 78.32 MT)

By alluding to Psalm 78 in his present situation, Jesus is making a pointed response to his audience. They are asking, "What sign will you perform then, that we may see it and believe you? What work will you do?" (6.30). Despite their earlier eagerness to "sieze him and make him king," they are now not ready to believe that Jesus is the Messiah without a sign. This is an outrageous request, given that Jesus has already fed them with five loaves. They want something like the manna, but first, they have already received a miraculous feeding, and second, Jesus asserts that they are blind to the typological nature of the manna:

> Moses did not give you the bread from heaven, but my Father gives/is giving (δίδωσιν—present tense!) you the true bread from heaven.

Their fault lies in not understanding who Jesus is and why he has come—not in a failure to recognize anything about the elements of the not-yet-instituted eucharist. They do not see what is before them: that the longed-for salvation has come in the person of Jesus. The central question concerns the identity of Jesus and his superiority to the types of the Old Covenant. (This in itself may mark John's Gospel as late, and Casey would no doubt protest that such a question has no *Sitz im Leben* within the ministry of Jesus, but only within the controversy between the nascent Church and the synagogue in the late first century.) It is the same question that the Jewish redactors of the Passover seder also stumbled over by expunging the figure of Moses and by prohibiting the christological exegesis of the rituals of the meal. "We do not conclude (sc. typologically interpret) the Pascha with *afiqoman*"—that is, we must not interpret the Passover's elements by identifying lamb with the matzah bread, thereby linking the original lamb with the Messiah, and claiming, as Christians did, that the new Exodus had happened through the Messiah's death.

We recall that after the episode with the Samaritan woman at the well, when Jesus' disciples brought him food, he replied by defining his food "of which you do not know":

My food is to do the will of him who sent me, and to finish his work. (Jn. 4:32)

This understanding of metaphorical bread is taken up again in John 6, and in light of John 4, we may be entitled to link 6.33 and 6.38:

For the bread of God is he who comes down from heaven (καταβαίνων ἐκ τοῦ οὐρανοῦ) and gives life to the world. (6.33)
For I have come down from heaven (καταβέβηκα ἐκ τοῦ οὐρανοῦ), not to do my own will, but the will of him who sent me. (6.38)

With Richard Bauckham, I recognize that John 6:53–56 speaks of Jesus' body in eucharistic terms,[5] but there is nothing here about transmogrified bread; not even anything about "setting bread apart for holy use." That is simply not what John 6 is about. It is about the need for Israel to recognize Jesus as the Messiah, understand what time it is in Israel's history, and stop responding to the generosity of God with unbelief and rebellion. Jesus applies to himself the language of "bread" and "food" in order to confront Israel with its failure to receive him as their Messiah and to indict them for their ingratitude.

In this connection, Robert Eisler suggested that a pun was at work in Jesus' statements in John 6. When Jesus' statement that "the bread which I shall give is my flesh . . ." (6:50) is back-translated into Aramaic, the word "flesh" would have been *biśrā,* בִּשְׂרָא = σάρξ, "meat"; this suggestion has found acceptance by some scholars.[6] Eisler suggests that this is a deliberate pun on the homophone בִּשְׂרָא, *biśrā'* "glad tidings," "good news," εὐαγγέλιον.[7] The suggestion must be considered with caution, since, as with all retroversions into Aramaic, there is considerable uncertainty; and the author of the fourth Gospel did not preserve the pun in Greek. The scholarly use of Aramaic retroversion has advanced considerably since Eisler's day, and the proposal of unverifiable one-word puns

---

[5] "[T]he eucharist can be relevant to a reading of the text [sc. John 6:53–56 and its immediate context] only insofar as the eucharist is understood precisely as an expression of faith in the crucified Jesus and as a symbol of participation in his life. Then the text can function to teach participants in the eucharist what the sacrament is actually about. At the same time, it is vital to recognize that while the eucharist is the communal rite that focuses what this text is about in the life of the church, the meaning of the text exceeds the eucharist. The primary meaning is both more basic and more extensive than the sacramental overtone." Richard Bauckham, *Gospel of Glory: Major Themes in Johannine Theology* (Grand Rapids, MI: Baker Academic, 2015), ch. 5.

[6] E.g., Jacob Neusner, Bruce Chilton, and William Albert, *Three Faiths, One God: The Formative Faith and Practice of Judaism, Christianity, and Islam* (Leiden: E.J. Brill, 2002), 133.

[7] Eisler, "Das letzte Abendmahl," 187.

is frowned upon by modern scholars.[8] Nonetheless, it is a provocative suggestion which fits well with other known instances of Aramaic paronomasia in the sayings of Jesus (e.g. *gamlā'* "camel" and *qalmā* "gnat" in Mt. 23:24; Πέτρος and πέτρα, Mt. 16:18; cf. other instances suggested by Duncan Derrett[9]). Eisler finds confirmation of the pun in the words of John 6.52: ὁ ἄρτος (*laḥma* = food) ὅν ἐγὼ δώσω, ἡ σάρξ (*biśrā* = σάρξ or εὐαγγέλιον) μου ἐστίν, "the food which I give to you, is my gospel," followed by 6.63: "it is the spirit that makes alive; the (ἡ σάρξ = *biśrā*) avails nothing. The words (τὰ ῥήματα) which I have spoken (i.e. my *biśrā*) to you are spirit and life."[10] If Eisler is correct about Jesus' use of paronomasia in these verses, this suggests that Jesus is faulting his audience for misunderstanding, not the transformation of bread in the not-yet-instituted eucharist, but what his place in the story of Israel is.

MISUNDERSTANDING AS A TOPOS IN JOHN'S GOSPEL

This interpretation gains further corroboration from a pattern in John's Gospel: there are many instances of Jesus' interlocutors misunderstanding him.[11] As Bauckham notes, the fourth Gospel's "frequently riddling character is not meant, as some scholars think, to enable informed readers to feel superior to characters in the Gospel who do not understand the riddles, but rather to tease the intelligence and to entice its readers into its world of multidimensional meaning."[12] A fair amount of scholarly writing has now been produced on misunderstandings in the fourth Gospel.[13] This is not the place to treat of all of them; for our purpose, it is sufficient to examine the sayings of Jesus

---

[8] Casey speaks of "the elevation of supposed puns to the level of a major tool when they could not be properly verified." Casey, *Aramaic Sources*, 253.

[9] E.g. Duncan Derrett, "John 9:6 Read with Isaiah 6:10; 29:9," *Studies in the New Testament* vol. 6 (Leiden: E.J. Brill, 1995), 2–5. The same volume contains other suggestions of puns by Jesus.

[10] Eisler, "Das letzte Abendmahl," 188.

[11] "The writer of John's Gospel is constantly putting two things together. He deploys the power of metaphor, symbol, and allegory, which illumine something by referring to it as something else. He creates correspondences between different parts of his narrative. He tells stories such that they have more meanings than the literal one. He is a master of irony who constantly has his characters say more than or even the opposite of what they mean. What Jesus says in metaphor and symbol the characters misunderstand, thereby foregrounding the question of its true meaning." Richard Bauckham, *Gospel of Glory*, ch. 7.

[12] Bauckham, *Gospel of Glory*, ch. 7.

[13] Chief among these are D.A. Carson, "Understanding Misunderstandings in the Fourth Gospel," *Tyndall Bulletin* 33 (1982), 59–91, and Oscar Cullman, "Der johanneische Gebrauch doppeldeutigen Ausdrücke als Schlüssel zum Verständnis des vierten Evangeliums," *TZ* 4 (1948), 360–372; repr. in *Vorträge und Aufsätze 1925–1962* (Tübingen: Mohn/Zürich: Zwingli, 1966), 176–186. See also C.H. Dodd, *Historical Tradition in the Fourth Gospel* (Cambridge: Cambridge University Press, 1963), 318 and Rudolf Bultmann, *The Gospel of John: A Commentary*, trans. G. R. Beasley-Murray, ed. R.W.N. Hoare and J.K. Riches (Oxford: Blackwell, 1971), 127f.

to which an interlocutor responds, in direct speech, with an overly literal or overly physical misunderstanding.

In 2:19–22, Jesus tells his audience: "Destroy this temple, and in three days I will raise it up." The Jews reply, "It has taken forty-six years to build this temple, and will you raise it up in three days?" Jesus' interlocutors misunderstand him as referring to the literal Temple. In 3:3–4, Jesus tells Nicodemus, "unless one is born again, he cannot see the kingdom of God." Nicodemus replies, "How can a man be born when he is old? Can he enter a second time into his mother's womb and be born?" In 4:10–11, Jesus tells the Samaritan woman, "If you knew the gift of God, and who it is who says to you, 'Give me a drink,' you would have asked him, and he would have given you living water." She replies, "Sir, you have nothing to draw with, and the well is deep. Where then do you get that living water?" In 4:31–34, Jesus tells his disciples, "I have food to eat of which you do not know." The disciples respond with the question, "Has anyone brought him anything to eat?" In John 6:41–42, Jesus declares that he is the "bread which came down from heaven." The Jews react to this by asking, nonplussed, "Is this not Jesus, the son of Joseph, whose father and mother we know? How is it then that he says, 'I have come down from heaven'?" (Note that his audience does not have difficulty with Jesus' claim to be "bread," but with the claim to have come down from heaven.) In John 7:33–35, Jesus promises that "I shall be with you a little while longer, and then I go to him who sent me. You will seek me and not find me, and where I am you cannot come." The Jews: "Where does he intend to go that we shall not find him? Does he intend to go to the Dispersion among the Greeks and teach the Greeks?" In John 8:21–22, Jesus declares that "I am going away, and you will seek me, and will die in your sin. Where I go you cannot come." The Jews respond: "Will he kill himself, because he says, 'Where I go you cannot come'?" In John 8:31–33, Jesus promises, "If you abide in my word, you are my disciples indeed. And you shall know the truth, and the truth shall make you free." The Jews respond: "We are Abraham's descendants, and have never been in bondage to anyone. How can you say, 'You will be made free'?" In John 11:11–12, Jesus explains that "Our friend Lazarus sleeps, but I go that I may wake him up." The disciples, mistaking the euphemistic reference to Lazarus' death for a claim that he is experiencing much-needed rest, reply: "Lord, if he sleeps he will get well."

Our concern is with Jesus' reference to his flesh as "bread" and his interlocutors' misunderstanding of him as meaning that he would "give them his flesh to eat," an assumption of cannibalism. The question is whether this passage's form and logic can be used to underwrite a "real presence" view of the eucharist. At first glance, it might seem so. Jesus does affirm that that "I am the bread" and "my flesh is food indeed" and "unless you eat the flesh of the Son of Man and drink his blood, you have no life in you"—a statement that the Jews misunderstand as a sort of cannibalism. Surely, we ought to take these words as an assertion of the real presence of Christ in the eucharistic elements? In reply, we should ask whether any of the other explicit misunderstandings in the fourth Gospel can be rightly interpreted in this way. When we examine them, we find that in every case the misunderstood words—living water, born again, food to eat, freedom, waking Lazarus up—have primary reference, not to rituals or sacraments, but to the historical events that underwrite those sacraments: the rebirth of Israel ("born again"); Jesus' obedience and suffering for the salvation of Israel ("my food is to do the will of my Father in heaven"); his ascension into heaven ("I am going away"); and the consequent resurrection of his people also ("I will wake up Lazarus"). In every instance, the misunderstanding of Jesus' interlocutors is conveyed in terms expressive of the most simple-minded literalism; indeed, that is the rhetorical signal by which the evangelist gives us to know that they are mistaken. In most of these passages, "the point at which Jesus apparently ceases to hope for comprehension from his auditors is the point at which he begins to speak of his death-and-exaltation."[14]

As Bauckham reminds us, "the primary meaning must be one that makes sense within the narrative context." And within that context, it is beyond impossible for Jesus to hope that his hearers might understand a sacrament that he had not yet instituted. Are there "sacramental overtones"? No doubt. John wrote his Gospel after the institution of the eucharist. But within the narrative, insofar as Jesus' words purport to communicate his intended meaning to his hearers (in however riddling a manner), that meaning must be sought in the events of his death-and-exaltation on behalf of Israel as Israel's Messiah. If Israel is in a proper relation to her Messiah, then she ought to share in all these events—and thereby be "born again," flow with "living waters," and "eat Jesus' flesh." The failure to understand is in every instance concerned with the identification of Jesus as the Messiah and the proper description of his Messianic vocation to die for Israel. The eucharistic overtone is secondary.

This means that the *Sitz im Leben* of John 6 is not the early church, but Jesus' ministry. The question in view is not sacraments, but whether Jesus is the Messiah. There are overtones of the manna stories, but the text does not address the mechanics of the eucharist. For that, we must turn to Paul's first epistle to the Corinthians.

---

[14] Bauckham, *Gospel of Glory*, ch. 7.

Chapter Seven

The Festal Meal in Corinth

So far, I have argued for a particular conception of how the eucharist works: it is a ritual meal by which the people of God participate in a salvific event of the past and anticipate salvific events in the eschatological future, all by virtue of sharing in the Messiah to whom those events have happened. More specifically, I have argued that this is how first-century Jews understood the workings of the Passover; that Jesus developed the eucharist out of the Passover, so that we ought to assume its workings to be the same. I have argued, following David Daube, that the choice of bread and wine as the elements of the ritual was intended by Jesus primarily as a means of self-identification as Israel's Messiah and a disclosure of his purpose to accomplish a new Exodus event by his impending death. I have argued all these things in two main ways: first, from extra-biblical evidence (rabbinic sources, Melito of Sardis, etc.) and second, by appeal to passages within the Bible, showing that they fit with this conception of the eucharist: that they speak of the Messiah as incorporating his people; that the New Testament is concerned with Jesus' self-disclosure and identity; and that the eschatological focus of the eucharist is of a piece with the New Testament's presentation of salvation generally.

We now turn to what I hope will be the coup de grace: the evidence of the apostle Paul's first letter to the church of Corinth. This epistle, especially in chapters 10 and 11, is the fullest discussion of the eucharist within the pages of the New Testament. And because of this, it is the foundation upon which most Christian sacramentology has historically been built. But I have not built this way: my argument up to this point has been constructed from other materials. I will now lift up my hypothesis, as with a crane, and lower it onto the foundation of 1 Corinthians. If the edifice I have built fits snugly onto this foundation, the fit will be a strong confirmation of my argument.

WHAT SACRAMENTOLOGY DOES PAUL PRESUPPOSE?

Although 1 Corinthians contains important evidence of NT sacramentology, this evidence is mostly indirect. The only reason we are able to read the Apostle Paul's instructions concerning the Lord's Supper is that the church of Corinth was abusing it. Indeed, the Corinthians were behaving in ways that perhaps no church since has ever behaved. I have seen much that I disagree with in the eucharistic practice of many churches, but never a display of open contempt for the poor, with gluttony and drunkenness. Paul's words are occasional, elicited by the abuses of the Corinthian church and aimed at correcting those abuses. He has not written for us a systematic or exhaustive explanation of the eucharist. Rather, his responses to the Corinthians' problems reveal his apostolic presuppositions; he corrects their behavior in terms of his core assumptions about the Lord's Supper: what sort of meal it is; how it works; and what its antecedents are.

As we approach 1 Corinthians, it will be helpful to review Pauline soteriology. Sharing in Jesus' death and resurrection is what Paul means by "salvation." His apostolic strivings, self-discipline, and sufferings are all aimed at the attainment of that resurrection. Further, Paul understands his sufferings as a "filling up what is lacking in the sufferings of Christ" (Col. 1:24), "sharing in his sufferings" and "being conformed to his death" (Phil. 3:10). For Paul, the death of Jesus was the event in which our old nature, sin, and the Torah with its condemning sentence against us were all put to death, and the resurrection of Jesus was the inauguration of a new life on the other side of all that (Rom. 6).

For Paul, salvation is a sharing both in these events that took place just after Passover in 33 CE, and also eventually in the future resurrection or the age to come, *ha'olam haba'*. Note that even this future hope is a hope of sharing in something that already happened to Jesus: he was the firstfruits, so that he experienced the resurrection first, and received a glorified body that our bodies will one day resemble (1 Cor. 15). Throughout all his letters, Paul teaches an event-centered view of salvation: "if Christ is not raised, then we are still in our sins" (1 Cor. 15). The entire transition out from under the curse of the Torah, through the death of the flesh, and into grace and the hope of the resurrection is *effected by what happened in and through Jesus*. For Paul, the honorific title of "Messiah" ("Christ") is an incorporative concept: it is *in Christ* that God's people are saved.[1]

---

[1] This has somehow managed to be controversial within Pauline studies. For the best defense of Paul's incorporative concept of the Messiah, see N.T. Wright, *Paul and the Faithfulness of God*, ch. 10.

For if we have been united together in the likeness of his death, certainly we also shall be in the likeness of his resurrection, knowing this, that our old man was crucified with him, that the body of sin might be done away with, that we should no longer be slaves of sin. (Rom. 6:5–6)

To be sure, there are various aspects to this: forensic justification, mystical union, the indwelling of the Holy Spirit. For our present purposes, it is enough that all these other aspects of salvation in the fullest sense are dependent for their efficacy on whether Christians share in Christ and the *events* that he experienced in 33 CE. In Ephesians 3, Paul speaks of the salvation of the church as consisting in the "κοινωνία of the mystery"—the sharing in the long-awaited redemptive events that have now been revealed, whereby God accomplishes his "eternal purpose" and makes a public display to the defeated "principalities and powers." For Paul, the goal of preaching the gospel is that "you may be blameless in the day of our Lord Jesus Christ," and Paul is confident that this will come true because "God is faithful, by whom you were called into the sharing (κοινωνία) in his Son, Jesus Christ our Lord." (1 Cor. 1:8–9) Thus, in the life of each individual disciple the eschatological vindication ("blameless in the day of our Lord Jesus Christ") is something that hinges on that disciple's *sharing in* Jesus and the events by which he already inaugurated that salvation.

Since Paul talks this way so frequently and pervasively, it should come as no surprise that he theorizes the eucharist also in terms of participation in Christ and all that he went through:

I speak as to wise men; judge for yourselves what I say. The cup of blessing which we bless, is it not the communion (κοινωνία) of the blood of Christ? The bread which we break, is it not the communion (κοινωνία) of the body of Christ? (1 Cor. 10:15–16)

The word κοινωνία is also used in Philippians 3 for "sharing in" the sufferings of Christ; the same word is used in Ephesians 3 and 1 Corinthians 1:8–9. Eating the ritual meal is a way of sharing in the corporate body of the Messiah and thereby also in the death and resurrection which that body already underwent.

To summarize our argument so far: We have shown that Jesus used the bread to identify himself as the Messiah expected by Israel; that he used the wine to tell his disciples that he would shortly die as a new Passover sacrifice effecting a new exodus; that the concept of the Messiah in the New Testament was an *incorporative* one by which the Messiah included his people in himself; and now, that the apostle Paul speaks of the eucharist according to this same incorporative idea, so that the ritual meal is a means of sharing in the Messiah and the events of his new exodus that he accomplished by his death and resurrection.

This way of thinking about the eucharist was laid down already in the language of Passover. Paul uses this language quite explicitly, not only to remind his readers of the pattern of that earlier salvific event and subsequent ritual meal, but also to characterize both Christ and the eucharist as Paschal: "Christ our Passover lamb is sacrificed for us; therefore let us keep the feast . . ." (1 Cor. 5:7–8) We could scarcely conceive of any more thoroughly Jewish way of thinking about the eucharist.

STEWARDS OF THE MYSTERIES?

One passage frequently cited as evidence for a clerical monopoly of the eucharist is 1 Corinthians 4:1, where Paul speaks of Christian leaders ("Paul, or Apollos, or Cephas," 3:22) as "stewards of the mysteries of God" (οἰκονόμους μυστηρίων θεοῦ). The passage is made more difficult by the common use of the term "mysteries" in Eastern Orthodoxy to denote what the Western church has generally referred to as "sacraments,"[2] supported by the usage of the church fathers as early as Ignatius of Antioch (d. 108). Nonetheless, it is a mistaken usage, perhaps influenced by the use of the Greek word μυστήριον to denote religious rituals, such as the rites of Demeter at Eleusis or the initiation of worshippers of the "great gods" of Samothrace, or the

---

[2]This usage is as early as the apostolic fathers (Ignatius and Irenaeus), and quite prevalent in Chrysostom, for example, "those who share in the mysteries unworthily" (τῶν ἀναξίως κοινωνούντων τοῖς μυστηρίοις) as shorthand for 1 Cor. 11:27's "eat this bread or drink the cup of the Lord unworthily" in his *In dictum Pauli: Oportet haereses esse* 2062: 074, Migne, *Patrologia Graeca* 51, 259. The usage persists to this day. Cf. Protopresbyter Michael Pomazansky, *Orthodox Dogmatic Theology* (Platina, CA: St Herman of Alaska Brotherhood Press, 1994): "Thus the activity of the Apostles was full of mystical elements (*mysterion*). Among them the central or culminating place was occupied by *sacred rites*. Therefore it is entirely natural that in the Church's life the series of special and most important moments of grace-given ministry, the series of sacred rites, gradually acquired preeminently the name of 'mysteries.' St. Ignatius the God-bearer, an immediate disciple of the Apostles, writes concerning deacons that they likewise are 'servants of the *mysteries* of Jesus Christ' (Epistle to the Trallians, par. 2). These words of St. Ignatius overturn the assertion of Protestant historians that in the ancient Church the concept of 'mysteries' or 'sacraments' was supposedly never applied to the Church's sacred rites . . . In the Mysteries, prayers are joined with blessings in one form or another, and with special acts. The words of blessing accompanied by outward sacred acts are, as it were, spiritual vessels by which the grace of the Holy Spirit is scooped up and given to the members of the Church who are sincere believers. Thus, *'a mystery (sacrament) is a sacred act which under a visible aspect communicates to the soul of a believer the invisible grace of God.'*" (Emphasis in the original.) Nonetheless, this usage is not found in the Bible itself; note Pomazansky's admission that sacred rites "gradually acquired . . . the name of 'mysteries'"—that is, they did not have that name originally.

A similar but slightly divergent definition is offered by John D. Zizioulas, *Lectures in Dogmatic Theology* (London: T & T Clark, 2008), 137, where he acknowledges the sense of the word as meaning "a fact revealed in history," but nonetheless speaks of "mysteries and sacraments" as though it were a hendiadys: "The identity of the Church has to be set out by examining the mysteries and sacraments that make the Church present within our historical experience." This idea is foreign to Paul's way of speaking: the Church as the people of God consummated in union with Christ is for Paul a historical fact, to be sure, but there is no idea of its being "made present" by rituals.

baptism of blood in Mithraism.³ The apocryphal Wisdom of Solomon uses μυστήρια to denote pagan rituals,⁴ but the word is never used in Scripture to refer to Jewish rituals. Instead, the word most frequently refers to the secret decrees or plans of God which are to be revealed as they are worked out in history (Dan. 2:28, Wis. 2:22), or to other secret plans, for example, of an army (2 Macc. 13:21) or of a king (Jdt. 2:2). And that is indeed the sense of the word in 1 Corinthians 4:1, in keeping with the other instances in the Corinthian correspondence:

> But we speak *the wisdom of God in a mystery*, even the hidden wisdom, which God ordained before the world unto our glory . . . (1 Cor. 2:7)

> And though I have the gift of prophecy and understand all *mysteries* and all knowledge; and though I have all faith, so that I could remove mountains, and have not love, I am nothing. (1 Cor. 13:2)

> For he who speaks in a tongue speaks not to men, but to God; for no man understands him, but in the Spirit he speaks *mysteries* . . . (1 Cor. 14:2)

> Behold, I show you a *mystery*: We shall not all sleep, but we shall all be changed. (1 Cor. 15:51)

These μυστήρια are matters of God's secret will, revealed only to a privileged few spiritual persons (1 Cor. 2:6–16), concerning what he would do in history. This is also how Jesus uses the word in the gospels when explaining his reason for speaking in parables: "To you [disciples] it is given to know the mysteries of the kingdom of heaven; but to them, it is not given . . ." (Mk. 4:11, Mt. 13:11, Lk. 8:10) Paul's usage of the word in the Corinthian letters is fully consistent with that in Ephesians 3:5–7 (". . . the mystery of Christ, which in other ages was not made known to the sons of men, as it has now been revealed by the Spirit to his holy apostles and prophets: that the Gentiles should be fellow heirs, of the same body, and partakers of his promise in Christ through the gospel . . ."). Indeed, in not one of the twenty-seven instances in the New Testament does the word denote baptism or the eucharist. The one instance where it is used of one of Eastern Orthodoxy's rituals is Ephesians 5:32, where it refers to marriage. John Calvin famously excoriated the Vulgate translation of Jerome for rendering μυστήριον here with the Latin

---

³Cf. LSJ sv. μυστήριον. This usage is common and prevalent throughout all ages of Greek literature, from Heraclitus 14 and Herodotus 2.52 to the Attic tragedians (Aeschylus fr. 479 and Sophocles fr. 804) to Hellenistic inscriptions (IG 5(1).1390.2, 1st c. BC) and papyri (PMag.Leid.W. 3.42, 2nd/3rd c. AD).

⁴Wis. 14:15 "For a father afflicted with untimely mourning, when he hath made an image of his child soon taken away, now honoured him as a god, which was then a dead man, and delivered to those that were under him ceremonies (μυστήρια) and sacrifices."

sacramentum,⁵ and he was correct to do so, since the context shows that Paul means that marriage corresponds to the union of Christ and the Church, which has been revealed as the climax and goal of history.

Paul speaks of the eucharist not as a prerogative or monopoly of the clergy, but as something that is done by the people of God, just as the Passover was. That is why it is important for the people of God to *eat together*. Indeed, it is so important that Paul says "it is not the Lord's supper" if the Corinthians do not wait for each other. The pericope concerning the eucharist in 1 Corinthians 11 begins with the words, " . . . when you come together in assembly . . ." (συνερχομένων ὑμῶν ἐν ἐκκλησίᾳ, 11:18) and ends with "Therefore, my brothers, when you come together to eat (συνερχόμενοι), wait for one another" (11:33). The unity of the people of God by sharing in the meal is the goal of Paul's entire argument. Nothing in the Pauline literature suggests that any deficiency in the prayers of consecration or in the ordination of the celebrant could render the eucharist "invalid." But failure of the people of God to eat together does so.

This is consistent with the way the Passover worked: God's salvation of Israel was accomplished by making a distinction between the Israelites and the Egyptians, and this distinction was marked by the Israelites' participation in a ritual meal from which non-Israelites were barred.⁶ And this distinction continued in the Passovers celebrated in the land.

Paul consistently speaks of the eucharist as a festal meal, the same sort of thing as Passover: "Christ our Passover is sacrificed for us. Therefore *let us keep the feast* (one word in Greek: ἑορτάζωμεν)" (5:7–8). The church's participation in Christ is by participation in the meal. This is something that they must *do*, and *do together*, as the people of God. The Supper must not be divided into separate and unequal meals eaten by different factions or individuals. Failure to eat the meal together makes it impossible for it to function as a distinguishing mark of God's people (and thereby as a means of salvation from the world). The protection depends upon the unity of God's people in one assembly (Gk. ἐκκλησία, Heb. עֵדָה), which is why in 11:20 Paul stresses the idea of coming together *in one place* (συνερχομένων οὖν ὑμῶν ἐπὶ τὸ αὐτό).

---

⁵"The thing which misled them was the term sacrament. But, was it right that the whole Church should be punished for the ignorance of these men? Paul called it a mystery. When the Latin interpreter might have abandoned this mode of expression as uncommon to Latin ears, or converted it into 'secret,' he preferred calling it *sacramentum*, but in no other sense than the Greek term μυστήριον was used by Paul. Let them go now and clamour against skill in languages, their ignorance of which leads them most shamefully astray in a matter easy and obvious to every one." John Calvin, *The Institutes of the Christian Religion*, trans. H. Beveridge. (London: T&T Clark, 1863), IV.19.36.

⁶Unlike many of the benefits of Israelites, participation in the Passover was not extended to resident foreigners (Ex. 12:43–48). Circumcision was an absolute necessity for male participants.

The failure to eat together is a symptom of the members' larger failure to live with each other in love and kindness. They "despise the church of God" and "shame those who have nothing." The aim of Paul's argument is to convince the Corinthians to correct their behavior and eat the meal together rather than separately. If we are to take Paul's language seriously, we must understand how the sharing of food and drink by the people of God gathered together—not the words of consecration or the faith of the individual—is in fact the very thing that "turns the trick." Plutarch reports that "The Romans have a saying of that pleasant and friendly man, Sossius Senecio, who said, when he had dined alone, that he had eaten, but not dined today, since he was always longing for the sharing (κοινωνίαν) of the meal and the delightful companionship" (*Quaest. Conv.* VII. prol. 697c).[7] The distinction is a relevant one, and it tells against any theorizing of the eucharist as something that operates by the physical act of eating. Paul's one-word exhortation ἑορτάζωμεν, "let us keep the feast" (1 Cor. 5:8), is something much closer to Sossius Senecio's desire: it is not a mere feeding, but a ritual meal. In short, the eucharist works in the same way the Passover worked because it is the same sort of thing as the Passover.

SHAME AND PRAISE

A ritual meal does its work in part *socially*, as a marker of who is in and who is out. For this reason, Paul addresses the Corinthians in terms of *shame* and *praise*, using verbs that denote these social realities:

> Do you despise (καταφρονεῖτε) the *ekklesia* of God and put to shame (καταισχύνετε) the have-nots? What shall I say to you? Shall I praise (ἐπαινέσω) you? In this matter I do not praise (ἐπαινῶ) you.

This sort of rhetoric has been addressed in the scholarship primarily as a feature of Greco-Roman society.[8] Paul uses it extensively throughout the whole letter, but especially in connection with the question of women's

---

[7]Plutarch, Quaest. conv. 7 prol. (697c). Cited in Matthias Klinghardt, "A Typology of the Communal Meal," in Hal Taussig, and Dennis Smith, *Meals in the Early Christian World* (New York: Palgrave MacMillan, 2012), 9–22 at 14.

[8]Cf. Derek M. McNamara, "The Rhetoric of Honour and Shame in 1 Corinthians 1–6" (U. of South Africa, 2008) and "Shame the Incestuous Man" in *Neotestamentica* vol. 44, No. 2 (2010), 307–326; A.H. Snyman, "1 Corinthians 1:1–18 from a rhetorical perspective," *Acta Theologica* 2009, 130–144; also Timothy K.H. Chong, *Strategies in Church Discipline from 1 Corinthians: A Chinese Perspective* (Bloomington, IN: Westbow, 2016), especially ch. 5, "Paul as Disciplinarian"; Ben Witherington III, *Community and Conflict in Corinth: a Socio-Rhetorical Commentary on 1 and 2 Corinthians* (Grand Rapids, MI: Eerdmans, 1996), passim.

headcoverings and hair in the earlier section of chapter 11, just before his discussion of the Lord's Supper.

It may seem a basic question, but it is rarely asked: Given the context of social shame-rhetoric, just why does Paul re-narrate the institution of the eucharist at the Last Supper (11:23–26)? Paul's particles indicate the logical connection: Ἐγὼ γὰρ παρέλαβον . . . "*For* I received from the Lord (11:23) . . ." There follows the narrative of the institution before the drawing of conclusions introduced by the Greek conjunction ὥστε: *"As a result,* whoever eats the bread unworthily . . ." The institution-narrative is included in order to give a reason for Paul's preceding condemnation of the Corinthians practices described in 11:17–22 (before the γὰρ of 23), and to provide the grounds for his immediately subsequent warning that unworthily (ἀναξίως) eating or drinking makes a person "guilty of" (ἔνοχος) the body and blood of the Lord.

Christ's sacrificial death was *for others*, and is the norm of both what it means to be an apostle and a Christian believer. Paul claims to be faithfully executing his office for the benefit of the Corinthians, not for his own sake, and he uses the institution-narrative of the Last Supper as a reminder that the Corinthians also ought to be living for others, not for themselves. As Anthony Thiselton puts it,

> the "splits" of chs. 1–4 undermine the heart of the gospel. Similarly, the practices which surround the sharing of the meal which (in Paul's view) points above all to the "for others" of the Lord's death undermine the very heart of why the worshiping community celebrates the Lord's Supper at all. Like apostleship, "remembering" and "showing forth" the Lord's death is a matter of conduct and lifestyle, not simply of words and ecclesial ritual. As in Israel's participation in the Passover, assembled believers are brought "there" to the cross, to allow it once again to reshape their mind-set and lifestyle.[9]

Since Paul has just explained that the Lord's Supper "proclaims the death of the Lord" (11:27), the statement that those who consume it unworthily are guilty of the body and blood should be understood as meaning that those who mistreat the members of the body (fellow believers) are liable to punishment just as though they had participated in the killing of Jesus. One must choose: either one is included in Christ, and manifests his self-sacrifice for the members of his body, or one is against Christ, and thus on the side of those who killed him.[10] This equation is all the more plausible coming from Paul, whom the risen Christ had asked, "Saul, Saul, why are you persecuting me?" when

---

[9] Anthony Thiselton, *The First Epistle to the Corinthians: A Commentary on the Greek Text* (Grand Rapids, MI: Eerdmans, 2000), 851.

[10] A similar antithesis is seen in Hebrews 10:29: "Of how much worse punishment will he be thought worthy who has trampled the Son of God underfoot, counted the blood of the covenant by which he was sanctified a common thing, and insulted the Spirit of grace?"

he was on his way to arrest and kill Jesus' followers (Act 9:4). No one knew better than Paul that offences against the church were counted as offences against Jesus himself. We see here a powerful aspect of the corporateness of the Messiah: to offend against the members of the people of God is to offend against their king.

NOT DISCERNING THE BODY

This offence takes the form of "not discerning the body" (μὴ διακρίνων τὸ σῶμα—11:29)—but this translation obscures the sociological nature of the offence in question. The verb διακρίνω does not mean "to recognize an object." It means *distinguishing* those who are a member of a group from those who are not by recognizing which persons are "in" the group and treating them as such. The verb comes from the root κριν-, to "sift," thus etymologically "to make a distinction between" two groups.[11] The LXX often uses διακρίνειν to translate Hebrew verbs of separating: e.g. בָּחַן in Job 12:11 (separating gold from base metals via smelting); פָּרַשׁ in Leviticus 24:12, of distinguishing courses of action. Indeed, even when it is used in the sense of "judging," it appears that the judging involves this sense of "making a distinction between" (1 Kings 3:9). Of course, that etymological meaning may or may not be at work in a given passage. But there are good reasons to think that it is at work in 1 Corinthians 11.

The same verb is used in the Spirit's instructions to Peter in Acts 10 when he is about to meet three Gentile men: "Behold, three men seeking you. But get up and go downstairs and go with them, making no distinction (μηδὲν διακρινόμενος), because I have sent them" (Acts 10:20). While many translations take the verb here to mean "doubting," it is better understood according to Peter's own usage in Acts 15:9, as he explains to the Jerusalem church that "God has made no distinction (οὐδέν διέκρινεν) between us [sc. believing Jews] and them [sc. believing Gentiles], purifying their hearts by faith." There is to be no distinction between different groups of Christians, because the proper distinction lies between Christians and the world. The Corinthians' sin amounts to misplacing this distinction and placing it between different groups of Christians, dividing the body of Christ into rich and poor. "If we distinguished (διεκρίνομεν) ourselves [sc. from the world], we would not be condemned (κατακριθῶμεν) with the world." (11:31) The operation in view

---

[11]Cf. Pierre Chantraine, *Dictionnaire Etymologique de la Langue Grecque* (Paris, 1968), 585 explains that the root denotes a sieve: "La racine, signifiant 'séparer,' s'est prêtée à des emplois divers: le sens de 'cribler' (cf. lat. *cribrum*) n'est qu'exceptionnel en grec. Le sens de 'juger' est une autre spécialisation qui a tenu une place importante en grec, mais en général κρίνω et ses dérivés ne présentent pas le sens précis et juridique de δικάζω, etc."

should be familiar to us: it is the same as the original Passover, which distinguished Israel from Egypt and condemned the latter.

The form this condemnation took is also the same as in the Exodus: supernaturally inflicted death. "Because of this [failure to draw the boundaries of the people of God properly], many among you are weak and sick and some are asleep [i.e. dead]." (11:30) If we are looking for a mechanism by which the eucharist operates, I submit that we have found it here: the communal meal, as an acted sharing in the salvific sacrificial death of the Messiah, marks the people of God as the ones who are to be spared God's deadly judgment, leaving those outside the Christian community exposed to that wrath. It is inflicted by God's own power.

This *modus operandi* should look familiar to us. In Exodus 11:4–7, YHWH announces that the Passover will work the same way:

> Then Moses said, "Thus says the Lord: 'About midnight I will go out into the midst of Egypt; and all the firstborn in the land of Egypt shall die, from the firstborn of Pharaoh who sits on his throne, even to the firstborn of the female servant who is behind the handmill, and all the firstborn of the animals. Then there shall be a great cry throughout all the land of Egypt, such as was not like it before, nor shall be like it again. But against none of the children of Israel shall a dog move its tongue, against man or beast, that you may know that the Lord does *make a difference* (יַפְלֶה) between the Egyptians and Israel."

Despite some unfortunate confusion among lexicographers, the hiphil of פָּלָה means "to make a difference between." HALOT gives only Exodus 9:4 and 11:7 as instances of this usage of פָּלָה, which its editors mistakenly connect to פלא, "to do something wonderful."[12] The error is very old: in Exodus 8:23 ("And I will put a division between my people and thy people") and 9:4 ("And the LORD shall sever between the cattle of Israel and the cattle of Egypt"), the LXX uses παραδοξάσω, showing that its translators assumed the word was from פָּלָא, and translated it overly literally according to this mistaken etymological sense, i.e. something like "I will marvelously glorify." In fact, the verb וְהִפְלֵיתִי in Exodus 8:22 is the Hiphil perfect of פָּלָה; cf. the Akkadian verb *palāku*, "to draw boundaries, to delimit, to divide" and the noun *pilku*, "boundary, border."[13] Hayim Tawil connects the Akkadian *palāku* with BH פלג, but misses the connection with פלה.[14] Thus, we should translate, "the Lord makes a difference between the Egyptians and Israel." The *discrimen*, the means by which this difference is marked, is the ritual meal itself. In Egypt, the Israelites' obedience to YHWH's command to eat the Passover was the

---

[12]HALOT, sv. פָּלָה.
[13]CAD vol. 12, 49–50 and 373.
[14]Tawil, *An Akkadian Lexical Companion*, 295 sv. פלג.

means by which they were able to escape the angel of death that killed the firstborn of the Egyptians.

In Corinth, however, the same procedure cannot be followed, for the people of God have not united to eat the meal commanded by Jesus but have divided among themselves and are eating separate meals—meals which, because they do not include all the people of God, cannot serve as a *discrimen* marking out God's people and distinguishing them from the world. The sickness and death that ought to have been reserved for unbelievers falls instead on many among the Corinthians themselves. Failing to keep the feast commanded by Jesus, "each takes his own meal" (ἕκαστος γὰρ τὸ ἴδιον δεῖπνον προλαμβάνει, 11:21)—and thereby many find themselves being "condemned with the world" (11:32) and falling to sickness and death. Chrysostom comments, "Owing to their disorder, it was no more than a private supper."[15] The shared meal offers protection by the blood of Christ; the private meal (τὸ ἴδιον δεῖπνον) gives none, because it does not mark the boundary between the people of God and those outside.

It is important to note that this does not mean that the rich in the Corinthian church had sacramental protection, so that only the poor were deprived and left vulnerable to condemnation "with the world." Rather, the entire protective function of the meal was lost, leaving all alike exposed to God's judgment, and especially those committing the abuse. Failure to join together in corporate solidarity left the entire community indiscriminately exposed to wrath.

PARTICIPATION IN EVENTS ACROSS TIME

As we have seen in our analysis of the Passover and the Last Supper, the available first-century Jewish conception of how sacramental meals worked was as a means of sharing in an event either future or past. Paul does not argue for this idea; rather, he presupposes it in arguing for *other* ideas. The central passage, long one of the most metaphysically challenging for Christian theologians, is 1 Corinthians 10:1–5:

> Moreover, brethren, I do not want you to be unaware that all our fathers were under the cloud, all passed through the sea, all were baptized into Moses in the cloud and in the sea, all ate the same spiritual food, and all drank the same spiritual drink. For they drank of that spiritual Rock that followed them, and that Rock was Christ. But with most of them God was not well pleased, for their bodies were scattered in the wilderness. (1 Cor. 10:1–5)

---

[15]Chrysostom, *Homily 27 on 1 Corinthians*, ad loc.

Now, on the face of things, it appears impossible that the Israelites of the Exodus should have "drunk from Christ," since he was not yet born. What impossible feat of time-traveling is this? But when we consider the analogy that Paul is making, things become clearer. Paul is making an argument to combat the Corinthians' presumption. Specifically, he wants them to fear the judgment of God on their immorality. But something is hindering the Corinthians from having this healthy fear: namely, they take false confidence in their experience of baptism and the eucharist. Paul deploys his argument about the sacraments of the Exodus in order to demolish this false confidence.

The Corinthians' problem is the opposite of most modern Christians' problem: in our day, it is difficult to persuade people that the sacraments have power or efficacy at all. They are "mere symbols" in the minds of many. For the Corinthians, however, it is obvious that the eucharist is a sharing in Christ, and Paul is able to appeal to that obviousness by asking his rhetorical questions ("is it not . . . ?") in 10:16. But first he feels the need to remind them that this sacramental participation in the Messiah does not make them more secure than Israel in the past. For participation in the Messiah was the future aspect of the Exodus, even as escape from Egypt was its present aspect. The Israelites of the Exodus had participation in Christ, too, he says. Yet they were not for that reason able to sin presumptuously and get away with it. He makes this argument in order to counter the Corinthians' presumption, lest they should say, "We have sacramental participation that is better than that of Israel of old."

The crucial point for our purposes is not something Paul says, but the presupposition without which he could not say what he does say; the foundation taken for granted as the given behind his entire argument: to wit, Paul's argument would founder if his Corinthian readers could say, "Ah, but our eucharist works *differently* from the original Passover meal of Israel in the Exodus!" If there were a difference of *modus operandi* between the eucharist on the one hand and the Passover on the other, then Paul's Corinthian readers would be able to reply to Paul's argument: "Yes, God scattered the bodies of those who drank from the rock and ate the manna. But he will not do that to us, because our sacraments make us share in Christ in a different way!" It is a presupposition of Paul's argument that there is essential similarity, not difference, between the participation in Christ enjoyed by the Israelites in the Exodus and that which the Corinthians have. Paul underscores this similarity by assimilating the Exodus to the experience of the Corinthian church using transferred diction: No Israelite who experienced the Exodus would have said that he had been "baptized" in the cloud and the sea. Rather, Paul has taken a description of unity and incorporation appropriate to the experience of the Corinthian church and applied it polemically to the Israelites of the Exodus.

Likewise, the description of the Israelites' food (βρῶμα) and drink (πόμα) and the rock (πέτρα) as "spiritual" (πνευματικός, 3 times) is a rhetorical use of intentional anachronism, an application to the Exodus of a word that was important to the Corinthians as a description of their own status and experience of participation in the Messiah through the Holy Spirit (1 Cor. 2:13, 2:15, 3:1, 9:11, 12:1, 14:1, 14:37, 15:46). The participation in Israel's Messiah which the Exodus generation enjoyed consisted in the fact that *they were Israel*, and the Messiah-to-come was thus *theirs*, to be united to them as their representative and head in the ways we surveyed in chapter 4.[16] They were Messiah-people *avant la lettre*.

In Romans and Galatians, Paul argues that Israel has been redefined around the Messiah: he contrasts those who are "of the works of the law" with those who are "of the faith of Christ." This is not a claim that God has scrapped the constitution of Israel, as though his people were now defined by sharing in the Messiah although they had not been so defined earlier. Rather, God's intention all along was that Israel would be the Messiah-people. The difference between the generation of the Exodus and the generation contemporary with Paul is that the former were the people of a Messiah who had not yet come, while the latter were the people of a Messiah who had already come. The inheritance was never by anything other than belonging to the Heir by faith. And this is Paul's argument concerning Abraham in Galatians 3 and Romans 4. Thus, in 1 Corinthians 10:1–5, Paul is able to argue by analogy: if the people who shared in the Messiah in the Exodus were liable to punishment for their disobedience, then we also ought to fear, lest we also be punished in a similar way. There is a difference of time, but not a difference in the mode of connection to the Messiah.

This way of understanding Paul's argument in 1 Corinthians 10:1–5 also solves an associated puzzle: namely, that Paul compares the sacramental communion of the Corinthian church with things that we might not otherwise have considered "sacramental" at all: the manna and the water from the rock. Seen from the perspective of those who ate the manna and drank the water, these events did not bear an obvious connection to the Messiah who would only come 1,500 years later. If an Israelite had been asked about the manna or the water from the rock, they would perhaps have associated them with Moses, or with YHWH, but not with the Messiah. Such a connection is apparent to Paul and his readers only in retrospect, in light of Jesus' identification with the YHWH of the Exodus. This might strike us as an audacious move, but it is one that was also made in Jude 5 with respect to the very same Exodus: "Jesus, having saved the people out of the land of Egypt, afterward destroyed

---

[16] *Vide supra*, ch. 4, 73–78, sections on *Union with Christ* and *Sharing in the Messiah*.

those who did not believe."[17] We may trace a line from 1 Corinthians 10:1–2 straight to Melito of Sardis and the Improperia.

Since Paul conceives of the relationship between the eucharist and Jesus' death as being analogous to that between the Passover and the Exodus, we are in position to understand what he means by the statement that "As often as we eat this bread and drink this cup, we proclaim the Lord's death until he comes." The statement is linked with an explanatory γὰρ to the immediately preceeding statement attributed to Christ: "do this, as often as you drink it, unto my memorial (εἰς τὴν ἐμὴν ἀνάμνησιν)." There are two crucial and oft-misunderstood terms here: "memorial" and "proclaim."

First, the concept of ἀνάμνησις. Contrary to much of the Reformed tradition, this does not primarily denote the remembering of Jesus by those who eat the Supper. Rather, in keeping with the idea of a *zikkarōn* in the Old Testament,[18] and with the close cognate μνημοσύνη in the New Testament, the intent is primarily to remind God, not the human participants. Joachim Jeremias was correct to say that εἰς τὴν ἐμὴν ἀνάμνησιν could be accurately glossed as "so that God may remember me."[19] As Richard Kearney points out,[20] the precise phrasing (εἰς μνημόσυνον) occurs in Psalm 112:6 (LXX 111:6): "The righteous shall be in everlasting remembrance"—as opposed to the wicked, who "shall perish." Similar eschatological remembrance by God is seen in Psalm 109:15 ("let their sins be before the Lord continually, that he may cut off the memory of them from the earth") and again in Psalms 37 and 69, "where the memory of God refers not just to creatures remembering their Creator in rituals and liturgies but also the Creator recalling creatures, making the past present before God in a sort of eternal re-presentation which endures into the future and beyond."[21] We see this sort of memorial in the New Testa-

---

[17]Whether this identification was made by Jude himself or by his later readers is a question of textual criticism; at any rate, it was thinkable by early Christians. In my view, Ἰησοῦς is the *lectio difficilior* here. It is attested in codex Vaticanus (B) and Alexandrinus (A), and supported by the Vulgate, Ethiopic, and Coptic versions, and by Origen. These are important and early witnesses. The ninth-century Athos manuscript Ψ, codex Sinaiticus (א), and the Sinai manuscript 1241 give κύριος, but it is likely that this is an emendation of the original text meant to ease the very chronological difficulty which we are discussing here. It does so at the cost of blunting Jude's argument. Cf. Anthony Hanson, *Jesus Christ in the Old Testament* (Eugene: Wipf and Stock, 2011), 165–167. Richard Bauckham disagrees, judging instead that the reading Ἰησοῦς is a scribal clarification of the ambiguous κύριος. Richard Bauckham, *Jude, 2 Peter* (Waco, TX: Word, 1983), 43. Either way, it is clear the early church identified Jesus with the κύριος of the LXX.

[18]This term is used of the Passover, of the stones of the priest's ephod, of the offering of money on the day of atonement, of the grain offering involved in the test for jealousy, of the stones in the Jordan where Joshua and the Israelites crossed over, and of various records written in books. (Ex. 12:14, 13:9, 17:14, 28:12, 30:16; Lev. 23:24; Num. 5:18, 10:10, 16:40, 31:54; Jos 4:7; Est. 6:1; Isa 57:8; Zec. 6:14; Mal. 3:16).

[19]J. Jeremias, *Eucharistic Words*, 252.

[20]Richard M. Kearney, "Re-Imagining God" in J. Caputo and M. Scanlon, ed. *Transcendence and Beyond: A Postmodern Inquiry* (Indiana University Press, 2007), 61.

[21]Kearney, "Re-Imagining God," 61.

ment in Jesus' words about the woman who anointed him with oil: "Assuredly, I say to you, wherever this gospel is preached in the whole world, what this woman has done will also be told as a memorial to her (εἰς μνημόσυνον αὐτῆς)" (Mt. 26:13 and Mk. 14:9) In Acts 10:4, the alms of Cornelius are said by the angel to have "come up for a memorial before God (εἰς μνημόσυνον ἔμπροσθεν τοῦ θεοῦ)." As a result of this remembrance, God is about to act to save and bless Cornelius and his household. In the original Passover, what mattered was that God (or his angel of death) saw and acted on the blood on the doorposts. Was Israel also commanded to remember? To be sure, and all the rituals of Passover to this day are aimed at inscribing the Exodus indelibly in the consciousness of every Jewish child. Yet in Egypt, it was not the Isaelites' consciousness, but the Lord's response to his own commanded memorial (*zeker*) that effected salvation for the Israelites and destruction for their enemies. In Paul's understanding, the eucharist operates not by the followers of Jesus thinking about it, but because it marks them as the people defined by Jesus' sacrificial death, which God remembers and honors and to which he responds with action in history.

I say "action in history" because the Lord's Supper is framed by its origins in Jesus' sacrificial death and the expectation of the eschatological vindication of the people of God at Jesus' coming. This is the significance of Paul's explanation that by eating and drinking the Lord's Supper the Corinthians "proclaim (καταγγέλετε) the Lord's death until he comes." This does not mean that while we eat and drink, we make an oral recital of Christ's death and remember it, although that should certainly be done as well, just as a similar recital of the events of the Exodus was certainly done in the course of celebrating Passover. Rather, Paul's phrasing is telling: he uses ὁσάκις with aorists of "eat" and "drink" (ἐσθίητε . . . καὶ . . . πίνητε), and follows them with another aorist, of the verb "proclaim" (καταγγέλετε). Thus, it is *by eating and drinking* that Christ's death is proclaimed. The community defined by this eating and drinking is a community with its origin in Jesus' death and its goal in Jesus' coming: those are the two events of salvation, one past and one future, into which the eucharist inscribes the participants. It is an inter-advental meal, eaten between the first and second comings of the Messiah. As Morna Hooker puts it, "The ritual based on the original story—the celebration of the eucharist—has now itself become a drama enacted by the community—a drama which proclaims Christ's death until he comes."[22]

In this connection, E.M.B. Green suggests that this verb καταγγέλλετε is a verbal echo of the biblical regulations of the Passover.[23] Exodus 13:8's verb,

---

[22] Hooker, *The Signs of a Prophet*, 52.
[23] E.M.B. Green, Address given at the Oxford Conference of Evangelical Churchmen, September, 1961.

"you shall tell your son" (*wehiggadta l^ebin^eka*) is rendered in the LXX as καὶ ἀναγγελεῖς τῷ υἱῷ σου. This is, of course, the verb from which the term *Haggadah*, "narration," is derived. The verb in 1 Corinthians 11:26 is very similar: "you proclaim (καταγγέλλετε) the Lord's death until he comes," but it is not quite the same. Paul's word, καταγγέλλω occurs only in II Maccabees, and not in the canonical books of the LXX,[24] but we do find הגד translated with ἀπ-άγγελλω. It is possible that the same Hebrew thought underlies both Greek verbs. If so, Green is likely right that "it is this technical term that is in Paul's mind when he speaks of 'shewing forth' the death, not of the Passover lamb at the paschal repast, as he had been used to doing as a Jew; but of the Lamb of God at the eucharist, as he told the *Haggadah* of the new Exodus."

Understood in these very Jewish terms, Paul's description of the eucharist in 1 Corinthians 11 conforms perfectly to the understanding for which we are arguing: it is a narratival ritual meal that involves the participants in the saving events which it symbolizes.

INTROSPECTION IN CORINTH?

It is sometimes alleged that 1 Corinthians 11:28 imposes a requirement of introspective "self-examination." Yet an examination of the lexical range of the verb in question (δοκιμάζω) reveals that it always concerns an outward and objectively knowable test.[25] Paul is not telling his Corinthian readers to "look inside themselves," but to demonstrate the behavior that is the hallmark of the true people of God: love for one another, unity, eating together at the same table.

---

[24]2 Macc. 8:36—"So he [Nicanor] who had undertaken to secure tribute for the Romans by the capture of the people of Jerusalem proclaimed (κατήγγελλεν) that the Jews had a Defender . . ." Likewise, in 2 Macc. 9:17, as the arch-villain Antiochus lies dying, he attempts to buy his life by offering to convert: "He also would become a Jew and would visit every inhabited place, proclaiming (καταγγέλλοντα) the power of God." It is noteworthy that in both of these instances, an enemy of the Jews admits the might of God *malgre lui*. I suppose it may be possible that this flavor is at work in Paul's usage in 1 Cor. 11:26: "Yes, we admit by our Supper that our Lord died, but this is only 'until he comes.'"

[25]Demosthenes 18.266 says "I am being examined for a crown," and then talks about how he is judicially innocent of all crimes. This is not introspective. Again, in Plato's *Laws*, 759D, some officers called "Expounders" are being examined. The scrutiny in question, the test indicated by "*dokimazo*," is "to see that a man is healthy and legitimate, reared in a family whose moral standards could hardly be higher, and that he himself and his father and mother have lived unpolluted by homicide and all such offences against heaven." In other words, it is again objective, not a matter of "looking into one's being." Again, in Thucydides 6.53, we see criminal informers being tested; in this case, "*dokimazo*" indicates a double-checking of the facts of their reports. Or in Xenophon, *Memorabilia* VI.1, we find talk of testing friends, where the test involves asking whether a person is "master of his appetites, not under the dominion, that is, of his belly, not addicted to the wine-cup or to lechery or sleep or idleness" and whether he is a debtor or quarrelsome.

2 Corinthians 13:5 is sometimes cited as corroboration for an introspective meaning of this verb, but a proper understanding of the situation in that passage reveals the opposite. The verse reads:

> "Examine yourselves as to whether you are in the faith. Test (δοκιμάζετε) yourselves. Do you not know yourselves, that Jesus Christ is in you?—unless indeed you are disqualified (ἀδόκιμοι)."

But the interpretation of this verse as a prescription of introspection does not fit the context of 2 Corinthians 12–13, let alone the context of 1 Corinthians 11. The verse is part of a larger argument of a particularly poignant and elegant character—and this argument of Paul's is only comprehensible if δοκιμάζω and its cognates have reference to objective matters mentioned in the immediate context, and not to introspection.

We may begin by noting that 2 Corinthians was written by Paul at a time when his credentials as an apostle were under attack by enemies in Corinth who were promoting false doctrines of hyper-spirituality and consequent antinomianism. This is the letter in which Paul is driven to his "insane" boasting about his service to Christ. The apostle is heartbroken. He loves the Corinthians, and hates having to discipline them and make them sorrowful (2 Cor. 2:1–2). But he is nonetheless motivated by a fierce and jealous love for them: he wants them, not their possessions (2 Cor. 12:14). He is heartbroken because his love for them is not reciprocated. They question the genuineness of his apostolic authority, so that he has to assert it.

These are the two parties to the quarrel: Paul on the one hand, with aspersions cast on the legitimacy of his office; and the Corinthians on the other, who have made their much-vaunted spiritual nature look very dubious by their evil deeds. Both of these parties are potential objects of testing. Both are fit objects for our little verb δοκιμάζω. And that is precisely what Paul plans to do.

In the course of answering the "super-apostles" who were undermining his work, Paul makes the telling observation—itself sufficient to undermine any introspective notion of δοκιμάζω—that "this one is not δόκιμος, who commends himself, but he whom the Lord commends." (10:18) But the real testing comes at the end of the letter. In 12:20–13:1, we are told explicitly that during his impending third visit to Corinth, both Paul and the Corinthians are about to be tested as to whether they are in Christ, or whether they are disqualified. For the Corinthians, the test involves whether Paul shall find them "not as I wish"—with "contentions, jealousies, outbursts of wrath, selfish ambitions, backbitings, whisperings, conceits, tumults." He is afraid that "many who have sinned before have not repented of the lewdness which they have practiced." At this point, readers rightly recall the man who had his father's wife, and the

Corinthians' "puffed-up" boasting about such behaviour, which they thought "spiritual."

For Paul, however, the test involves proof of his authority, which the Corinthians doubt. They are under the influence of false teachers, who have put it about that Paul only writes impressive-sounding letters, and that no one should be scared of him. In response to this, Paul threatens to use his apostolic power, the power of Christ. He has done so before (12:11–12), and now he warns (13:2) that "if I come to you again, I will not spare you . . ." Why not? ". . . since you seek proof of Christ speaking in me" (ἐπεὶ δοκιμὴν ζητεῖτε τοῦ ἐν ἐμοὶ λαλοῦντος Χριστοῦ). The word "proof" is δοκιμή, close cognate with δοκιμάζω. Paul knows perfectly well that he is an apostle. But his own consciousness of it is neither here nor there, because *it is not proof.* What matters is that the Corinthians be convinced of Paul's authority by the demonstration of the power of God. The assumption is that if he spares them—if he does not administer consequences by the power delegated to him as an apostle of Christ—then the Corinthians will continue to think that he has no such commission from Christ. So he will not spare them. He will use his power. And this will constitute his δοκιμή; it will show that he is δόκιμος. Thus he says (13:6), "But I trust you will know that we are not ἀδόκιμοι."

What about the Corinthians? Paul's fear is that he will find them "not as I wish." But that is not his hope. His hope is that they will clean up their act, and that he will not be forced to apply his power against them. Thus, following immediately after the threat of punishment, the next sentence is set off with δέ: "But (δὲ) I pray to God that you not do any evil thing."

There follows a clause which is now clear in light of the bilateral testing Paul has in view. Why does he pray that they not do any wrong?—"not so that we may appear δόκιμοι, but so that you may do what is good, and we may be as though ἀδόκιμοι." Paul wants to arrive in Corinth and find the Corinthians so thoroughly reformed in their behavior, that he will not have to produce proof (δοκιμή) of his authority. Indeed, he goes on to say that if he finds them better, he will not be able to use his power: "For we are not able to do anything against the truth, but on behalf of the truth."

Thus Paul's desire is that the Corinthians should be δόκιμοι by their abandonment of the gross sins he listed in 12:20–21, even if it means, as it must, that he will appear disqualified (ἀδόκιμος) by not displaying his power. Thus, "we are glad when we are weak and you are strong" (13:9).

Paul concludes his exhortation by stating, "Therefore I write these things being absent, lest being present I should use sharpness, according to the authority which the Lord has given me for edification and not for destruction."

In all this, introspection plays no part. When Paul urges the Corinthians to "δοκιμάζετε" themselves, he means "correct your behaviour in such a way that you pass the test when I come to see you." As for Paul, in his preferred outcome, he will be "as ἀδόκιμος," because he will have made no visible, objective display of the "sharpness" of his apostolic power. Both tests are about one party displaying something that the other party can observe.

SHARING IN CHRIST

But if the Supper does not work by introspection, how does it work? For in Corinth of all places, there was no doubt that it worked. It is the Corinthians to whom Paul addresses his "is it not?" questions about the Supper as a means of sharing in Christ's body and blood, questions which are counting on the assent of the readers to the truth of this claim. So obvious is this claim of "sharing in" Christ via a meal that Paul can use it to drive home the (surprisingly) contested claim that eating things sacrificed to idols is an act of disloyalty to God, since it is a "sharing in" the idols, even as eating the Lord's Supper is an act of "sharing in" Christ.

Paul's arguments by analogy with pagan sacrifices (1 Cor. 10:20) and with Jewish sacrifices in the Temple (1 Cor. 10:19) are only possible if the eucharist works the way other meals work. What is special about it is not the way it connects its participants to a person, but the person to whom it connects them.

ESCHATOLOGICAL EXPECTATION

"We proclaim the Lord's death *until* he comes"—This statement sketches the outlines of the story into which the eucharist inscribes its participants. It is eschatological through and through: it has a diachronic forward movement in time from an initial act (Jesus' death) to an anticipated final consummation (Jesus' coming). In this respect, the eucharist as described in 1 Corinthians 11 is a Jewish ritual meal like the Passover: it treats its participants as members of Israel, but Israel redefined around the Messiah. Where the Passover had the Exodus from Egypt as the constitutive event marking the birth of Israel as a people, and looked forward to their entry into the land, the eucharist looks back to the cross and forward to the coming of Christ. It is the distinguishing hallmark of Israel as a people that she, unlike all other peoples on the earth, had been placed into a relationship with YHWH and had received from him promises concerning the Messiah. Jesus died *as Israel's Messiah*; and since he is inclusive of his people, they too share in the resurrection that followed after his death. The mark of their inclusion is participation in the ritual meal which he instituted.

If the Corinthians fail to make the distinction between the members of the Messiah's body and the world outside of the Messiah, if they treat the one bread not as food for the one body, but in such a way that the weaker and poorer members of that body are humiliated, then the Corinthians will be found to be like Israelites who had failed to paint the blood on their doorposts.

Chapter Eight

Experiencing the Lord's Supper Today

Following Daube and Eisler, I have argued that we should see Jesus' words and actions in the Last Supper in their Passover context as an act of Messianic self-identification. I have urged that the Pauline doctrine of participation in Christ via the eucharist makes good sense within the same context of Jewish covenantal soteriology and eschatological expectation that is presupposed by Jesus' words over the wine and bread. Due appreciation of these ideas has the potential to shape Christian approaches to questions of eucharistic praxis. The answers suggested by this approach differ from those that have historically been given by theologians on the basis of philosophical ontology or other considerations of medieval and Reformation-era sacramentology.

I have in mind such questions as these: Who should partake? May children be admitted to the Lord's Supper? If so, at what age and on what conditions? Is it appropriate to force-feed, or administer the eucharist to an infant or nursing child? Do nursing children receive the benefit of the eucharist vicariously, through their mother's milk? Do unborn children *in utero* partake through the umbilicus? If an adult member willfully refuses to partake of the Supper, is he excluded from the Supper in the same way as a person who has been formally excommunicated? If a person is unable to consume the bread and wine because of illness, does she miss a benefit? How should the remaining eucharistic elements be handled after the service is over? Must they be consumed? Is it appropriate to dispose of them as we would any other food?

The answers that we give to such questions will vary greatly with our view of the eucharist itself: how it works, what its purpose is, and whether our practice is grounded upon the historical actions of Jesus. If we consider the eucharist primarily as an action performed by individuals, with benefit tied to consumption of the elements, as though they were medicine or containers for invisible grace (i.e., as Hugh of St. Victor did) or occasions for the exercise of mental faith, this framing of the questions will lead us to one set of answers. If we consider the eucharist as a ritual modeled on the Passover, and working in terms of covenant and history, as a meal eaten by the people of God, then we will find a different set of answers.

WHO SHOULD PARTAKE?

How do we determine who is included and excluded at, say, a birthday party or a wedding reception? If an infant, a babe-in-arms, is at the feast, do we say, "But he wasn't included because he did not eat the cake"? Of course not. In no other festal meal is inclusion or exclusion determined in such a manner. The child's presence and participation according to his ability—even if that ability is only to sleep in a sling on his mother the entire time—is welcomed, because he is included as a guest at the wedding or birthday party. But if the host, or his parents, prohibits him from eating even though he is at the party, a small child will understand—and understand rightly—that he is being excluded.

Many theologians analyze the ritual meal as though it were merely a digestive event, or a mental event with an edible sideshow. Both of these approaches are reductive. They fail to do justice to the nature of human beings as social animals. As in the Old Testament feasts, the social dimension of the eucharist is not merely incidental to its operation. Participation in any social function involves not only performing the actions appropriate to the occasion but also, even more importantly, relating to the other participants as person to person. Indeed, the performance of actions in the social event is always considered *within the context* of the social relations in question: for instance, if I am hosting a wedding banquet for my daughter, and steak is the main course, a refusal by one of the guests to eat with me may be construed as a way of refusing relationship or as an expression of hostility. But if a friend declines to share in the steak because he is a known vegetarian, his refusal will be inoffensive and gladly accommodated.

A glance at the rhetoric and arguments of 1 Corinthians 11 shows that Paul assumes that the Lord's supper works in this social way. Paul's concern that the participants "wait for one other" (11:33) and not "despise the church of God" and "shame those who have nothing" (11:22); the entire discussion's context immediately following a similarly social topic, the covering of women's heads (11:2–13); and Paul's use of praise and shame language (11:2, 4, 6, 14, 17, 22)—all make clear that the social dimensions of the eucharistic gathering are, for Paul, essential to the proper celebration of the ritual meal.

In other aspects, however, the eucharist as it has developed in the Christian tradition is closer to the biblical sacramentology. One such aspect is the matter of legislated quantities. Approaching the eucharist as a social and festal meal like Passover relativizes the question of how much participants must eat and drink. The Bible is largely silent on such questions about the eucharist, leaving them to be settled by custom and long use without theoretical consideration. The rabbis of the Tannaitic and Amoraic periods were, by contrast, exclusively concerned with such practical questions in connection with Passover, since they approached the ritual meal as a matter of covenantal obedience. They legislated the quantities of Passover foods that had to be consumed in order to fulfill the *mitzvot* of Passover, stipulating that each person must eat an amount of bread "equal to the size of an olive" (m.Pes. 70a) and that enough wine must be provided that all might have four cups; there should be enough meat that all might have some, yet not so much that any should be left over. The rabbis decreed what was required to eat the Passover "under one roof" and ruled on the minimum requirements for participation: for instance, if one fell asleep, did he continue participating? (We saw the answer earlier, in chapter 1: the rabbis distinguish between a doze, which does not end a man's participation, and a full sleep, which does.) There is some basis for such legislation of particulars: the instructions in Exodus 12 do contain many more specifics ("under one roof" and "roasted with fire"; "with your loins girded, your shoes on your feet, and your staff in your hand . . ."; "what remains until the morning you shall burn with fire") than any of the New Testament's instructions concerning the eucharist. Jesus' words of institution and Paul's summary of his tradition concerning the Lord's Supper leave us with no basis at all for prescribing any minimum or maximum quantities, or for measuring attention or alertness: these questions are matters of etiquette, not of sacramentology proper.

A CORPORATE MEAL

It is common today for members of the Church to abstain from one of the eucharistic elements voluntarily. A member might be in perfectly good standing, not excommunicated, but have gluten allergies or a history of alcoholism. If Christ's body and blood are locally present in the elements, such a person abstaining from one of the elements would fail to receive the benefit of the eucharist, and would be "excommunicating himself" to some extent. But if the eucharist is viewed as a festal meal and inclusion or exclusion is reckoned in the same way that we usually reckon participation in a meal, then there may be some awkwardness, but no severe problem. What would we say of an Israelite in Egypt for the original Passover who was on a vegetarian diet, and thus could not partake of the roasted lamb? Or a Nazirite in the early church who had vowed to abstain from wine? (We see Nazirite vows by Jewish Christians in Acts 21:23–26.) I believe the answer in both these cases is simple: they were included as full members of the congregation and participants in their respective ritual meals, eating or drinking what did not conflict with their special condition. And each would have fully received the benefit of the meal he shared in: escape from Egypt or union with Christ in his death and resurrection.

Approaching the eucharist as a festal meal also eliminates any need for speculations about babies consuming via nursing or *in utero*. The case of Samson, sometimes adduced as evidence that the unborn child shares in the mother's consumption of food,[1] is actually not at all similar, since there is a great difference between prohibiting certain foods to a Nazirite and commanding certain foods to be served at Passover. A vow of abstention is indeed a matter of individual consumption; inclusion in a feast is not.

The apostle Paul is in full agreement with this way of considering the eucharist. Notice how he speaks: "I do not want you to be partakers (κοινωνοὺς) with demons. You cannot drink the cup of the Lord and the cup of demons; you cannot partake of the Lord's table and of the table of demons" (1 Cor. 10:20–21). This is not mere metonymy, as though by "cup" and "table" Paul really meant "the wine in the cup" and "the bread on the table." Rather, the participation (κοινωνία) that Paul is concerned about is participation in the festal meal and thereby in the Messiah and the eschatological people of God who share in his death and resurrection. For that reason, Paul denotes that participation by the most appropriate terms, namely, the physical implements that are the means of sharing in the meal: the cup that is passed from hand to hand among the participants; the table around which they all sit. (Yes, he does speak of the actual elements when he says that "all partake of that one bread" in 1 Cor. 10:18, but even that is a means of expressing the gathered church's unity manifested by their common participation in the meal.) In the Pauline sacramentology, eating together is essential. "Do you not have houses to eat and drink in?" he asks the abusive rich in Corinth.

The practice of reservation or keeping back part of the sacrament from distribution and consumption, has ordinarily been done for two purposes: to

---

[1] Cf. James B. Jordan, *Judges: A Practical and Theological Commentary* (Eugene, OR: Wipf and Stock, 1999), 232. ". . . if the fetus is to avoid sacramentally unclean food in the womb, then the fetus also participates in the sacramental food of Holy Communion in the womb. When Samson's mother ate grapes, they went to her baby as well as to her. When a Christian woman eats Christ's flesh and drinks his blood, these go to her baby also. When the baby is born, he is separated from the spiritual protection of the womb, excommunicated as it were, and must be baptized into the Church before he can once again partake of the Lord's Supper." Jordan is considering the eucharist as something other than a festal meal, an event, and is viewing the benefits of the Supper as contained in the elements, so that they are passed from the mother to the child along with (and in the same manner as?) nutrition. The resulting need to explain the baby's birth as "excommunication" can only be characterized as an epicycle produced by a mistaken idea of just what participation in sacrificial meals involved.

administer to the sick when they are unable to attend worship with the rest of the congregation, and to display for adoration in a pyx, in an adoration chapel. The latter use seems to depend wholly upon a "real presence" theory of the eucharist's operation, and cannot be justified if the eucharist is properly understood as a festal meal, and especially if the communal aspect of it is essential to its operation. If in the Pauline sacramentology, the assembled congregation shares in Christ by eating bread and drinking wine together, then adoration of the elements removes the communal aspect without which, for Paul, the eucharist is no longer a means of participation in Christ.

WHAT TO DO WITH THE LEFTOVERS?

The disposal of the elements that remain after the celebration also poses no problem once we realise that the eucharist does its work as a festal meal, and not as medicine or containers for grace. The bread and wine have not become Christ; there is no presence of Christ locally in the elements. Rather, the meal in which they are consumed is a means of sharing in his death and resurrection. Therefore there is no need to consume them all, as though some of Christ's body and blood would be wasted otherwise. At the same time, crass treatment of the elements—throwing them in the trash—should be avoided, because it would naturally be construed as disdain for the festal occasion in which they were used.

There is likewise a question over what sort of bread to use. The Book of Common Prayer bears the scars of English contentions over the use of wafers: the Elizabethan 1552 rubric required "unleavened, and rounde" wafers; the 1559 edition followed John Calvin's preference for "ordinary bread," ordering that

> ... to take awaye the superstition, whiche any person hath, or myghte have in the breade and wyne, it shall suffice that the breade be suche as is usual to be eaten at the table, with other meates, but the beste and purest wheate breade, that conveniently may be gotten. And yf anye of the breade or wyne remaine, the Curate shall have it to hys owne use.[2]

The 1662 edition, however, eliminated this instruction, and wafers are now the prevailing custom in Anglican churches around the world, as well as in the Roman Catholic Church.

The difficulty with wafers is that they sever the symbolic link that Jesus intended to establish. As Calvin puts it, "Christ wished to testify by an external symbol that his flesh was food. If he exhibited merely an empty show

---

[2]Brian Cummings, ed. *The Book of Common Prayer: The Texts of 1549, 1559, and 1662* (Oxford University Press, 2011), n. 140.

of bread, and not true bread, where is the analogy or similitude to conduct us from the visible thing to the invisible?"[3] We may differ from Calvin concerning what Christ wished to testify by the bread's symbolism, but his point remains: if the bread is not bread, then the semiotic content of the food is lost, and the symbolic meaning of the ritual is changed.

Whatever other symbolism may be affected by the change to wafers, it certainly diminishes the force of Paul's argument in 1 Corinthians 10:16–17: "The bread which we break, is it not a participation of the body of Christ? Because the bread is one (ὅτι εἷς ἄρτος), we the many are one body, for we all have a share of the one bread." The force of this argument is somewhat hamstrung by the fact that English does not map its vocabulary onto Greek one-for-one. For Greek uses ἄρτος to mean either "bread" or "loaf" (e.g., the πέντε ἄρτους with which the five thousand are fed in Mt. 14:17, Mk. 6:38, Lk. 9:10, Jn. 6:9). Paul's argument is not merely an appeal to the fact that all are eating the same meal; rather, he appeals to the unified loaf that is quite literally "broken" into pieces in the act of distribution to the gathered congregation. If this loaf be replaced with wafers which have never been unified, but were shaped and baked as separate pieces, Paul's argument can no longer appeal to the fact that all partake of the "one loaf." A powerful piece of symbolism is thus lost by the use of wafers.

Paul's argument makes explicit appeal to the fact that the one loaf is distributed to many participants. He says this in the context of a larger argument against sharing in sacrifices made to idols (1 Cor. 10:14–22). The appeal to the oneness of the bread and the oneness of the ecclesial body of those who share in that one bread is driven by the need to contrast this faithful community with those who are unfaithful and are sharers of demons (δαιμονία, 10:20–21). The concluding line of Paul's argument (1 Cor. 10:22) is a quotation of Deuteronomy 32:21:[4]

| "They provoked me to jealousy (παραζήλωσαν) by what is not a god; they enraged me by their idols." (Dt. 32:21) | Or do we provoke the Lord to jealousy (παραζηλοῦμεν)? We aren't stronger than he, are we? (1 Cor. 10:22) |

As Richard Bauckham notes, "Paul here attributes the divine jealousy to Jesus Christ."[5] Paul also has prepared his readers for this argument by his adap-

---

[3] John Calvin. *Institutes of the Christian Religion*, trans. H. Beveridge. IV, 17.14.
[4] On this echo, cf. Richard Hays, *The Conversion of the Imagination: Paul as Interpreter of Israel's Scripture* (Grand Rapids, MI: Eerdmans, 2005), ch. 1, n. 29.
[5] Richard Bauckham, *Jesus and the God of Israel* (Grand Rapids, MI: Eerdmans, 2008), ch. 2, "Biblical Theology and the Problems of Monotheism."

tation of the Shema two chapters earlier in 1 Corinthians 8:6. Since the Shema ("Hear, O Israel, YHWH our God, YHWH is one," Dt. 6:4) was understood as a credal statement against idolatry or split loyalties, binding Israel to follow YHWH alone, Paul's repeated use of the word "one" in his argument against idolatry in 1 Corinthians 10:17–22 should be understood as a way of framing the issue of idol sacrifices as a matter of loyalty to Jesus Christ (and thereby to YHWH). Note also the echo of Deuteronomy 32:17 ("They sacrificed to demons, not to God," δαιμονίοις καὶ οὐ θεῷ) in 1 Corinthians 10:20 ("the things which the Gentiles sacrifice, they sacrifice to demons, not to God," δαιμονίοις θύει καὶ οὐ θεῷ). The one loaf is thus a vivid symbol of the congregation's loyalty to YHWH through their sharing in Christ, and thereby worshipping the one God of Israel: one loaf, one people, one Messiah, one God. The same imagery is at work in the prayer over the bread in the Didache, but with an additional idea introduced: the one loaf was brought together out of many grains of wheat.

> As this broken bread was scattered over the hills and was brought together becoming one, so gather your Church from the ends of the earth into your kingdom. (Didache 9)[6]

The central tenets of early Christianity are symbolically bound up in the single unified loaf.

By contrast, there is no need for contention over whether to use leavened or unleavened bread, since neither choice derogates from the biblical symbolism. The bread ritual at the Last Supper would of course have been unleavened, but that on the road to Emmaus would presumably have been leavened, or if it was not, it was not significant that it was so, since it was not Passover any longer. The apostle Paul's exhortation to "keep the feast, not with the old leaven nor with the leaven of wickedness and evil, but with the unleavened bread of sincerity and truth" (1 Cor. 5:8) is specifically Paschal imagery, written in the context of advice to the Corinthians to expel the sexual immoral man from their midst. Here we must avoid conceiving of "leaven" as modern yeast, packaged in a jar or bag. That is not how bread was leavened in the ancient world. Instead, each new batch of dough was made to include a bit of old dough, already alive with yeast cultures from the air. There was thus a very real continuity from one loaf to the next. When Paul urges the Corinthians to purge out the old leaven, he is referring to the custom of burning all leaven before the Passover, thus symbolically making a clean break with their pre-Exodus past and representing the newness of Israel as God's people. But

---

[6] *The Didache*, trans. M.B. Riddle in *Ante-Nicene Fathers*, Vol. 7, ed. Roberts and Donaldson. (Buffalo, NY: Christian Literature Publishing, 1886).

it is not likely that the earliest Jewish Christians would have made unleavened bread beyond the week of Passover; their celebrations of the eucharist were most likely with leavened bread such as was ordinary at all other times.

WINE OR JUICE?

The Paschal background also allows us to answer the question of whether to use wine or grape juice.

Fermentation is a chemical process that begins at the moment when yeast from the skin of a grape makes contact with fructose from the inside of the grape. Pasteurization and refrigeration are able to arrest fermentation by killing the yeast and preventing its further growth. This process was first applied to grapes by a Wesleyan Methodist minister, Thomas Bramwell Welch, in 1869. Yet the Wesleyan Methodist Connection had already published a rubric in the first edition of their Discipline instructing that "unfermented wine only should be used at the sacrament."[7] Thus Welch was supplying a need felt by the church in his day, driven by theological and ethical concerns.

If we could confront Socrates and Odysseus with Welch's grape juice and ask them what it is, they would reply using the Greek word for wine, οἶνος, which denoted both fermented and unfermented drink made from grapes. But it would be a grave mistake to allow our understanding of wine in Jesus' day to be shaped by nineteenth-century temperance movements. The Passover was certainly celebrated with wine, not with new grape juice. The Torah's regulation of all the pilgrim feasts for which Israelites were required to go to Jerusalem expressly authorizes the use of tithes "for wine and strong drink," *bayayin ubaššēkar* (Dt. 14:26), where the term *šēkar* denotes "intoxicating drink" (HALOT) made from barley or wheat (cf. Akkadian *šikārum* and Arabic *sakar*, both of which denote beer or ale). Wine is paired with other alcoholic drinks.[8] Why? The verse concludes " . . . and you shall rejoice (*wešāmaḥtā*), you and your household." Deuteronomy 14:26 moves directly from permission for purchasing alcoholic beverages to the purpose for which alcohol was made: The power of wine to elevate the mood of the participants is an expected benefit of the feast—a intended feature, not a problem. Isaiah's description of the eschatological banquet as "a feast of wine on the lees" (Is. 25:6) also rules out new wine; indeed, the word "lees" or "dregs" (Heb. *šemārîm*) is used metonymically to denote "old wine" as opposed to new: wine that has not been separated from the dregs by a sieve, but has been left

---

[7] Karen Tucker, "The Lord's Supper," *American Methodist Worship* (New York: Oxford University Press, 2006), 151.

[8] The Hebrew *šēkar* is behind the Greek σίκερα, paired with wine (οἶνος) in Luke 1:15 to denote the beverages to be avoided by John the Baptist, a Nazirite from his infancy.

to age, with the fragments of grape skin and their fermentation-causing yeast still at the bottom of the skin or cask. The narrative of Jesus' miracle at the wedding at Cana (Jn. 2:1–12) distinguishes between inferior (ἐλάσσω) wine and good (καλόν) wine—that is, between wine which is newer and weaker and that which is stronger and more aged. Indeed, the coup de grace in the narrative is the fact that Jesus turns water, not into weak and poor-tasting drink, but into a well-aged and strong vintage such as would normally be offered at the start of a celebratory feast, when its powerful effect would be most needed and appreciated.

ONE CUP OR MANY?

The question of whether to use one common cup or several cups, one for each participant, does not admit of easy solution by appeal to Jesus' last Passover meal with his disciples. The sequence of four cups in the Mishnah does not solve the problem, since such terms as "the first cup" or "the third cup" are ambiguous: Do they denote a single common cup that was passed around? Or did each participant in the Last Supper have his own cup before him, so that "the first cup" referred to the drinking that each did from his own vessel? The balance of the rabbinic evidence is in favor of a single cup shared round to each participant: twice the Mishnah describes the *paterfamilias* presiding over the cup with the formula "The [first, second, etc.] cup has been mixed for him. Now he . . . [says a prescribed prayer or performs other liturgical actions]." (*m.Pes.* 10.2 and *m.Pes.* 10.7) Jeremias suggests that this reflects also the usage at other communal meals, such as were described in the rabbinic sources concerning *berakoth* ("blessings"): "On festal occasions it remained the general practice for the cup of blessing to be passed to all the participants after the one who had said the blessing had drunk from it."[9] There was thus a symbolic association of the blessing with the cup, so that to share in the one was to share in the other. Since this shared cup was the practice on other occasions, it would be surprising if the same practice were not also operative at Passover. Some of the earliest rabbinic sources (*Tosefta Ber.* 5.10 and *Derek Ereṣ* 9, even earlier than the *Mishnah*), however, reflect scruples and controversy about using a single cup and enjoin instead the use of individual cups for each participant. It is impossible to know whether these sources also reflect first-century practice, or whether, as seems more likely to me, the practice of the common cup was the original one. If the latter, it is possible that alongside aesthetic and hygienic considerations the rabbis also desired to differentiate Jewish practice from the early Christians' common cup. In other

---

[9]Jeremias, *Eucharistic Words*, 69.

words, the apparent abandonment of the common cup by the rabbis may be another instance of the strife between the two sister religions.

Evidence for the use of a single cup in the eucharist is even earlier than the earliest Jewish sources for the use of multiple cups in the Passover. Consider the argument of Ignatius of Antioch (c. 108):

> So then, be diligent to use (χρῆσθαι) one eucharist. For there is one flesh of our Lord Jesus Christ, one cup into union with his blood, one altar, as there is one bishop, together with the presbytery (πρεσβυτερίῳ) and deacons, my fellow-servants—that whatsoever you do, you may do it in accordance with God. (*Letter to the Philadelphians*, 4)[10]

All other objects to which "one" is applied in this passage—the body of Jesus, the altar, the bishop—are each singular count-nouns. It is unlikely that Ignatius would have included "one cup" in the list if the eucharist had been celebrated with multiple individual vessels, one for each participant.

Perhaps more important is the symbolic connection which the cup bears to Jesus' sufferings. Jesus' refusal of the fourth cup at the Last Supper continued on the cross as he refused the proffered sponge of spiced wine (Mk. 15:23). Within the context of the Passover, this cup represented the kingdom of God. But Jesus had consistently used the cup as a symbol of suffering, both in his prayers in Gethsemane (Mk. 14:36, Mt. 26:39, Lk. 22:42) and in his response to the request of the sons of Zebedee (Mk. 10:38, Mt. 20:22). The kingdom comes through suffering and death. The disciples who shared the cup at the Last Supper had been told that they would sit on thrones judging the twelve tribes of Israel, but that they would first drink the cup of suffering and martyrdom (Mk. 10:39). Jesus' response to the sons of Zebedee describes the sharing of "the cup that I drink," not the coordinated drinking of other similar cups. If Christians' participation in the ritual meal is a sharing in Jesus' own sufferings and death rather than an experience of some other different sufferings, then the use of a common, shared cup helps underscore that fact.

HISTORICAL TRUTH IS ECUMENICAL

The use of shared bread and a shared cup highlights the horizontal and social dimension of the eucharist. The eucharist in the NT churches was not an occasion for private interiority or pietistic meditation, but a fully social and communal sharing in the ritual meal by "right use"—eating and drinking *together*—of its commanded elements. The participants' eyes were open, as

---

[10] *Ante-Nicene Fathers*, Vol. 1. Edited by Alexander Roberts, James Donaldson, and A. Cleveland Coxe (Buffalo, NY: Christian Literature Publishing Co., 1885).

they would have been at any other social meal, because the presence of other participants was part of what made it a festal occasion.

At the same time, the actions of Christ at the Last Supper not only underwrote and instituted the repeated eucharist, but also identified Jesus as the Messiah whose death as a new paschal sacrifice effected a new Exodus and rescued a new Israel constituted of his disciples ("Christ our Passover is sacrificed for us. Therefore let us keep the feast . . ."). This renewed people of God shares in the events of Jesus' death by sharing in the ritual meal ("Is it not a participation in the blood of Christ?"). At the same time, they are marked out as those who will share in his resurrected glory at his coming ("we declare the Lord's death until he comes").

Though they may be unaware of the antecedent Paschal symbolism by which Jesus communicated with his disciples at the Last Supper, all Christians nonetheless accept the things that he communicated by his words and actions against the background of this symbolism: all Christians believe that he is Israel's Messiah; all believe that his death was for his people; all believe that they themselves share in his death; all look to share in his resurrection and to reign with him in glory. There is good reason to hope that the pursuit of a historical New Testament sacramentology may eventually have the effect of uniting followers of Jesus around the table he has given them, so that each may "regard himself as though he personally had" been crucified and resurrected.

Bibliography

Amar, Joseph. "Book Review: Ephrem, a 'Jewish' Sage." *Theological Studies* 75.1 (2014): 209–210.
Bauckham, Richard. *Gospel of Glory: Major Themes in Johannine Theology.* Grand Rapids, MI: Baker Academic, 2015.
———. *Jesus and the Eyewitnesses.* Grand Rapids, MI: Eerdmans, 2008.
———. *Jesus and the God of Israel.* Grand Rapids, MI: Eerdmans, 2008.
———. *Jude, 2 Peter.* Waco, TX: Word, 1983.
Bauckham, Richard, ed. *The Gospels for all Christians: Rethinking the Gospel audiences.* Grand Rapids: Eerdmans, 1997.
Begbie, Jeremy. *Theology, Music, and Time.* Cambridge: Cambridge University Press, 2000.
Behm, Johannes. "κλάω." *Theological Dictionary of the New Testament* vol. 3, edited by Gerhard Kittel, 736. Grand Rapids: Eerdmans, 1965.
Biale, David. *Gershom Scholem: Master of the Kabbalah.* New Haven, CT: Yale University Press, 2018.
Bock, Darrel. *Luke.* Downer's Grove, IL: Intervarsity Press, 1994.
Boersma, Hans, and Matthew Levering, ed. *The Oxford Handbook of Sacramental Theology.* Oxford: Oxford University Press, 2015.
Bokser, Baruch. *The Origins of the Seder.* Berkeley, CA: University of California Press, 1984.
Bonner, Campbell, ed. *The Homily on the Passion by Melito Bishop of Sardis and Some Fragments of the Apocryphal Ezekiel.* Philadelphia: University of Prennsylvania Press, 1940.
The Book of Common Prayer 1662. Oxford: Oxford University Press, 1989.
The Book of Praise: Anglo-Genevan Psalter. Hamilton: Canadian Reformed Churches, 1984.
Bouyer, Louis. *Eucharist: Theology and Spirituality of the Eucharistic Prayer.* Notre Dame: University of Notre Dame Press, 1968.
Bradshaw, Paul. *Eucharistic Origins.* London: SPCK, 2004.

———. *The Search for the Origins of Christian Worship: Sources and Methods for the Study of Early Liturgy.* London: SPCK, 2002.
Brisson, Luc. *How Philosophers Saved Myths: Allegorical Interpretation and Classical Mythology*, translated by Catherine Tihanyi. Chicago: University of Chicago Press, 2004.
Browe, Peter. *Die eucharistischen Under des Mittelalters.* Breslau: Müller and Sieffert, 1938.
Brumberg-Kraus, Jonathan. "Performing Myth, Performing Midrash." *Meals in Early Judaism: Social Formation at the Table*, edited by Susan Marks and Hal Taussig. New York: Palgrave MacMillan, 2014.
Bultmann, Rudolf. *The Gospel of John: A Commentary.* Translated by G. R. Beasley-Murray. Oxford: Blackwell, 1971.
Calvin, John. *The Institutes of the Christian Religion.* Translated by Henry Beveridge. London: T&T Clark, 1863.
Carmichael, Calum, ed. *Collected Works of David Daube vol. 2: New Testament Judaism.* Berkeley, CA: The Robbins Collection, 2000.
Carmichael, Deborah Bleicher. "David Daube on the Eucharist and the Passover Seder." *Journal for the Study of the New Testament* 42 (1991): 45–67.
Carson, D.A. "Understanding Misunderstandings in the Fourth Gospel." *Tyndale Bulletin* 33 (1982): 59–91.
Casey, Maurice. *An Aramaic Approach to Q.* Cambridge: Cambridge University Press, 2002.
———. *Aramaic Sources of Mark's Gospel.* Cambridge: Cambridge University Press, 2004.
———. *Is John's Gospel True?* London: Routledge, 1996.
———. *Jesus of Nazareth: An Independent Historian's Account of His Life and Teaching.* New York: T&T Clark, 2010.
———. "No Cannibals at Passover." *Theology* 96 (1993): 199–205.
———. *The Solution to the Son of Man Problem.* London: T&T Clark, 2009.
Chantraine, Pierre. *Dictionnaire Etymologique de la Langue Grecque.* Paris: Librairie Klincksieck, 1968.
Chauvet, Louis-Marie. *The Sacraments: The Word of God at the Mercy of the Body.* Collegeville, MN: Liturgical Press, 2001.
Chilton, Bruce. *A Feast of Meanings.* Leiden: E.J. Brill, 1994.
———. *Types of Authority in Formative Christianity and Judaism.* New York: Routledge, 1999.
Chong, Timothy K.H. *Strategies in Church Discipline from 1 Corinthians: a Chinese Perspective.* Bloomington, IN: Westbow, 2016.
Colautti, Federico. *Passover in the Works of Josephus.* Leiden: E.J. Brill, 2002.
Cross, Frank Leslie. *Early Christian Fathers.* London: Duckworth, 1960.
Cullman, Oscar. "Der johanneische Gebrauch doppeldeutigen Ausdrücke als Schlüssel zum Verständnis des vierten Evangeliums," *Theologische Zeitschrift* 4 (1948): 360–372; repr. in *Vorträge und Aufsätze 1925-1962*, 176–186. Tübingen: Mohn/Zürich: Zwingli, 1966.

———. "La signification de la Sainte-Cène dans le christianisme primitif," *Revue d'Histoire et de Philosophie religieuses* (Strasbourg, 1936), translated by J.G. Davies in O. Cullmann, Oscar, and F.J. Leenhardt. *Essays on the Lord's Supper*. Atlanta, John Knox Press, 1958.

Cummings, Brian ed. *The Book of Common Prayer: The Texts of 1549, 1559, and 1662*. Oxford: Oxford University Press, 2011.

Dalman, Gustaf. *Jesus-Jeshua*, translated by Paul Levertoff. New York: MacMillan, 1929.

Daube, David. "A Baptismal Catechism." *Collected Works of David Daube vol. 2*, edited by Calum Carmichael, 501–502. Berkeley, CA: The Robbins Collection, 2000.

———. "He That Cometh." *Collected Works of David Daube vol. 2*, edited by Calum Carmichael, 438–439. Berkeley, CA: The Robbins Collection, 2000.

———. "Judas." *Collected Works of David Daube vol. 2*, edited by Calum Carmichael, 795–799. Berkeley, CA: The Robbins Collection, 2000.

———. "Two Incidents after the Last Supper" in *Collected Works of David Daube vol. 2: New Testament Judaism*, edited by Calum Carmichael, 441–446. Berkeley, CA: the Robbins Collection, 2000.

de Lange, Nicholas. "Jewish Use of Greek in the Middle Ages: Evidence from Passover *Haggadoth* from the Cairo Genizah." *The Jewish Quarterly Review* 96 (Fall 2006): 490–497.

Delitzsch, Franz. *The Delitzsch Hebrew Gospels*. Marshfield, MO: Vine of David, 2011.

Derrett, Duncan. "John 9:6 Read with Isaiah 6:10; 29:9." *Studies in the New Testament*, vol. 6, 2–5. Leiden: E.J. Brill, 1995.

Dodd, C.H. *Historical Tradition in the Fourth Gospel*. Cambridge: Cambridge University Press, 1963.

Dordek, Eliyahu ed. *Koren Mishna Sdura Bartenura*. Jerusalem: Koren Publishers, 2015.

Driver, G.R. "Hebrew Poetic Diction." *Congress Volume: Copenhagen 1953*, *Supplements to Vetus Testamentum* vol. 1, 26–39. Leiden: E.J. Brill, 1953.

Eisler, Robert. "Das Letzte Abendmahl." *Zeitschrift für die Neutestamentliche Wissenschaft* 24 (1925): 161–192 and 25 (1926): 5–37.

Elis, Niv. "Why Israeli Dairy Cows Eat Kosher for Passover." *Jerusalem Post*, April 6, 2014.

Elwood, Christopher. *The Body Broken: The Calvinist Doctrine of the Eucharist and the Symbolization of Power in Sixteenth-Century France*. Oxford: Oxford University Press, 1999.

Evans, Craig. "Feeding the Five Thousand and the Eucharist." *John, Jesus, and History volume 2: Aspects of Historicity in the Fourth Gospel*, edited by Paul N. Anderson, Felix Just, and Tom Thatcher, 131–138. Atlanta, GA: Society of Biblical Literature, 2009.

Finkelstein, Louis. "Pre-Maccabean Documents in the Passover Haggadah." *Harvard Theological Review* 35 (1942): 291–332 and 36 (1943): 1–38.

Fishbane, Michael. *The JPS Bible Commentary: Haftarot.* Philadelphia, PA: Jewish Publication Society, 2002.
Flesher, Paul V.M., and Bruce Chilton. *The Targums: A Critical Introduction.* Leiden: E.J. Brill, 2011.
Flusser, David. "Some Notes on Easter and the Passover Haggadah." *Immanuel* 7 (1977): 52–60.
Foerster, Werner. "ἐπιούσιος." *Theological Dictionary of the New Testament,* vol. 2, edited by Gerhard Kittel, 590–599. Grand Rapids, MI: Eerdmans, 1964.
France, R.T. "The Servant of the Lord in the Teaching of Jesus." *Tyndale Bulletin* 19 (1968): 26–52.
Gill, Katherine. "Transcript of the Marburg Colloquy." *Great Debates of the Reformation,* 77–107. New York: Random House, 1969.
Glaser, Mitch. "Passover in the Gospel of John," in *Messiah in the Passover,* edited by Darrell Bock and Mitch Glaser, 70–72. Grand Rapids, MI: Kregel, 2017.
Glatzer, Nahum. *The Passover Haggadah.* New York: Schocken, 1989.
Godet, Frederic. *Commentary on the Gospel of John.* London: T&T Clark, 1881.
Gottheil, Richard, and Samuel Krauss. "Greek Language and the Jews." *The Jewish Encyclopedia,* vol. VI, 85–88. New York: Funk & Wagnalls, 1906.
Grossfeld, Bernard. *Two Targums of Esther.* Edinburgh: T&T Clark, 1991.
Guggenheimer, Heinrich. *The Jerusalem Talmud. Second Order: Moʻed Tractates Pesaḥim and Yoma.* Berlin: Walter de Gruyter, 2013.
Hageman, Elizabeth, and Katherine Conway. *Resurrecting Elizabeth I in Seventeenth-Century England.* Vancouver: Fairleigh Dickinson University Press, 2007.
Hall, Stuart. "Melito in Light of the Passover Haggadah." *Journal of Theological Studies* new series XXII part 1 (April 1971): 29–46.
———. *On Pascha and fragments.* Oxford: Clarendon Press, 1979.
Hanneken, Todd. "A Completely Different Reading of Melito's Peri Pascha." *Meqorot: The University of Chicago Journal of Jewish Studies* 3 (1997): 26–33.
Hanson, Anthony. *Jesus Christ in the Old Testament.* Eugene, OR: Wipf and Stock, 2011.
Harrison, Jane Ellen. *Themis:A Study of the Social Origins of Greek Religion.* New York: Cambridge University Press, 2010.
Hays, Richard. *The Conversion of the Imagination: Paul as Interpreter of Israel's Scripture.* Grand Rapids, MI: Eerdmans, 2005.
———. *Echoes of Scripture in the Gospels.* Waco, TX: Baylor University Press, 2016.
———. *Reading Backward.* Waco, TX: Baylor University Press, 2014.
Holifield, E. Brooks. *The Covenant Sealed: The Development of Puritan Sacramental Theology in Old and New England, 1570–1720.* Eugene: Wipf and Stock, 2002.
Hooker, Morna. *Jesus and the Servant.* London: SPCK, 1959.
Instone-Brewer, David. *Traditions of the Rabbis from the Era of the New Testament vol. 1: Prayer and Agriculture.* Grand Rapids, MI: Eerdmans, 2004.
———. *Traditions of the Rabbis from the Era of the New Testament vol. 2A: Feasts and Sabbaths: Passover and Atonement.* Grand Rapids, MI: Eerdmans, 2011.
Jastrow, Marcus. *A Dictionary of the Targumim, the Talmud Babli and Yerushalmi, and the Midrashic Literature.* New York: Judaica Press, 1903.

Jaubert, Annie. *The Date of the Last Supper.* Staten Island: Alba House, 1965.
Jeremias, Joachim. *The Eucharistic Words of Jesus.* Minneapolis: Fortress, 1966.
———. *The Lord's Prayer.* Minneapolis: Fortress, 1969.
———. *The Prayers of Jesus.* ET London: SCM, 1967.
Jordan, James B. *Judges: A Practical and Theological Commentary.* Eugene: Wipf and Stock, 1999.
Kearney, Richard M. "Re-Imagining God." *Transcendence and Beyond: A Postmodern Inquiry,* edited by J. Caputo and M. Scanlon. Bloomington: Indiana University Press, 2007.
Keener, Craig. *The Gospel of John: A Commentary.* Grand Rapids, MI: Baker Academic, 2003.
Klawans, Jonathan. "Was Jesus' Last Supper a Seder?" *Bible Review* 17:5 (October 2001).
Klinghardt, Matthias. "A Typology of the Communal Meal." *Meals in the Early Christian World,* edited by Hal Taussig and Dennis Smith, 9–22. New York: Palgrave MacMillan, 2012.
Köstenberger, Andreas. "Was the Last Supper a Passover Meal?" *The Lord's Supper: Remembering and Proclaiming Christ Until He Comes,* edited by Thomas Schreiner and Matthew Crawford, 6–30. Nashville, TN: B&H, 2011.
Krauss, Samuel, and Immanuel Löw. *Griechische und Lateinische Lehnwörter im Talmud, Midrasch und Targum.* Berlin: Georg Olms Verlag, 1898.
Krivoruchko, Julia. "Greek Loanwords in Rabbinic Literature: Reflections on Current Research Methodology." *Greek Scripture and the Rabbis*, edited by Timothy Law and Alison Salvesen, 193–216. Leuven: Peeters Publishers, 2012.
Kulp, Joshua. "The Origins of the Seder and Haggadah." *Currents in Biblical Research* 4.1 (2005): 109–134.
Lachs, Samuel Tobias. *A Rabbinic Commentary on the New Testament.* Hoboken, NJ: Ktav, 1987.
LeCroy, Timothy R. "The Role of Corpus in the Eucharistic Theology of Paschasius Radbertus." Ph.D. diss., Saint Louis University, 2012.
Leithart, Peter. *The Priesthood of the Plebs.* Eugene: Wipf & Stock, 2003.
Lieberman, Saul. *Hayerushalmi Kifshuto.* Jerusalem: Darom, 1934.
———. *Hayerushalmi Kiphshuto.* New York: The Jewish Technological Seminary of America, 1995.
Lietzmann, Hans. "Jüdische Passahsitten und der ἀφικόμενος." *Zeitschrift für die Neutestamentliche Wissenschaft* 25 (1926): 299–303.
———. *Messe und Herrenmahl—Eine Studie zur Geschichte der Liturgie* (Berlin, Verlag Walter de Gruyter, 1926), translated by Dorothea Reeve as *Mass and Lord's Supper: A Study in the History of the Liturgy.* Leiden: E.J. Brill, 1979.
Loehe, Wilhelm. *Questions and Answers to the Six Parts of the Small Catechism of Dr. Martin Luther.* Columbia: W.J. Duffie, 1893.
Lohse, Bernhard. *Das Passafest der Quartodecimaner.* Gütersloh: Bertelsman, 1953.
Macy, Gary. "Medieval Theology of the Eucharist and the Chapel of the Miracle Corporal." *Vivens homo* 18 (2007): 59–77.
Malina, Bruce. *The Palestinian Manna Tradition.* Leiden: E.J. Brill, 1968.

Marmorstein, Arthur. "Miscellen I: Das letze Abendmahl und der Sederabend." In *Zeitschrift für die Neutestamentliche Wissenschaft* 25 (1926): 249–253.
Marshall, I. Howard. *Last Supper and Lord's Supper*. Grand Rapids: Eerdmans, 1980.
Marshall, Mary J. "Re-examining the Last Supper Sayings in Light of the Hebrew Scriptues." *Jesus and the Scriptures: Problems, Passages, and Patterns*, edited by Tobias Hägerland, 193–214. London: T&T Clark, 2016.
Maxfield, T.H.W. *The Words of Institution; A Study of the Hebrew Background of the Holy Communion Service*. Cambridge: W. Heffer & Sons, 1933.
McGowan, Andrew. *Ascetic Eucharists*. Oxford: Oxford University Press, 1999.
———. "Rethinking Eucharistic Origins." *Pacifica* 23 (June 2010): 173–191.
McKnight, Scot. *Jesus and His Death*. Waco, TX: Baylor University Press, 2005.
McNamara, Derek M. "The Rhetoric of Honour and Shame in 1 Corinthians 1–6." PhD diss., U. of South Africa, 2008.
———. "Shame the Incestuous Man." *Neotestamentica* 44.2 (2010): 307–326.
McNamara, Martin. *Targum Neofiti 1: Exodus*. Collegeville, MN: Liturgical Press, 1994.
Metzger, Ernest. "*Quare?* Argument in David Daube, after Karl Popper." *Law for All Times*, edited by Ernest Metzger, 27–58. Lawrence, KS: University of Kansas School of Law, 2009.
Meyer, Ben F. *Critical Realism and the New Testament*, Eugene, OR: Pickwick Publications, 2009.
Meyer, Rudolf. "σάρξ." *Theological Dictionary of the New Testament*, vol. 7, edited by Gerhard Kittel and Gerhard Friedrich, 116. Grand Rapids: Eerdmans, 1971.
Michaels, J. Ramsey. *The Gospel of John*. Grand Rapids, MI: Erdmans, 1971.
Monks of Solesmes. *Gregorian Missal*. Solesmes: Les Editions des Solesmes, 1990.
Narinskaya, Elena. *Ephrem, a 'Jewish' sage: A Comparison of the Exegetical Writings of St. Ephrem the Syrian and Jewish Traditions*. Turnhout: Brepols, 2010.
Neusner, Jacob, and Baruch Bokser. *Yerushalmi Pesahim* vol. 13. Chicago: University of Chicago Press, 1995.
Neusner, Jacob, Bruce Chilton, and William Albert. *Three Faiths, One God: The Formative Faith and Practice of Judaism, Christianity, and Islam*. Leiden: E.J. Brill, 2002.
Newman, Julius. "The Righteous of the Nations of the World." *De Fructu Oris Sui: Essays in Honour of Adrianus van Selms*, edited by I.M. Eybers et al., 130–144. Leiden: E.J. Brill, 1971.
Niemand, Christoph. "Jesu Abendmahl. Versuche zur historischen Rekonstruktion und theologischen Deutung." *Forschungen zum Neuen Testament und seiner Umwelt* LPhThB 7 (2002): 81–122.
Nodet, Etienne. "On Jesus' Last Supper." *Biblica* 91 fasc. 3 (2010): 348–369.
O'Connor, James. *The Hidden Manna: A Theology of the Eucharist*. San Francisco: Ignatius Press, 2005.
Oesterley, W.O.E. *The Jewish Background of the Christian Liturgy*. Oxford: Peter Smith, 1925.
Osborne, Grant. *The Hermeneutical Spiral: A Comprehensive Introduction to Biblical Interpretation*. Downers Grove: Intervarsity Press, 2010.

Perriman, Andrew. *The Future of the People of God: Reading Romans Before and After Western Christendom*. Eugene: Cascade Books, 2010.

Pesch, Rudolf. *Das Abendmahl und Jesu Todesverständnis*. Basel: Editiones Herder, 1978.

Peters, E.F. *The Origin and Meaning of the Axiom: "Nothing Has the Character of a Sacrament Outside of the Use."* Fort Wayne, IN: Concordia Theological Seminary Press, 1993.

Petuchowski, Jakob Josef. "'Do this in remembrance of me' (1 Cor 11:24)." *Journal of Biblical Literature* 76.4 (Dec. 1957): 293–298.

Pietrowski, Mieczysław. "Eucharistic Miracle in Buenos Aires." *Love One Another* 17 (2010). http://www.loamagazine.org/nr/the_main_topic/eucharistic_miracle_in_buenos.html.

Piotrowski, Nicholas. "Johannes Oecolampadius: Christology and the Supper." *Mid-America Journal of Theology* 23 (2012): 131–137.

Pitre, Brant. *Jesus and the Jewish Roots of the Eucharist*. New York, NY: Crown, 2016.

———. *Jesus and the Last Supper*. Grand Rapids: Eerdmans, 2017.

Pomazansky, Michael. *Orthodox Dogmatic Theology*. Platina, CA: St. Herman of Alaska Brotherhood Press, 1994.

Prosic, Tamara. *The Development and Symbolism of the Passover to 70 CE*. London: T&T Clark, 2004.

Rahlfs, Alfred. *Septuaginta: Editio altera*. Stuttgart: Deutsche Bibelgesellschaft, 2006.

Roberts, Alastair. *A Musical Case For Typological Realism*. Birmingham, AL: Theopolis, 2016.

Rodger, Alan. "Law For All Times: the Work and Contribution of David Daube." *Law for All Times*, edited by Ernest Metzger, 3–23. Lawrence, KS: University of Kansas School of Law, 2009.

Scholem, Gershom. *From Berlin to Jerusalem*. Translated by Harry Zohn. New York: Schocken, 1980.

Schuster, Ruth. "Israel's Safari Animals Are Keeping Kosher for Passover, and Loving It." *HaAretz*, April 10, 2017.

Schweizer, Eduard. "σῶμα κτλ." *Theological Dictionary of the New Testament,* vol. 7, edited by Gerhard Kittel and Gerhard Friedrich, 1059. Grand Rapids: Eerdmans, 1971.

Segal, Alan. "Paul's Jewish Presuppositions." *The Cambridge Companion to Paul*. Cambridge: Cambridge University Press, 2003.

Shepardson, Christine. *Anti-Judaism and Christian Orthodoxy: Ephrem's Hymns in Fourth-Century Syria*. Washington, DC: Catholic University of America Press, 2008.

Sicker, Martin. *A Passover Seder Companion and Analytic Introduction to the Haggadah*. Lincoln: iUniverse, 2004.

Smallwood, E. Mary. *The Jews Under Roman Rule*. Leiden: E.J. Brill, 1976.

Smith, Barry. "The Chronology of the Last Supper." *Westminster Theological Journal* 53:1 (1991): 29–45.

Smith, Dennis, and Hal Taussig. *Many Meals: the Eucharist in the New Testament and Liturgy Today.* London: SCM Press, 1990.

Snyman, A.H. "1 Corinthians 1:1–18 from a Rhetorical Perspective." *Acta Theologica* 29.1 (2009): 130–144.

Sperber, Daniel. *A Dictionary of Greek and Latin Legal Terms in the Mishnah, Talmud and Midrashic Literature.* Ramat-Gan: Bar-Ilan University Press,1984.

———. *Nautica Talmudica.* Ramat-Gan: Bar-Ilan University Press, 1986.

Spinks, Bryan. *Do This in Remembrance of Me: the Eucharist from the Early Church to the Present Day.* London: SCM Press, 2013.

Stacey, David. "The Lord's Supper as Prophetic Drama," in *The Signs of a Prophet*, edited by Morna Hooker, 80–95. Eugene: Wipf and Stock, 1997.

Stewart-Sykes, Alistair. *The Lamb's High Feast: Melito, Peri Pascha and the Quartodeciman Paschal Liturgy at Sardis* (Supplements to Vigiliae Christianae xlii). Leiden: E.J. Brill, 1998.

———. "Melito's Anti-Judaism." *Journal of Early Christian Studies* Volume 5, Number 2 (1997): 271–283.

Stone, Darwall. *A History of the Doctrine of the Holy Eucharist,* vol. I. London: Longmans, 1909.

Strabo, Walafrid. *De ecclesiasticarum rerum exordiis et incrementis* (PL 114.936a). Patrologia Latina. Edited by J.-P. Migne. 217 vols. Paris, 1844–1864.

Tabory, Joseph. *The JPS Commentary on the Haggadah.* Philadelphia, PA: Jewish Publication Society, 2008.

Tabory, Joseph. "The Passover Eve Ceremony—An Historical Outline." *Immanuel* 12 (1981): 32–43.

Taussig, Hal, and Dennis Smith. *Many Tables.* Eugene: Wipf & Stock, 2001.

Taussig, Hal, and Dennis Smith, ed. *Meals in the Early Christian World.* New York: Palgrave MacMillan, 2012.

Tawil, Hayim. *An Akkadian Lexical Companion for Biblical Hebrew.* New York: Ktav, 2009.

Thiselton, Anthony. *The First Epistle to the Corinthians: A Commentary on the Greek Text.* Grand Rapids: Eerdmans, 2000.

Tov, Emmanuel. "The Septuagint between Judaism and Christianity." *Textual Criticism of the Hebrew Bible, Qumran, Septuagint: Collected Essays*, 449–70. Leiden: E.J. Brill, 2015.

Tucker, Karen. *American Methodist Worship.* New York: Oxford University Press, 2006).

van Staalduine-Sulman, Eveline. *The Targum of Samuel.* Leiden: E.J. Brill, 2002.

Walters, J. Edward. *Ephrem the Syrian's Hymns on the Unleavened Bread.* Piscataway: Gorgias Press, 2012.

Warning, Rainer. *The Ambivalences of Medieval Religious Drama.* Stanford: Stanford University Press, 2001.

Werner, Eric. "Melito of Sardis, the First Poet of Deicide." *Hebrew Union College Annual* 37 (1966): 191–210.

———. *The Sacred Bridge,* vol. II. New York: Ktav, 1984.

Witherington III, Ben. *Community and Conflict in Corinth: a Socio-Rhetorical Commentary on 1 and 2 Corinthians.* Grand Rapids: Eerdmans, 1996.
Wright, N. T. *Jesus and the Victory of God.* London: SPCK, 1996.
———. *The Meal Jesus Gave Us.* London: SPCK, 2014.
———. *The New Testament and the People of God.* London: SPCK, 1991.
———. *Paul and the Faithfulness of God.* London: SPCK, 2013.
Yuval, Israel. "Easter and Passover as early Jewish Christian Dialogue." *Passover and Easter: Origin and History to Modern Times*, edited by Paul Bradshaw and Lawrence Hoffman, 98–123. Notre Dame: University of Notre Dame Press, 2000.
———. *Two Nations in Your Womb.* Berkeley: University of California Press, 2008.
Zahn, Theodor. *Das Evangelium des Johannes.* Leipzig: A. Deichert, 1908.
Zemel, Alan. "Haggadah as Argument." *Argumentation* 12 (1998): 57–77.
Zizioulas, John D. *Lectures in Dogmatic Theology.* London: T & T Clark, 2008.
Zoll, Rachel. "Reform Rabbi Michael J. Cook Says Jews Are Handicapped by Not Knowing New Testament." Associated Press, April 8, 2006.

General Index

abstention from one of the elements of the eucharist, 141–42
afikomen/afiqoman: date of origin, 26, 56; Eisler's etyomology, 25, 47; hidden and recovered, 24–25, 56, 73, 82; as a name for a piece of unleavened bread, 26, 56; and other Greek verbs of "coming," 64; Rabbinic explanations of the meaning of, 26, 52–54; spelling, 49; traced to Greek ἀφικόμενος, 25, 63
Amalarius of Metz, 104–5, 105n22
Aramaic, 2; bilingual interference behind the Greek of the gospels, 2, 40; original language of the Lord's Prayer, 58, 84
Archelaus, 21
ascetic eucharists, x
R. Ashi, 8

Bauckham, Richard, 1–2, 111, 116, 116n12, 118, 132n17, 144
Bede, The Venerable, 17n14
Begbie, Jeremy, 82–83
Behm, Johannes, 32–33
Belgic Confession, 99–100, 102
Billerbeck, Paul, 6
Bleicher Carmichael, Deborah, 28n44, 60, 62, 64

blood: life in the, 91; "of the covenant," 79; poured out, 91–92
Bock, Darrel, 88n34
body: members of Christ, 73
Bokser, Baruch, 42, 46, 49
Book of Common Prayer, 100, 143
Book of Kells, 104
Bouyer, Louis, xn2
Bradshaw, Paul, xn2, 16n8
Bradshaw, William, 101
bread: afflicted, 80; of angels, 25; compared to flesh, 72; of limbs, 25; meanings in the Old Testament, 71; representing the church, 25, 73; representing Israel, 56, 73; representing the Messiah, 24–25, 28, 30, 33; required to be interpreted at Passover, 23; and salt, x; symbolism already known to Jesus' disciples, 28, 33–34
de Brés, Guido, 99
Brumberg-Kraus, Jonathan, 81

Calvin, John, 101, 123–24, 143–44
Casey, Maurice, 2, 3n9, 19, 22n31, 23–24, 32, 38–39, 40, 58, 64n82, 84, 92, 111, 116n8
Chauvet, Louis-Marie, 109–10
Cleopas (Clopas), 14, 90

clericalism, 124
communities, gospels as products of discrete, 1–2
Chilton, Bruce, 1–2, 92
covenant, 40, 84
Cranmer, Archbishop Thomas, 100, 108–9
Cullmann, Oscar, x, 41
Cumanus, procurator of Judea, 21
cup: for Elijah, 82; common vs multiple, 147–48; as means of κοινωνία, 142; specifically named in the Passover, 16, 42, 86–88

Dalman, Gustaf, 17n12, 18, 32
date of Last Supper, 17
Daube, David, 5, 8, 22n31, 24, 27, 28–30, 34n63, 37, 46, 47, 51, 56, 60, 68–69, 72–73, 80, 85, 88, 95; his scholarly method, 28–29
deictic. *See* "this"
Driver, G. R., 30n51

Eisler, Robert, 6, 24–28, 47, 56, 63, 64, 68–69, 72–73, 115–16
elements. *See* bread; wine
R. Eliezer b. Ḥasama, 75, 80
Elizabeth I on the eucharist, 12
Ephrem of Nisibis (the Syrian), 38, 66–68; use of exegetical traditions from the Targums, 66
eschatology, Jewish, 13;
in the Lord's Prayer, 59
eucharist: connection to Passover, 93–94; Jewish narrative meaning of, 11–12; metaphysics of, 12
events, sharing in past or future, 75
exile, end of, 90
the Exodus as theme for Passover, 13

fetus, communion of, 142n1
Finkelstein, Louis, 45n20
fish in the eucharist, 15n5
Foerster, Werner, 57
France, R. T., 91n40
Francis (Pope), 106

R. Gamaliel, 22n31, 23, 42, 78–79, 83, 109–10
Glatzer, Nahum, 48–49
Goguel, Maurice, 22
Goldberg, R. Nathan, 51
Green, E. M. B., 133–34

Hachenburg, Johann, 103
haggadah, Passover 35, 41–56; *Dayenu*, 43–46; earliest manuscripts of, 42; expurgation of Moses' name from, 46; four sons, 47; Greek loanwords in, 66n87; vorlage of καταγγέλετε, 134
Hallel psalms, 16, 87, 88n34
Harrison, Jane, 81
Hays, Richard, 14, 79n11, 98
Heidelberg Catechism, 102
R. Hillel, 23, 37, 42, 82n19
R. Ḥiyyah, 26, 53–54
Holifield, E. Brooks, 101
Hooker, Morna, 91n40, 133
Hugh of St. Victor, 95, 139

idol-sacrifices, 145
Instone-Brewer, David, 8n16, 42n10, 51, 87

Jastrow, Marcus, 48n28, 50, 64
Jaubert, Annie, 17n14
Jeremias, Joachim, 16, 19, 22–23, 32, 58–59, 89, 62, 84, 89, 132, 147
Jerome: 20, 57, 58, 123–24; translation of ἐπιούσιος as *supersubstantialem*, 57n56; translation of μυστήριον as *sacramentum*, 123–24
Johanan ben Zaccai, 99
Jordan, James B., 142n1
R. Joshua ben Hananiah, 20
Judas of Galilee, 21
Judas Iscariot, 34

Kearney, Richard, 132
Kiddush meal, 17
Klawans, Jonathan, 18n16
Krauss, Samuel, 48n27–28

Krivoruchko, Julia, 49n32
Kulp, Joshua, xi, 42n10, 46, 54

Lachs, Samuel Tobias, 9n19
lamb, the Passover, 55–56; blood sprinkled, 79
leaven, 145
leftovers, disposal of, 143
Lieberman, Saul, 54
Lietzmann, Hans, x, 26, 52, 53, 55, 68, 87n33
Liturgical texts, gospel accounts of Last Supper as, 1–2
Löw, Immanuel, 48n28
the Lord's Prayer, 57–60; Aramaic original, 58–59; Coptic versions, 59
Luther, Martin: licking up spilled wine, 103; at Marburg Colloquy, 29; translated ἐπιούσιος as *täglich*, 57

Macy, Gary, 106n27
Malina, Bruce, 74–75, 80–81
manna, 43–45, 60, 74–75, 80–81, 113–14, 130–31
Marburg Colloquy, 29, 29n49
Marmorstein, Arthur, 26–27, 68
Maxfield, T. H. W., 15
McGowan, Andrew, 16n8
McKnight, Scot, 18n16, 19n19, 33, 79n10
meals in the Greco-Roman world, xi
Melito of Sardis, 45, 60–66; structure of *Peri Pascha*, 62; uses ἀφικόμενος as epithet of Christ, 63
Messiah: participation in, 76, 121, 137–38, 149; as theme of Passover, 14
Metzger, Ernest, 29
Meyer, Rudolf, 32
mice eating wafers, 104
miracles, eucharist attested by, 106–7
misunderstanding, a topos in John's gospel, 116–18
mold growing on wafers, 106–7
mystery, eucharist as, 13n3, 105–6, 121, 122–24

mystery religions, Greek, 14, 22n34, 24, 122–23

Nazirite, 141–42
Nevin, John Williamson, 101
Niemand, Christoph, 18n16
Nodet, Etienne, 17n14

Oecolampadius, 29
Oesterley, W. O. E., 17
olive, size of, 141
one kind, communion in. *See* abstention from one of the elements of the eucharist

Paschal lamb. *See* lamb, the Passover
Paschasius Radbertus, 97, 105–8
Passover: details show that Last Supper was, 16; eve of, 17–18; halakhah concerning dozing during, 8; omission of its details from the gospels, 3–4; political nature of, 20–21; rebellions during, 21; seen as a type of the eucharist, 37, 145; slaughtering of lambs, 3
Passover lamb. *See* lamb, the Passover
Passover seder: date of development, 51
Perkins, William, 101
Perriman, Andrew, 91n39
Pesch, Rudolf, 32
Petuchowski, Jakob, 20n20, 42, 46n21
Piotrowski, Nicholas, 29n49
Pitre, Brant, 31, 40, 57n54, 59–60, 85
Pomazansky, Michael, 122n2
Prosic, Tamara, 42n13
Prudentius, Pontificale of, 43

Quartodecimans, 61–62, 65

Ratramnus of Corbie, 74, 108
real presence, 74, 76, 80, 85, 96–98, 103–4, 117–18
ritual performance, 78–83
Roberts, Alastair, 82–83
Rodger, Sir Alan, 28

sacraments: Augustinian *signum/res*, 97; containers for invisible grace, 95–96; in Exodus, 131; and Israel's story, 11; overtones in John 6, 118; and Pauline soteriology, 78; Reformed doctrine of, 99–101; *sacramentum* as translation for μυστήριον, 124; and time, 82–84; used, not gazed upon, 108–9

Samaritans: daughters are unclean menstruants from birth, 9; do not use vessels in common with Jews, 9

Scholem, Gershom, 27

seder. *See* Passover seder

Segal, Alan, 42n13

self-identification by Jesus, 28, 30–35

Septuagint, rejected to preclude Christian exegesis, 47

shame, 140

sharing in the Messiah. *See* Messiah, participation in

showbread, 85

sign of invisible grace, 102–3

R. Simeon, 53

Sitz im Leben as criterion of authenticity, 2, 38, 40, 114, 118

Smith, Barry, 17n14

Smith, Dennis, xi

Sossius Senecio, 125

Sperber, Daniel, 48n28

Spinks, Bryan, 18n16

stercorianism, 105

Stewart(-Sykes), Alistair, 45, 65–66

Tabory, Joseph, 42n12, 50, 87

Talmud (*Bavli* and *Yerushalmi*): date of production, 7

Targums, Palestinian, 74–75, 92

Taussig, Hal, xi

Tawil, Hayim, 128

Theognis: 1.940, 53

the 39 Articles of Religion, 108n33, 109

"this" (deictic), 5, 22, 25, 79, 80

Thiselton, Anthony, 126

Tosefta: date of production, 6

transubstantiation, 76, 110

wafers, 143–44

Werner, Eric, 43, 45, 63–64

Westminster Larger Catechism, 100

wine: as blood, 71–72; dregs or lees, 146; mixed with myrrh at Jesus' crucifixion, 89; as punishment, 72; used in Passover, 86–90

Wright, N. T., 8n16, 11, 30n50, 77n8, 83, 90–91

Yuval, Israel, 43n14, 45, 62

Zahn, Theodor, 17

Zemel, Alan, 81

Zizioulas, John, 122n2

Zwingli, Ulrich, 29

Ancient Greek Terms

ἀδόκιμος, 136–37
ἄζυμα, 4
ἀνάγαιον, 4
ἀνάμνησις, 132
ἀναξίως, 126
ἄρτος, 144
ἀφικόμενος, 25
δεικνύμενα, 81, 109
διακρίνω, 127
δοκιμάζω, 134–36
ἔθυον, 3
ἐκκλησία, 124
ἐκχυννόμενον, 91
ἐν τῷ πάσχα, 19
ἔνοχος, 126
ἐπίκομον/-ος, 25, 50–51
ἐπικώμιος, 52
ἐπιούσιον, 26, 57–59
ἑορτὴν, κατὰ, 19
ἑορτάζωμεν, 124
ἔσμεν, 74
ἐτύθη, 73
ἴδιον δεῖπνον, 129
ἰχθύες, 15n5

General Index

καθ' ἡμέραν, 57
καθημερινός, 57
κατὰ ἑορτῆν. See ἑορτῆν, κατὰ
καταγγέλετε, 133
κοινωνία, 74, 76, 78, 121
λογίζεσθε, 78
λοιπόν, 9
μέρος, 76–77
μυστηρίον, -ων. See mystery, eucharist as; mystery, religions, Greek
οἶνος, 146
ὀφειλέταις, 58
ὀφειλήματα, 58
οὐχί, 76
ὀψάρια, 15n5
παραζηλόω, 144
παρασκευὴ τοῦ πάσχα, 17–19
πάσχα, 4, 73
ποτήριον μετὰ τὸ δειπνῆσαι, 42
ποτήριον τῆς εὐλογίας, 42
σάββατα/-ον, 4
σκυθρωποί, 98
συ εἶπας, 34
συγχρῶνται, 9
συνερχόμενοι, -ων, 124
υἱὸς τοῦ ἀνθρώπου, 34

Hebrew and Aramaic Terms

אפיקומן, *'afiqomen*, 25–26, 47–56
בְּשָׂרָא *biśrā'*, 32, 115–16
גַּמְלָא *gamlā*, 116
גֶּשֶׁם *geshem/gshem*, 32
גּוּף *gūph/gūphā/guphi (gufi)*, 25, 28, 30–33
דַּיֵּנוּ *dayenu*, 43–46
זִכָּרוֹן *zikrōn*, 132–33
זֶמֶר *zemer*, 53
חָבוּרָה *ḥaburah*, 8, 16, 54
חֵלֶק *ḥēleq, khélek*, 76
יַיִן *yayin*, 146
קַלְמָא *qalmā*, 116
לֶחֶם אֲבִירִים *leḥem abhirim*, 25
לֶחֶם פָּנִים *leḥem panîm*, 85
מָחָר *maḥar*, 58
מַצָּה *matzah* (unleavened bread). See bread
מפטירין *maftîrîn* ("concluding"), 54–55
מרנא תא *maranatha*, 59
נֶפֶשׁ *nephesh*, 91
פטר *ptr*. See מפטירין *maftîrîn*
פָּלַח *palaḥ* and פְּלָא *pala'*, 128
שֵׁכָר *šēkar*, 146

Index of Ancient Literature

Old Testament

Genesis:
40:16–19, 71;
47:18, 30n51

Exodus:
2:24, 40;
12, 79, 141;
12:14, 40;
12:24–27, 83;
13:8, 23, 78;
16:8, 113;
16:22, 26;
24, 70;
24:8, 79;
25:30, 85;
29:31–35, 40

Leviticus:
17:11, 91;
24:12, 127

Numbers:
9:11, 23;
15:8–15, 40

Deuteronomy:
14:26, 146;
32:17, 145;
32:21, 144

1 Samuel:
10, 3;
20:1, 76

2 Samuel:
19:44, 76;
19–20, 77;
23:16–20, 71–72

1 Kings:
3:9, 127

Nehemiah:
9:37, 30n51

Job:
12:11, 127

Psalms:
14:4, 56;
37, 132;
53:4, 56;
69, 132;
75:8, 72;
78:23, 25;
78:24–25, 113;
78:29, 113;
78:32, 114;
109:15, 132;
112:6, 132;
114, 87;
145, 89

Isaiah:
25:6;
53:12, 91

Jeremiah:
49:12, 72;
51:7, 72

Lamentations:
4:21, 72

Ezekiel:
1, 55;
16:2, 55

Daniel:
2:28;
3:27–28, 32

Hosea:
7:8, 56

Habakkuk:
2:16, 72

Zechariah:
9:9–11, 90–91

Apocrypha and Intertestamental Literature

Judith:
2:2, 123

2 Maccabees:
8:36, 134n24;
13:21, 123

Wisdom of Solomon:
2:22, 123

Jubilees:
49, 86

New Testament

Matthew:
6:12, 58;
11:3, 25;
13:11, 123;
14:17, 15n5, 144;
16:16–17, 34;
17:4, 37;
20:22, 72, 148;
24:51, 77;
26:3–5, 21;
26:13, 133;
26:25, 34;
26:28, 91;
26:29, 89;
26:39, 72, 148;
26:55, 57;
26:64, 34n63;
27:11, 34n63;
27:62, 17

Mark:
2:23–28, 8;
4:11, 123;
6:38, 15n5, 144;
8:14, 15, 37;
8:29–30;
10:38, 72, 148;
10:39, 148;
11:3, 25;
14:1, 3;
14:9, 133;
14:12, 3;
14:14, 9;
14:36, 72;
14:17, 4;
14:20, 4;
14:24, 84, 91;
14:26, 89;
14:40, 15;
14:27, 39;
14:36, 148;
14:38, 39;
14:49, 57;
15:2, 34n63;
15:23, 89, 148;
15:42, 17

Luke:
4:16–21, 91;
7:19, 25;
8:10, 123;

9:10, 144;
9:13, 15n5;
9:33, 15;
12:46, 77;
19:47, 57;
22:19, 31;
22:20, 87;
22:42, 72, 148;
22:53, 57;
23:3, 34n63;
23:54, 17;
24, 69;
24:16–31, 14;
24:31, 98;
24:35, 97;
24:36–37, 98;
24:41–45, 15n5;
24:45, 98

John:
2:1–12, 147;
2:19–22, 117;
3:3–4, 117;
4:9, 9–10;
4:10–11, 117;
4:31–34, 117;
4:32, 115;
6, 111–18;
6:5, 112;
6:9, 144;
6:25, 113;
6:30, 114;
6:32–33, 58;
6:33, 115;
6:38, 115;
6:41–42, 117;
6:52, 113, 116;
6:53–56, 115;
6:63, 116;
7:33–35, 117;
8:21–22, 117;
11:11–12, 117;
13:1, 18;
13:8, 37, 76;
17:9–19;

18:8, 39;
18:37, 34n63;
19:14, 17–18;
19:23, 25

Acts:
1:6, 112;
5:34, 42;
9:4, 126–27;
10:20, 127;
15:5, 39;
15:9, 127;
7:2–53, 45;
11:31, 127;
21:23–26

Romans:
6:5–6, 121;
6:11, 78

1 Corinthians:
1:8–9, 121;
2:7, 123;
4:1, 13n3;
5–6, 73;
5:6, 25;
5:6–8, 73;
5:7, 56;
5:7–8, 124–25;
5:8, 145;
6:1, 57;
8:6, 145;
9:17, 13n3;
10:1–5, 129–30;
10:3–4, 80;
10:16, 13n3, 42, 56, 87, 130;
10:16–17, 73–74, 144;
10:16–18, 78;
10:17, 25;
10:17–22, 145;
10:21, 76;
11:2–13, 140;
11:18, 124;
11:20, 124;
11:21, 129;
11:22, 125, 140, 144;

170 *Index of Ancient Literature*

11:23–26, 126;
11:24, 31, 74;
11:25, 42;
11:28, 134;
11:30, 101, 128;
11:31, 127;
11:32, 129;
11:33, 124;
13:2, 123;
14:2, 123;
15, 120;
15:51, 13n3, 123

2 Corinthians:
5:15–16, 78;
12:11–12, 136;
13:2, 136;
13:5, 135;
13:6, 136;
13:9, 136

Ephesians:
3:5–7, 123;
5:32, 13n3, 123

Philippians:
3:10, 78, 121

Hebrews:
10:29, 79, 126;
10:37, 25

Jude:
1:5, 131–32

Revelation:
2:17, 75, 80;
14:17–20, 72

Dead Sea Scrolls

4Q531 fg. 40:1, 32

Damascus Document, 74

Rabbinic Sources

Mekhilta:
7, 20;
16.25, 75, 80

Mishnah:
date of production, 6;
m.Avot 4:6, 31;
m.Sanhedrin 10.1, 77;
m.Shabbat 7:2, 8;
m.Niddah 4:1, 9;
m.Kelim 1:1, 9;
m.Pesachim 4.1, 8.8, 18;
5.7, 53;
10.1, 18, 86;
10.2, 147;
10.3, 31;
10.5, 22n31, 23, 78;
10.7, 87, 147;
10.8, 47n25, 54

Tosefta:
t.Berakot 5.10, 147;
t.Derek Ereṣ 9, 147;
t.Pesachim 2.22, 23;
10.9, 31;
10.11, 52;
t.Sanhedrin 13.2, 77;
t.Shabbat 15.9, 92

Babylonian Talmud (Bavli):
b.Megillah 25a, 55;
b.Pesachim 115a, 23;
119b, 52;
b.Qiddushin 37a, 32;
b.Sanhedrin 90a, 77;
Derek Ereṣ 9, 147;

Palestinian Talmud (Yerushalmi):
y.Pesachim 10.4, 50;
y.Pesachim 10.7–8, 52–53

Midrashim and Other Jewish Sources

Avot de-Rabbi Nathan:
27, 31

Exodus Rabbah:
18.12, 20

Pirke Avot:
1, 77

Pirke de Rabbi Eliezer:
  28–29, 79

The Targums

Targum Jonathan:
  1 Samuel 5:4, 31n52;
  1 Samuel 31:10, 30n51, 31n52;
  Isaiah 8:6, 31n52

Targum Neofiti:
  Genesis 47:18, 31n52;
  Exodus 22:12, 32;
  Leviticus 1:8, 1:12, 8:20, 31n52

Targum Sheni (Esther):
  Esther 1.8, 31

Greek and Latin Authors

Dio Chrysostom:
  Oration 33.14.9, 50

Diogenes Laertius:
  Vitae Philosophorum II.128, 54

Epictetus:
  Diatribai 1.12, 77

Euripides:
  Cyclops 445, 54

Josephus:
  Antiquities 2.315–17, 60;
  3.10.5, 18;
  16.6, 17;
  20.105–12, 21n27;
  20.113–17, 21n27;
  War 1.88, 21n28;
  6.9, 21n29;
  2.12.1, 21;
  2.224–27, 21n27;
  2.228–31, 21n27

Marcus Aurelius:
  Meditations 4.14, 7.13, 77

Pindar:
  Nemean Ode 6.32, 48, 52;
  8.50, 52;
  Pythian Ode 10.6, 50n35, 52

Plutarch:
  Moralia 148B, 51;
  784B, 51;
  Quaest. Conv. VII prol. 697c, 125

Christian Authors

Augustine:
  City of God XI.3, 97n5

Didache:
  9.8, 73, 145;
  10.14, 59

Ephrem of Nisibis:
  H.Azym. 1.1–15, 67;
  2.7, 68;
  2.13–15, 67;
  6.4, 38;
  12.3–4, 67

Ignatius of Antioch:
  Epist. ad Philadelphios 4, 148
  The Improperia, 43–46, 82

Jerome:
  Comm. on Gospel of Matthew;
  6:11, 58;
  25:6, 20;
  Tract on Psalm 135, 58

Marlowe, Christopher:
  Doctor Faustus V.1, 96

Melito of Sardis:
  Peri Pascha, 61, 63–64, 82

Origen:
  De Oratione 27.7, 57

Paschasius Radbertus:
  De corpore et sanguine Domini xv–xvi, 105;
  viii, 106;
  Ep. Ad Frudegardum, 106

Rabanus Maurus:
  Poenitentiale 33, 107–8

Walafrid Strabo:
  De ecclesiasticarum rerum exordiis et incrementis 16, 107

About the Author

Matthew Colvin holds a PhD in classics from Cornell University. He is a presbyter in the Reformed Episcopal Church.